WOODTURNING

Woodturning

W. J. Wooldridge

B. T. BATSFORD LTD · LONDON

Dedication

To my wife's tireless encouragement, and my daughter's work on the manuscript

Acknowledgements

My special thanks to Stuart Pilkington, who cheerfully surmounted all difficulties in taking the photographs, and Frederick Longbottom, whose pleas to be taught the craft led the way to a lasting friendship and this book

First published 1982
© W. J. Wooldridge 1982

ISBN 0 7134 4045 7

Printed in Great Britain by
Butler & Tanner Ltd, Frome and London
for the publishers, B. T. Batsford Ltd,
4 Fitzhardinge Street, London, W1H OAH

Contents

CHAPTER ONE

Selection of Tools

The beginner will be tempted to equip himself with a full range of gouges: shallow, half-round, deep 'U' and long nose, plus skew and square ended chisels in a range of sizes, scrapers and the like. He will soon find, however, that like the golfer with his bulging bag of clubs, he will return again and again to a few well tried favourites. There are 21 gouges, chisels and scrapers in my rack, but I could manage comfortably with six, including at least two scrapers. So I recommend the following list of tools as necessary to handling most jobs the beginner will want to tackle, and only those marked with an asterisk would be essential at the outset.

$1\frac{1}{2}$in (3.81cm) skew chisel*

$\frac{1}{2}$in (12.7mm) square ended chisel*

$\frac{3}{8}$in (9.525mm) gouge – deep 'U'*

$\frac{5}{8}$in (15.875mm) gouge – shallow 'U'*

$\frac{1}{2}$in (12.7mm) gouge – long nose*

$\frac{1}{16}$in (1.587mm) parting tool – spearpoint*

1in (2.54cm) scraper – round nose/side cutting combination*

$\frac{1}{2}$in (12.7mm) scraper – round nose*

6in (15.24cm) dividers – spring, 1 pair*

A selection of tools. 1–3, scrapers; 4–6, gouges; 7, spearpoint, general purpose; 8, $\frac{1}{2}$in (12.7mm) chisel; 9, $1\frac{1}{2}$in (3.81cm) skew chisel

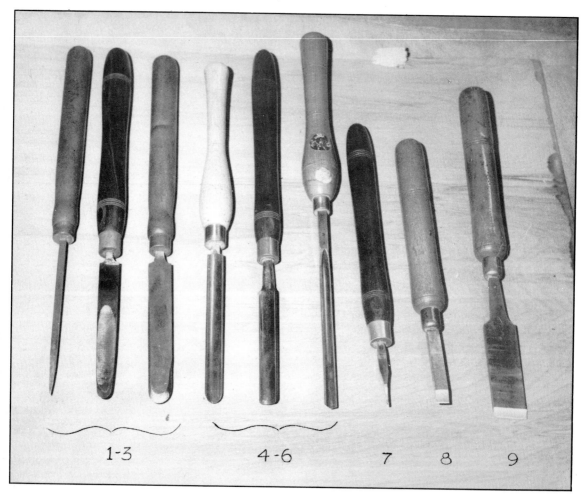

1-3   4-6   7   8   9

6in (15.24cm) callipers – spring, 1 pair inside*

6in (15.24cm) callipers – spring, 1 pair outside*

6in (15.24cm) rule, steel*

72in (182.88cm) measuring tape

hammer – plastic face

$\frac{1}{8}$in (3.175mm) gimlet or bradawl*

12in (30.48cm) screwdriver*

pencil, carpenter's – 1 medium, 1 soft*

8 × 2 × 1in (20.32 × 5.08 × 2.54cm) India oilstone, medium grade*

6in (15.24cm) conical oilstone – medium grade for gouges

1 set of carpentry bits – Irwin type. Sizes: $\frac{3}{8}$in (9.52mm); $\frac{1}{2}$in (12.7mm); $\frac{5}{8}$in (15.875mm); $\frac{3}{4}$in (19.05mm); 1in (2.54cm).* (The square shank to be removed and the screw point filed to a four sided pyramid as needed)

1 Set of jobbing drills, parallel shank, sizes ranging from $\frac{1}{8}$in (3.175mm) to $\frac{3}{8}$in (9.525mm)*

centre punch

wooden mallet or maul. (An early turning project, see Chapter 15)

6in (15.24cm) second cut half-round file

handle for above. (An early turning project, see Chapter 15)

12in (30.48cm) try square with sliding stock*

A number of these items will already be in the home workshop no doubt, but the turning tools proper will have to be bought. Sets of these are available from the main suppliers, but tend to be rather lightweight for serious turning. They also include some tools which are not often needed. It would pay, therefore, to buy individual tools where possible direct from the manufacturers, making up handles oneself as time goes on. Alternatively, one often sees secondhand tools offered for sale in woodworking magazines, another possible source of supply.

By whatever means you obtain them, be absolutely sure your tools are of high quality. There is nothing so infuriating as a tool which will not keep its edge and so requires constant resharpening. Woodturning tools last a very long time (it has taken 20 years to reduce my spearpoint parting tool from ten to two inches long!) so you can afford to buy the best, and only the best will please you.

A selection of tools. 1, mallet; 2, flat oilstone; 3, callipers, outside; 4, callipers, inside; 5, conical oilstone; 6, modified Irwin bit; 7, unmodified Irwin bit; 8, centre punch; 9, dividers

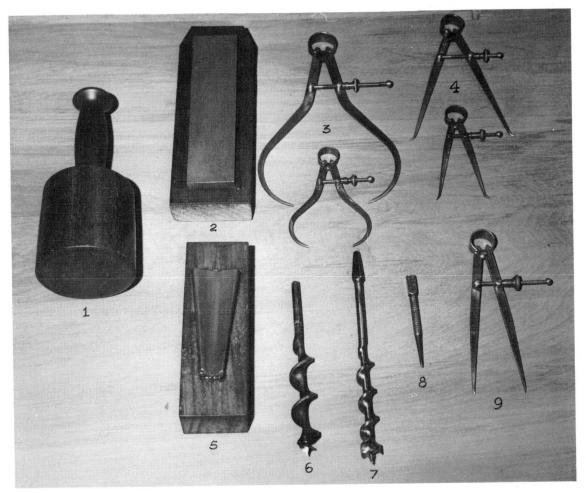

CHAPTER TWO

Selection of Lathe

Coronet Major 7635 lathe, incorporating grindstone and swivelling headstock. (By courtesy of the Coronet Tool Co., Derby)

These come in such a variety of sizes – and prices! – that it would be foolhardy to make any specific recommendations, but I do suggest that the beginner sets his sights on something of not less than $\frac{1}{2}$ horsepower capacity.

There is of course a variety of much smaller powered lathes available, such as those driven by electric hand drills, and quite reasonable standards of work can be achieved on them. They are of limited capacity, however, and the serious beginner will probably prefer purchasing, new or second-hand, a more practical, versatile machine.

The following criteria are suggested as a basis for making your selection:

36in (91.44cm) between centres. (A softball bat is 30in (76.20cm) long)

12in (30.42cm) capacity for faceplate work, with outside headstock turning facility desirable but not essential

three speed pulley giving say 750, 1200 and 2700 r.p.m.

$\frac{1}{2}-\frac{3}{4}$ h.p. motor, with the control switch accessible from the working position

No. 2 Morse taper sockets in head and tailstock spindles*

---

* Permits interchangeability of fittings between head and tailstocks, and use of wooden lathe turned fittings robust enough to withstand heavy usage.

The Author's bespoke lathe. ½p. motor, 5½in (13.97cm) centre, 36in (91.44cm) bed, 3-step pulley giving 750:1150:1700 r.p.m. No. 2 Morse taper head and tailstock fitting

Headstock assembly. Note the split phosphor bronze bearings adjusted by jubilee clips

The tailstock. Note the clamping arrangement, which allows the tailstock to be swung clear for long hole boring

The saddle and tool rest, clamped by one lever under the bed

Accessories should include:

two prong driving chuck or centre

four prong driving chuck or centre

screw chuck

4in (10.16cm) faceplate

6in (15.24cm) faceplate

ring centre

conical centre

revolving centre (see Chapter 15)

6in (15.24cm) tool rest
12in (30. 48cm) tool rest

½in (12.7mm) capacity Jacobs chuck

5 × ¾in (12.70cm × 19.05mm) medium grit carborundum wheel

These basic accessories will be augmented in course of time by fittings of your own making, following designs described in Chapter 15.

To make it easier for the reader to follow the terms used in describing later operations, a knowledge of the major parts of the lathe is essential. Let us proceed then to acquire it.

A DESCRIPTION OF THE MAJOR LATHE ASSEMBLIES

The lathe, which has a very long history, is probably one of the most useful woodworking tools evolved by man, and in its modern form unlikely to be improved upon. It consists basically of a bed, which may be flat or tubular, on which are carried the major fittings, comprising the headstock, tailstock and saddle.

The headstock is fixed to the bed, and used to support and drive the wood in both faceplate and spindle turning, by means of a mandrel carried in bearings and rotated by a pulley, belt-driven from a motor.

The mandrel is threaded externally at its forward end, for the attachment of a faceplate, and bored internally for Morse tapered or screw-in driving centres, for spindle turning.

The tailstock is adjustable along the length of the bed, and is used to support the end of the workpiece in spindle turning, by means of centres which fit into a poppet barrel, itself adjustable by means of a hand wheel. Locking levers for both the tailstock position on the bed, and the poppet in the tailstock , are provided.

Set on the lathe bed between the head and tail stocks, and also adjustable along the length of it, is the saddle. This is a platform supporting the tool rest holder, which is adjustable in any direction, and, like the saddle, provided with a locking lever. Some lathes dispense with the saddle, in which case the tool rest holder clamps directly on to the bed.

Provision is made with a number of lathes for faceplate turning to be done on the outside end of the headstock, the mandrel being threaded for this purpose. This extra facility allows for the turning of table tops and similar large articles up to a radial dimension equal to the height of the headstock axis from the ground.

A bracket to support the tool rest is incorporated in the design, or a separate stand for the purpose is provided.

Like all machinery, the lathe will give optimum service only if it is properly cared for. Bearings should be regularly lubricated; make a habit of oiling them each time you use the lathe, and give the bright metal parts a wipe with an oily rag at the end of the day's work. Likewise, put a drop of oil on clamping screw threads from time to time, but at all costs avoid getting it on your pulleys or belt.

One last precaution. If you must dry sand your work contrary to my recommended wet and dry method, take care to screen your motor from inducting the dust into its innards.

CHAPTER THREE

Working Area and Lighting

In setting up your workshop, careful thought should be given to the location of the lathe, remembering that extra wiring, lighting and power supply may need to be installed. To save unnecessary expense, therefore, the site chosen should be the right one from the start.

The following points will need consideration:

1. The lathe must be set up on a firm floor, preferably concrete, with at least four clear feet (1.5m) of space on the operator's side, including the end of the lathe if fitted with an outside headstock turning attachment.

2. As the height of the lathe is important in avoiding unnecessary fatigue for the operator, the bench height should be so adjusted that the centre line of the lathe through the head and tailstocks is approximately level with the position of the elbow with the arm resting at the side.

3. There should be a good natural light if possible, but, in any case, adjustable artificial lighting; an anglepoise type fitting can be particularly useful when turning hollow ware. Avoid single tube fluorescent lighting, however, as no shadow is thrown from this source of light, which can be a disadvantage when balancing profiles of curves and hollows, whilst at certain lathe speeds the moving parts will appear to be stationary, which might prove dangerous.

Consideration must also be given to the possibility of the motor noise creating a nuisance.

In addition to a rack for woodturning tools, described later, a shadow board handy to the lathe, with all the lathe

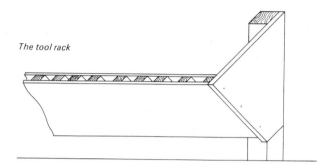

The tool rack

accessories and additional tools arranged on it, and shelving for stowing jigs, patterns, workpieces and oddments (which accumulate at an alarming rate), are also essential. As far as possible, however, keep your shelving out of range of flying chips and shavings.

The tool rack comprises a simple wooden frame made of two sheets of $\frac{1}{4} \times 12$in (6.35mm $\times$ 30.48cm) wide hardboard sandwiching $\frac{3}{4}$in (19.05mm) spacers set at graduated distances to take differing widths of tool blades, and set up at the back edge of the lathe bench. The frame is inclined forward towards the operator, and provided the tool handles are made of a variety of woods, each tool in its own slot is readily identified.

The frame should be left open at the bottom of course, so that the tools rest on the ferrules of their handles, and shavings are not trapped in the rack.

CHAPTER FOUR

Clothes and Comfort

Sensible clothes

The handguard against flying chips

Having made your choice of tools, lathe and workplace, there are just a few more points to cover before embarking on the exciting new experience of bringing steel and flying wood together.

You must feel free and unhampered. So:

1. Wear clothes which are comfortable, with no loose cuffs or scarves, but fastening securely at the neck. Nothing can be more irritating than a few chips of wood chafing inside a shirt.

   Be warned against wearing knitted woollen cardigans or similar attire though; wood chips and shavings have an affinity for them which only a stiff brush will master. Trouser turnups can be a nuisance too, but a simple safeguard from all these problems is to wear a zip fronted combination overall. It is far superior to a dust coat, fits snug to the body, can be worn over good clothes and is slipped off in a jiffy.

   You can of course save yourself a lot of annoyance from chips flying into your face and clothing by simply changing your grip at the tool rest. If the hand is opened with the fingers extended upwards, whilst still using the thumb and palm of the index finger to control the tool, you are stopping the fragments at source. This applies particularly in roughing down between centres.

2. Wear a mask *and* hat or cap when sanding, to protect the hair as well as the lungs from dust. Some woods can irritate the nasal passages and eyes, so on occasion even goggles are in order. (This is a problem I am not bothered by, however, as all my sanding is done with wet and dry paper. See Chapter 17.)

In some quarters there appears to be a tendency to consider woodturners as rather untidy men, scratching along with rough and ready methods and toil worn tools, but achieving a high standard and output notwithstanding. No doubt the harsh conditions under which they once laboured forced them into this mould, but let us not accept such traditional attitudes as the norm for ourselves.

Here then are some further suggestions:

3. Never finish work for the day without first cleaning down your machine and oiling its bearings. (The oil flows in easily when the metal is warm.)

4. Sharpen your tools and stow things away. The tidy, methodical turner will return his tools to the rack as each is finished with, and will have his workshop ready for an immediate start whenever he returns to it. This way he will rarely lose his smaller drills, callipers, pencils and the like, swept away with the accumulated shavings and rubbish of a weekly or less frequent clean-up. He will also know just where to put his hands on anything he needs.

5. Should the air in the workshop tend to be damp, causing tools to rust rapidly, the simple solution is to face a rectangular block of wood with heavy felt. This is impregnated with oil, and the metal parts of the tools used during the session rubbed over before they are stowed away. Once the habit of doing this is acquired, rust spots no longer trouble you, although a coat of varnish on all bright parts is my recommended long term solution.

CHAPTER FIVE

Tool Sharpening and Grinding Bevels

As sharp tools are the second most important factor in successful turning – the first being the all important bevel rubbing during cutting operations, of which more anon – I will now give them more detailed consideration.

The first thing to bear in mind is that unlike carpenter's tools such as gouges, chisels and plane irons, with which most of us are familiar, the woodturner's tools have no secondary bevel at the edge, although scrapers can be an exception. (See Chapter 15.)

Our gouges and chisels come from the manufacturer with machine ground bevels which are often unfit for use until they have been reshaped. The gouges sometimes have a bevel which is too long, so necessitating the presentation of the tool at an angle which is not suitable to most turners, whilst chisels, for reasons which no-one seems able to explain, are occasionally ground with convex bevels, quite the reverse of our needs, which is for a dead flat or even concave bevel.

The first operation with new tools will therefore probably involve regrinding the bevels. As most turners have their own preference in bevel angles, no hard and fast rule can be laid down, so until one has formed one's own opinion after some practical experience, an angle of approximately 45° for gouges and 25° for chisels may be used.

In grinding, for which a carborundum wheel 5–6 × 1 in (12.70–15.24 × 2.54cm) thick in a medium grit, and mounted on an arbour in the lathe, is quite suitable (goggles are recommended), there is the choice of flat grinding on the flat surface of the stone, or hollow grinding on its edge.

The advantage of hollow grinding is that when the tool is being oilstoned, the stone bridges the concave face of the bevel, and so makes contact with two points only: the edge and the back end of the bevel. This means that only a minimum amount of oilstoning is necessary to restore the edge, and there is no fear of the edge being rounded over.

Resharpening the edge of a flat bevel entails oilstoning the whole face of the bevel, so inevitably the edge tends to get rounded over. Repeated resharpening results in an edge so rounded that the bevel cannot be kept in contact with the wood surface as the edge cuts, so that sooner or later the tool digs in.

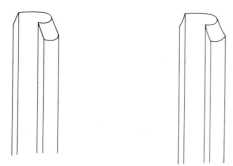

Left: *Gouge ground on side of wheel.* Right: *Gouge ground on edge of wheel*

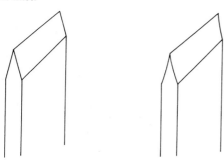

Left: *Chisel ground on side of wheel.* Right: *Chisel ground on edge of wheel*

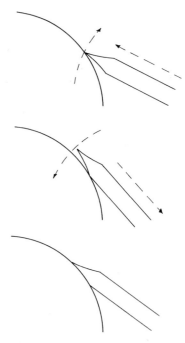

From top to bottom: *When the chisel contacts the grinder too near the tool's edge, move as arrows indicate. When the chisel contacts the grinder on the heel of the bevel, move as arrows indicate. Bevel of chisel in correct position on the grinder*

I have always hollow ground my tools because I find by this means they cut more cleanly, and I spend far less time oilstoning *and* grinding them.

The procedure is as follows:

CHISELS

Having set up the grindstone in the lathe, supported if necessary by the revolving centre, adjust the tool rest to a convenient height for bringing the tool bevel into contact with the edge of the stone at an angle of approximately 25°.

With the grindstone stationary, fix the position the bevel is to contact the stone, and grasp the tool at a point where the fingers will be against the back edge of the tool rest. (With most tool rests a more positive edge to control the fingers is presented if the rest is reversed. In this position the edge normally towards the wood is towards the operator, so offering a sheer straight edge to bear the fingers against.)

Without relaxing the grip on the tool with this hand, switch on, and lower the tool to the stone *after* having positioned the hand and tool in their original position against the rest. As soon as contact is made with the stone, and still grasping the tool as before, withdraw the tool from the stone, and check where it has marked the bevel. If the stone is grinding in the required place, return the hand to its position against the tool rest, with the tool resting on it. Lower the edge of the tool to the stone, and continue grinding. Should contact between the stone and bevel be too near the edge of the tool, ease it forward very slightly in the control hand and try again, adjusting hand pressure against the tool rest as required. Conversely, if the initial contact between tool and stone is too near the back end of the bevel, ease the tool back very slightly in the control hand grip, and try again.

Although this all sounds very difficult, it will be found possible after some experience that by exerting extra pressure, or by easing pressure of the fingers against the tool rest, the bevel can be brought to the exactly right position on the stone. Once the correct position has been found, the tool is moved laterally left and right across the face of the stone, by sliding the hand along the tool rest. This movement ensures that the entire edge of the tool is ground, and the stone is worn down uniformly across its face.

GOUGES – SQUARE ENDED

These are also best hollow ground, but, unlike the chisels, cannot be stationary in one place against the edge of the stone. However, the same techniques of using the control hand against the back of the tool rest, and setting the bevel at the approximate position on the stationary stone, still apply.

Having adjusted the grip to get the desired contact between stone and bevel, the gouge is rotated in the hand whilst keeping both in contact with the tool rest. Without altering the grip, the gouge is removed from time to time and grinding progress checked. Care must be taken not to over-rotate the tool, otherwise the corners will be ground away, and the gouge spoiled for bowl turning.

GOUGES – LONG NOSE

These, as the name implies, are rounded at the edge like a fingernail, and in grinding require an additional movement to the normal gouge. Whilst following the same procedure as before, the tool should be simultaneously traversed across the face of the stone inverted pendulum fashion. This ensures that the hollow grinding follows the curvature of the edge of the tool.

Hollow grinding the square end gouge. Note the reversed tool rest for controlling the hand, and the revolving centre adapter supporting the grindstone arbor

Hollow grinding the long nose gouge. Note the tilt and angle of the tool

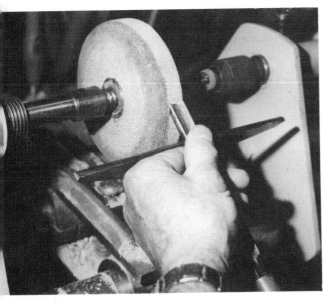

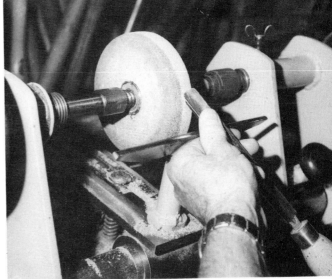

In all grinding operations the endeavour should be to remove the minimum amount of metal to achieve a bevel running up to the edge of the tool or just short of it, and under no circumstances to overheat the tool.

By maintaining overlong contact with the stone, or exerting heavy pressure on the tool whilst grinding, overheating may result. Should this happen, the temper of the steel will be lost, and it will become soft and useless until it has been retempered – a specialist's job.

It is therefore always advisable when grinding to have a tin of water on hand, to quench any tools which may need cooling off.

OILSTONING

Having now got a satisfactory bevel on the tools, the final step is to hone them to a fine, sharp edge.

As with most crafts, there is a variety of methods, and advocates for each of them. Some recommend holding the tool in one hand rested against a support, and passing the oilstone across its bevel with the other. A reverse procedure will be the choice of another expert, whilst I prefer to have at least one of the two articles anchored firmly in the vice.

To my mind, there is less chance of error if either the oilstone or the tool is gripped in the vice, so leaving both hands free to control the other, than if each is held in a separate hand to sharpen the tool.

I clamp my $8 \times 2 \times 1$ in ($20.32 \times 5.08 \times 2.54$cm) India medium cutting oilstone in the vice, and lay my chisel bevel flat on it, lubricated with an oil and paraffin mixture. By using both hands to control the tool, a few backward and forward strokes the full length of the stone soon produce a really fine edge.

For a final strop I use a 3in (7.62cm) wide strip of heavy leather, undressed side upwards, glued to a board and laid on the bench. It is kept lightly oiled, and when not in use hung on the workshop wall. Naturally, all stropping strokes are made away from the tool's edge to avoid cutting the leather.

With my gouges, I again lay the bevel flat to the stone at its centre, and by holding the blade in one hand and the end of the handle in the other, I swing the edge pendulum fashion along the stone, rotating it at the same time.

If it is a long nose gouge then the handle remains stationary, but if it is a square ended gouge the handle hand moves along the stone in unison with the blade hand, care being taken to maintain the handle at the same angle throughout. It may sound hard, but with a little practice it is surprisingly easy to hold the bevel at the one angle, so the edge is sharpened in a very short time.

The main point to remember in using oilstones is to apply plenty of lubricant to float off the metal particles from the surface of the stone. Once the oil has turned completely black it should be wiped away and a fresh oil mixture applied. If this is not done, the pores of the stone will rapidly clog up and its cutting action be diminished. (I would also suggest that before going to the oilstone to resharpen a tool during later turning operations, you dislodge the chips and shavings from your body and clothing which will otherwise scatter across the face of the stone. Another tip worth following is to reserve one face of the stone for gouges, which tend to hollow out the centre, and use the other side only for plane irons, skew chisels and the like.

An alternative method with gouges is to use a conical shaped stone, well oiled, especially made for them. The

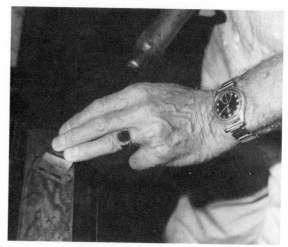

Sharpening the skew chisel. Notice the oil commencing to turn black

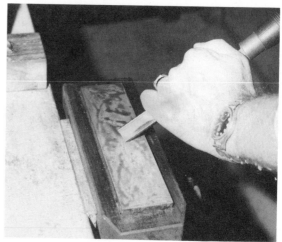

Sharpening the square end gouge with the oilstone secured in the vice

Sharpening the long nose gouge using an inverted pendulum motion

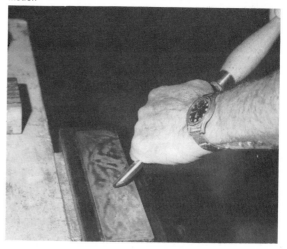

Sharpening the square end gouge using the conical stone in the vice

Sharpening the long nose gouge using the conical stone in the vice

Sharpening the long nose gouge with the conical stone, using the bench in support

concave shaped face of the stone fits the bevel curvature of the gouge which, if it is clamped in the vice or held firmly against the edge of the bench with the handle supported by the thigh, is quickly sharpened without the edge getting dubbed over. Or again, the stone can be let into a wooden block laid on the bench, and the gouge sharpened in the same way as the chisel described earlier.

The rounded sides of the conical stone are also very useful for removing burrs from the inside face of the gouge after grinding or honing. These are carefully removed by a light pass of the stone towards the edge, keeping it flat against the inner face – a very important detail.

After honing, test the edge by touching it against the face of the thumbnail. A sharp edge will check on contact, but a dull one will slide across the nail.

The slightest suggestion of shine from the edge of the blade indicates that a flat, and therefore blunt, area is reflecting the light and so requires attention.

In conclusion, never consider time spent sharpening tools as time wasted. Try to develop the habit, when pausing at some point in a turning session, of sharpening the tool in your hand and, to make the trip to the oilstone worthwhile, the couple of other tools lying on the bench. Tool sharpening time, indeed, is time saved in the long run. The sharper the tool, the more quickly, effectively and accurately it cuts, and with hollow ground bevels the job is done in a jiffy anyway!

So here we are at last, our tools freshly ground and sharpened, ready for the first preliminaries to actually turning . . . but before we proceed, a word or two about centres, faceplates and tool rests to help us get the maximum performance from them.

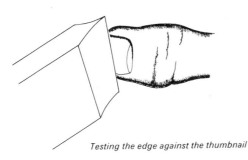

Testing the edge against the thumbnail

CHAPTER SIX

Centres and Faceplates

Display of centres, faceplates, screwchuck and internal tool rest

Before going into marking out and setting up work on the lathe, let us consider the devices used to support and rotate the wood whilst it is being shaped.

CENTRES

For turning spindles, a common task for woodturners in the days of the spinning wheel, the wood is held between centres: the headstock centre, often called the driving centre for obvious reasons, and the tailstock centre or dead centre.

The driving centre is also called the fork or prong centre or chuck, and consists of a two or four prong fitting with a point at its centre. The prongs are sharpened to a bevel, the edges being designed to bite into the wood and rotate it. The bevel or angle is fairly flat so as to reduce the splitting action of the fangs or prongs as the centre is driven into the wood.

The four prong driving centre, having greater driving power, does not need to be driven in so far, but in either case it is good practice, especially with hardwoods, to saw cuts about $\frac{1}{8}$in (3.175mm) deep across the centre hole to assist the fangs biting into the end grain. The driving edges

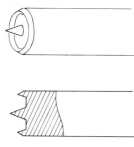

Sectioned view of the ring centre

or heat is generated. The pressure is taken on a fully enclosed ball race within the centre, which is formed with a conical point for supporting the wood.

Not being able to obtain one when I first took up woodturning twenty-odd years ago, I improvised it out of a thrust race from a car clutch, set in an oak housing which fitted over the tailstock poppet. Although it served its purpose, it was a pretty hefty affair, so later on I made a much simpler and more versatile device utilising a pair of small ball races one behind the other, into the centre hole of which I fitted centres to suit the job in hand. The fitting is easily made, and fully described in Chapter 15.

FACEPLATES

Faceplates are an essential accessory for what is called faceplate work. In this, the wood to be turned is secured, usually by screws, to the faceplate, and held in the vertical plane at the headstock, as opposed to spindle turning where the wood is held in the horizontal plane between the head and tailstock centres.

Faceplates come in a variety of sizes from 3in (7.62cm) up to 9in (22.86cm) diameter, depending usually on the capacity of the lathe concerned. I find my favourite one is 4in (10.16cm) in diameter; a size capable of handling the largest bowls my lathe will accept: 11in (27.94cm) diameter. They are designed to screw on to the headstock mandrel, and usually have two sets of screw holes: an inner set of three or four for smaller work, and an outer set for the maximum size of workpiece the lathe is designed for. The holes are arranged in a ring 90° or 120° apart, and are often sunk into webs formed on the back of the faceplate. This arrangement ensures that the heads of the screws are supported, and so must drive squarely into the wood. The central hole for the mandrel is usually open right through the front, and can be very useful for certain purposes, as I will describe later.

In faceplate work it is sound practice to centre-punch a positive mark alongside one screw hole in each of the inner and outer group of holes, so making it a master hole. The idea is that when the workpiece is screwed to the faceplate, a pencil mark is made on the wood alongside the master hole. If at any time later the workpiece is removed from the faceplate for some reason, and then screwed back on to it, the pencil mark and master hole being brought together will ensure that the workpiece will again run absolutely true.

When laying out the positions 120° apart for drilling the holes for tripod legs of hollow ware, lamp bases, etc., the three hole faceplate can be used in a similar way to an indexing head, with equally accurate results. (See Chapter 11.) Chapter 15 contains a description of a tool for accurately centering faceplate work.

and the point should always be kept sharp, and the clearance between them deep enough to allow them full penetration into the wood.

Although the centre should be accurately made, it is always advisable to mark one fang clearly with a centre punch or file. This mark, used in conjunction with a pencil mark on the end of the work, will always ensure that no eccentricity in the workpiece results from separating and subsequently rejoining the workpiece and centre.

At the tailstock end three types of centre are commonly used: a conical shaped 'dead' centre, a ring centre and the revolving centre. Basically they all do the same job of supporting the wood and, by pressure from the tailstock hand wheel, maintaining the wood in engagement with the driving centre.

In use the dead centre should have a well formed point, and be kept lubricated. I prefer candle wax for this: it is dry, clean to handle, and leaves no stains on the wood, but some use soap, oil or Vaseline.

The ring centre is formed with a central small point, surrounded by a flat area for exerting pressure on the wood, enclosed by a lip or ring which is sharpened at its forward edge. In use, the centre point engages in the end of the wood, the ring cuts a groove to support it against the lateral pressure of the tool, whilst the flat face bears against the end grain and so keeps the wood hard on to the driving centre.

It is lubricated in the usual way, but excessive pressure from the hand wheel will generate enough heat to char the wood and so build up a deposit on the flat face which will affect the centre's efficiency. Ring centres in various sizes also serve as useful guides when reducing dowel ends to set diameters.

Last but not least is the most expensive centre, and not every turner possesses one, but it does save you the chore of lubricating the point! This is the revolving centre, and, as the name implies, it turns with the wood, so that no friction

CHAPTER SEVEN

Tool Rests

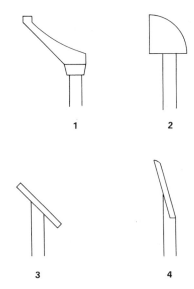

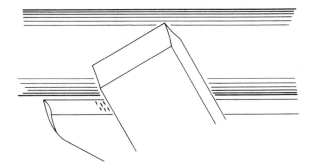

A tool rest being cut by the side of a new chisel before chamfering

Tool rests of various shapes; No. 4 is the best

As the sketches indicate, these come in a variety of shapes, not all of them perfect for their purpose. Too often they are made with a flat surface along the top forward edge, which means that at various stages of the work the tool sits on the back edge of the flat surface, moves on to the flat, and later, as the wood reduces in diameter and the tool handle is raised to maintain the bevel of the tool in contact with it, the tool is resting on the front edge. This means that the chisel or gouge changes its fulcrum point on the tool rest in three distinct movements, so upsetting the smooth manipulation of the tool – a bad feature.

Other rests consist of one plane surface inclined upwards at the front so that in use it causes the tool to behave in exactly the same way as that already described, only more so, because the width of the flat surface is so much greater. Again, a poor design.

Turners tend to have their own preferences in tool rests, as in bevel angles, but most appear to agree that a rounded edge over which the tool can roll is the best. So a rest with a straight or forward inclined front, with the top rounded down from a square edge, is the soundest choice.

If yours cannot be modified to this shape, I suggest you have your local garage workshop make one. With an oxy-acetylene cutting torch it is a relatively simple job to cut the blade of the tool rest from $2 \times \frac{3}{8}$in (5.08cm × 9.525mm) thick mild steel strip, and weld it to a bolt stud of the diameter of the tool rest holder. Once made, the top edge is easily ground or even filed to shape.

New chisels sometimes have quite sharp edges along their length, and as in paring cuts the chisel rests with one edge inclined into the tool rest, this sharpness prevents the free traverse of the tool, besides making nicks in the top of the rest. It is always advisable therefore to chamfer the corners along the length of new chisels with the grinder or oilstone before taking them into use.

The tool rest likewise should be checked from time to time, and the working surface smoothed off. Often when spindle turning it is a help just to rub a candle stub along the edge of the rest to ease the movement of the tool along it.

For long spindle work a wooden rest is the most practical answer, held on a spigot in the tool rest holder at one end, and clamped to the tailstock with an L-shaped bolt at the other. Being wood, it tends to take the impressions of tools used frequently in any one position, which can be an advantage in repetition work. In any case, the positions of various dimensional cuts are readily marked off along its length in pencil or chalk, and when the impressions along its edge are no longer needed, they are simply planed away.

You will find that the ordinarry tool rest has definite limitations when it comes to turning hollow ware, the tool having to be extended far beyond the tool rest as the hollowing out proceeds, so increasing vibration and loss of control at the cutting edge.

Those lathes designed with a faceplate turning set-up on the outside of the headstock are usually fitted with a swan-neck support for the tool rest, which projects the rest forward in bowl hollowing operations, but does nothing to solve the problems related to hollow ware such as jars, vases and containers being turned at the inside headstock position. My answer to this difficulty, which, I feel, is one the lathe manufacturers should have recognised and remedied long ago, is a simple welded angle iron rest used in combination with a modified scraper, which I describe in Chapter 15.

CHAPTER EIGHT

Marking Out and Setting Up: Spindle and Faceplate Work

Marking out the positions for the driving centre and dead centre in spindle turning, and for the faceplate or screw-chuck in faceplate work, may be done in several different ways according to choice or the initial shape of the work-piece.

SPINDLE TURNING – MARKING OUT

If the material is square in section, diagonals drawn across the ends from corner to corner will intersect at the centres. If, however, the workpiece is out of square, or irregular in shape, the dividers are set at roughly half its diameter, and with one leg held by the thumb against the edge, an arc is struck on the end face of the wood. This is repeated at various positions around the edge of the wood, making a series of arcs intersecting in the area of the centre, so that its exact position is readily seen. (A simple template made of plastic or celluloid is useful for finding the centres of irregular shaped pieces: see Chapter 15.)

If the material is already round, the centre can be gauged by eye, or the dividers used to mark.it, as described above.

SPINDLE TURNING – SETTING UP

Having marked the centres on the ends of the work, drill them to a depth of $\frac{3}{16}$in (4.765mm) with a small bradawl or $\frac{1}{8}$in (3.175mm) diameter drill. Now support the wood on the corner of the bench and drive the fork centre into the end with a wooden mallet. Never use a hammer for this: it will damage the centre and affect its fit in the headstock mandrel. A further word of caution: never drive the wood on to the driving centre whilst it is in the headstock; the headstock bearings are not designed to withstand that kind of abuse.

Now assemble the fork centre in the headstock mandrel, and set up the workpiece using the dead or revolving centre at the tailstock end. If the dead centre is used, give the hole in the wood a smear with candle wax beforehand.

Following this, clamp the tailstock, tighten the hand wheel until slight resistance is felt when the workpiece is rotated by hand, and clamp the tailstock centre.

Finally, adjust the tool rest to be just below the centre line of the work, and just to clear the workpiece when revolving it by hand. If the tool rest does not span the full length of the wood, set it in position to start at the tailstock end, and clamp it.

FACEPLATE TURNING – MARKING OUT

If the workpiece is square, diagonals drawn from corner to corner will intersect at the centre, but if the workpiece is irregular in shape, then proceed as for spindle turning. That is, set the dividers at roughly half the diameter, and with one leg held by the thumb against the edge of the wood, strike a series of arcs from different positions around it. These will intersect in the area of the centre, so that its true position can be easily determined.

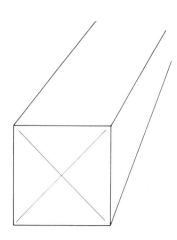

Spindle turning. Marking out diagonals using the rule and pencil

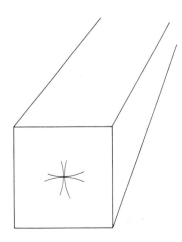

Spindle turning. Marking out arcs using dividers

Faceplate screwed to scribed circle on bowl

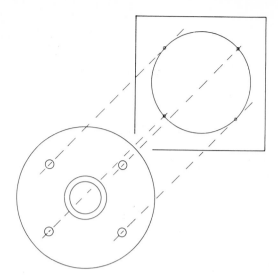

Diagram showing projection of faceplate screw holes on to the scribed circle of the workpiece

FACEPLATE TURNING – SETTING UP

Having marked the centre of the workpiece, strike with the dividers a circle of the same diameter as the position of the screw holes in the faceplate. Next, drill *one* hole on the circle for the first screw, and screw the workpiece to the faceplate. Now swing the faceplate on the screw until the marked circle is in position under the remaining screw holes of the faceplate. Mark their position on the circle, drill pilot holes and screw home the remaining screws.

The workpiece is now accurately centred and set up, ready for turning.

Starting Operations: Spindle Turning

Stance at lathe when roughing down with the gouge

Perhaps, before proceeding further, I should tell you there is one golden rule to observe in all spindle turning: when cutting a taper, always cut from the larger to the smaller diameter, or downhill. Imagine you are sharpening a pencil, and cut your taper in the same way. If you have any doubts, try it in the reverse direction, and see what happens!

But to continue. Start operations with a simple gouge and chisel exercise on a piece of 2–3in (5.08–7.62cm) diameter wood set up between the fork chuck and dead centre. Take care in centering the ends, drive the fork chuck in using a mallet on the bench, and wipe the dead centre hole with a stump of candle wax. The tailstock has been brought up with the dead centre wound well back to reduce vibration and, with the centre engaged in the hole, secured.

Any slack is now taken up on the hand wheel, the tension on the centre being tested by hand rotating the pulley or workpiece. It should not rotate freely, neither should it offer undue resistance to rotation by hand. After a few minutes' running, further slight tightening of the hand wheel may be necessary. Lastly, the tailstock centre is clamped, and then the tool rest adjusted.

The tool rest should be just clear of the widest part of the wood, and set at the dead centre end if too short to bridge the full length of the job. The quickest means of adjusting the distance of the tool rest from the wood is to push it into contact, and just ease it back until it no longer touches. It should be set at a height which allows the bevel of the gouge to rub with the tool held comfortably at the side – say a little below centre.

You will find with experience the most comfortable position to adopt, as so many variables are involved: the diameter of the work, your own height, the height of the lathe, angle of the tool bevel, even the shape of the tool rest. Perhaps a safe starting height for it would be a little below the centre line of the work.

THE GOUGE

Grasp the gouge firmly, but not tightly, by one hand at the end of the handle (as one may turn with equal facility left or right handed, no hard and fast rule is applied), and with the other grasp it, fingers over the top, thumb underneath, at a position where the meaty part of the hand and tool both rest on the tool rest, with the bevel of the gouge in contact with the wood.

Alternatively, the tool may be gripped by the fingers under and the thumb pressed into the groove of the blade, with the finger joints against the tool rest controlling the forward position of the tool. With experience you will find that this grip has more feel, and is especially suitable when only light cuts are being taken.

The body should be positioned so that the gouge is pointing obliquely in the direction of travel, with its shoulders tilted in the same direction.

Start the cut about 2in (5cm) from the tailstock end of the wood, and move in that direction. The tool is moved laterally along the tool rest, maintaining the angle which produces shavings, until the end of the cut is reached. It will be found that the gouge has a tendency to move of its own accord in the direction of cut, so apart from keeping the bevel rubbing, and maintaining the depth of cut, no real effort is required.

Returning to the point where the cut began, reverse the grip on the tool and direct it so that it is now pointed towards the headstock. With the gouge shoulders inclined in the same direction, and by bringing the bevel against the wood, ease the cutting edge down to produce shavings, and pare off towards the driving centre end. Try to keep an even projection of the tool with the control hand at the tool rest, with the tool's angle to the wood unchanged, so that the gouge removes shavings of uniform thickness, and the cylinder of wood remains of roughly parallel shape.

The gouge overgrip

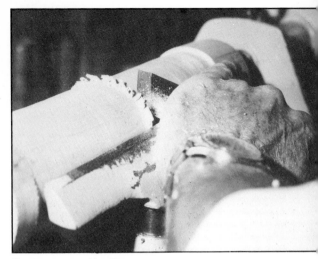

The skew corner raising fibres

The gouge undergrip

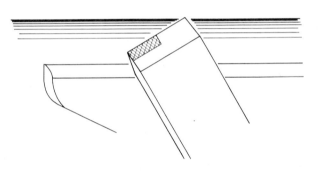

Diagram of skew showing correct cutting position. Note tool is tilted slightly on tool rest

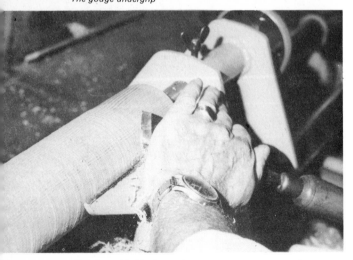

The skew chisel in the cutting position on wood

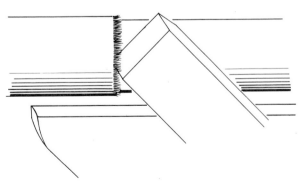

Diagram of skew corner raising fibres

The gouge may well leave a series of spiral grooves in the surface, deep or shallow according to the shape of the gouge and its smoothness of traverse along the wood, so these are removed, or planed off, by the following tool, the skew chisel.

THE SKEW CHISEL

As the name implies, the end of the skew chisel is angled, or skew, so that it can be held in the correct planing position without a change of stance for the operator. The long corner or point must be kept clear of contact with the wood in all planing cuts, otherwise a dig-in will result. The dig-in, a bogey haunting the pages of all woodturning manuals and, no doubt, the minds of most aspiring turners, is best understood if an actual dig-in is simulated with the help of a friend. With the motor switched off, adopt a normal skewing position on a cylinder of wood, and have a friend rotate the workpiece by hand. As the wood rotates, ease the chisel back, to allow the cutting area of the edge to move from the centre to the top of the blade. At the instant the point of the tool comes into contact with the revolving wood, it will dig-in. In this instance no harm will be done, but if the wood is flying round at say 2000 r.p.m. it will be a different story!

So, the correct planing position is obtained by pointing the tool, long corner to the top, obliquely in the direction of travel, having its bevel in contact with the wood surface, and using only that half of the cutting edge away from the point, i.e. the lower half.

The chisel is held in very much the same way as the gouge, and the cutting operation follows the same sequence, but to bring its bevel *and* cutting edge into contact the chisel must be tilted slightly on the tool rest.

By increasing the tilt of the tool a heavier cut results, and conversely, by reducing the tilt, the edge is eased out of the wood until finally the bevel only is rubbing. Should the tool be pushed too far up the face of the wood the cutting action will move down the lower half of the edge to the corner, and a build up of uncut fibres will follow. This is then remedied by drawing the tool back slightly, or reversing its direction of travel, so that the fringe of fibres is planed off and the smoothing of the surface completed.

The aim should be to have not only a smooth surface, which a sharp skew will always produce, but an even cut ensuring a uniform cylinder of wood. To achieve this, several passes along the high spots may be necessary, but be careful not to reduce the diameter below the required size.

The skew corner away from the point can be very useful too of course, as when cutting up to a shoulder. The corner would normally strike it before the cutting action of the lower half of the edge had reached it, so in this case the chisel is tilted slightly and moved up the face of the wood, to bring the corner into action, and the cut thereby taken all the way. This in turn may raise a feather of fibres at the shoulder, so a light parting cut is made at its base to sever them.

The corner of the skew is also used in turning over the end of a handle or in similar rounding operations. The bevel is kept rubbing, and the tool rotated to follow the desired degree of curve, the handle being raised and swung in towards the centre of the body as the cut progresses. It is also useful in removing spirals or ribbing formed by vibration in light spindle work.

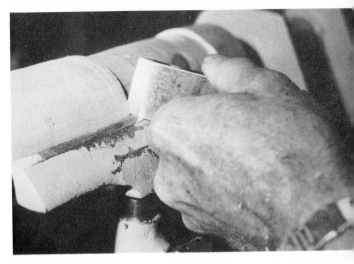

The skew chisel cutting in at the shoulder to remove fibres

Diagram of skew cutting in at the shoulder to remove fibres

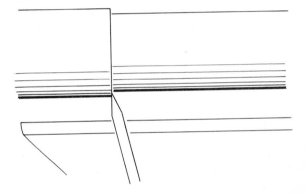

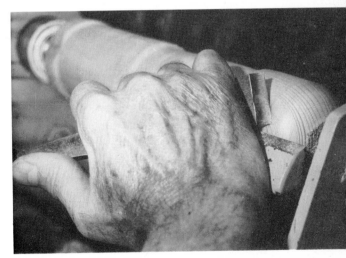

The skew chisel rounding the end of a cylinder. Note that the corner only is cutting

If the problem of handling the skew appears insurmountable (and I assure you it isn't!) a newly introduced tool called the Buckingham Skew will provide an easy solution. It is designed to lie flat on the tool rest whilst the cutting edge and bevel set diagonally across the end of the tool engage the wood. This ensures that the tool is fully supported by the rest and any tendency for the skew to dig-in is eliminated. By virtue of its design the tool can cut in one direction only, so if you wish to cut in both directions, as I hope you will, both left and right hand models are available.

RIBBING: ITS CAUSES AND REMEDIES

Ribbing can in fact be quite a problem, and may be due to a variety of causes. It occurs only in spindle turning, usually on small diameter work, so I will digress a little here and consider its possible causes and remedies.

If the tailstock centre is too tight it tends to bow the wood, so causing it to spring under the tool, in which case the centre is adjusted to be just tight and no more. Any slackness in the headstock bearing, or other loose parts such as the bolts securing the lathe to the bench, or a springy floor, can transmit vibrations, and should be checked.

Harder areas of wood, such as heart and sap wood in the same piece, tend, because of the unbalanced weight, not only to set up vibrations, but to bounce the tool, and ribbing sometimes results from this. It can even be that you have failed to clamp the tailstock centre, so that it holds the wood, but the poppet in which it is fixed is vibrating in the tailstock.

Various means are used to dampen vibration: a leather pad on the hand was often used in the old days, and several patterns of steadies have been devised, more recently in metal by lathe makers, but they all have some shortcomings. The metal ones tend to mark the wood, and even the wooden ones will scorch it if care isn't taken and wax or other lubricant applied at the point of contact.

In using the corner of the skew chisel to remove ribbing, the tool is gripped in its bevel rubbing position, with the fingers encircling the work and the thumb on top of the chisel, the hand thereby damping down the vibration whilst the tool rest and the other hand combine in controlling the movement of the tool. Only slight pressure of the encircling hand is needed, whilst the chisel corner undercuts the humps and levels out the hollows. Should this means fail, a narrow mouth gouge with its different cutting action may do the trick, but in the last resort garnet paper may have to be used.

The skew again comes into play when squaring off the ends of spindle work, or chamfering a corner or rounding a bead; whatever it is, the cardinal rule remains the same: the bevel rubbing and only the corner cutting. In squaring off ends the corner of the chisel is to the top and inclined slightly away from the surface, with the long point cutting whilst its bevel bears against the wood.

The same rule also applies in rounding beads. The point *or* corner of the skew chisel may be used, the sole criterion being that the cut must be made by the tip of the blade only, with the bevel bearing against the wood throughout the movement.

There are other uses for the long point too. It is used most often for marking out positions for sizing cuts for the parting tool; for forming a shoulder in spindle or faceplate work against which a gouge bevel may bear for its initial cut; cutting in rebates, or levelling side walls in hollowing out jars, etc., on the faceplate, this being done by a straight-in

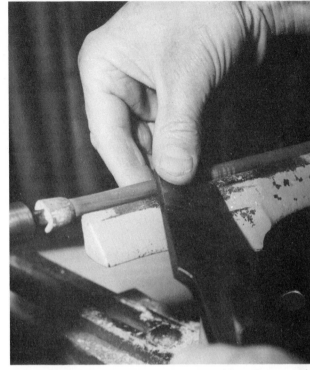

Supporting small diameter work with fingers around the workpiece

Supporting small diameter work by means of a steady clamped to the bench

scraping action, the point scraping whilst the side of the chisel aligns it against the side of the hole.

But to get back to the turning exercise. If the cylinder of wood is to be a certain diameter, or maybe have several different diameters along its length, proceed as follows.

LAYING OFF DIAMETERS

With the tool rest set a little below centre height, square up the tailstock end by making an incision about $\frac{1}{32}$in (0.794mm) from the edge and forming this into a shoulder by lightly scraping a step to the waste side of the cut. With the skew chisel held point down, bring its bevel against the shoulder thus formed on the end of the wood, with the bevel, *not* the tool, being aligned at right angles to the axis of the lathe.

Next, tilt the trailing edge, that is, the side opposite the cutting edge, slightly away from the wood's surface, but keeping the bevel and cutting edge against the shoulder. Now push the chisel in, maintaining the squareness of the cut across the end, whilst lifting the handle of the tool to bring its cutting edge arcing down to the centre.

In end squaring cuts it is preferable to use a conical rather than a ring centre. The tool can cut right across the whole end of the wood if a conical centre is used, whereas the ring centre encloses a small circle of wood which remains uncut, and must be removed later.

Having trued up the end, it can now be used as a datum or base line from which to span distances along the workpiece. So, set the dividers at the measurement to be laid off, if that is within the scope of the dividers in use, usually 6in (15.24cm), and with one leg hooked against the end of the wood, and the other supported on the tool rest with the point trailing slightly downwards, make a mark on the revolving wood. All subsequent measurements are taken from the same base line, the end of the workpiece, and *not* from the last line drawn. If this is not done, an accumulative error may result which could mean spoilt work, lost time and a waste of valuable wood.

An alternative to using dividers is to use a steel ribbon rule, engaging its hook on the end of the stationary work, and marking off the distances with pencil. Having done this, the pencil is held firmly against the mark, the lathe switched on and, presto, a circle is drawn.

PARTING DOWN

Once the workpiece is marked out, the next step is to part down at the various markings to the diameters required. These would be set down in a sketch or drawing for easy reference, otherwise a rash of pencilled rings on the workpiece could create some confusion and lead to mistakes being made.

If is is intended to make a number of identical articles, then a template of ply or hardboard is recommended. This could have a straight edge with lines at the points where dimensional cuts are to be made, each line being marked with its dimension, and the edge nicked to control the pencil, or sharpened brads set in the edge of the template could be used to transfer scratched markings to the wood, the template being marked at each brad with the dimension cut at that point. Alternatively, the template may be profiled as a female counterpart of the intended shape of the spindle.

There is also, currently available, a sizing tool which may be found very useful. This is a semi-circular fitting secured by two thumb screws to the end of a standard parting tool. The unattached end projects forward, and the distance between the cutting edge and the inside face of the sizing tool is adjusted to the diameter required. In use the sizing arm is rested on the top of the work, and the tool handle gently raised until the cut begins. By continued raising of

Marking off a workpiece using dividers. Note the slight downward tilt of the tool

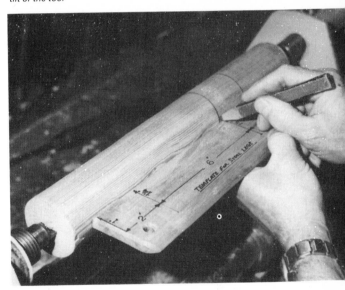

Marking off a workpiece using pencil and template

the handle the cut deepens until the sizing arm clears the wood and the job is done.

When a number of chair legs, banisters or items of identical design have to be made, a recently introduced copying attachment can prove of great help. It consists of a shaft carrying six or more adjustable sleeves to which are pivoted short arms or fingers. This assembly is set up at centre height behind the lathe, and a sample of the article to be copied is accurately centred and mounted in the lathe. The arms are next moved to align with the salient features of the design – maximum and minimum diameters, beads, coves, etc. – and adjusted so that they just touch the pattern and fall clear. The sample is rotated by hand a few times to ensure that the arms are correctly adjusted, and then removed from the lathe. The workpiece, having been previously rough turned, is set up, and the arms swung over to rest on the top of the wood. From there on, the wood is reduced with gouge and skew at each salient point, allowing the arms to drop clear as the profile of the workpiece emerges.

The parting down would be done with the narrow ended chisel or parting tool, making a groove sufficiently wide for the free entry of callipers ready set at the desired diameter plus $\frac{1}{32}$in (0.794mm), or $\frac{1}{16}$in (1.58mm) if you are not too confident, for finishing off later.

As the groove approaches finished size, the tool is held in position with the hand and forearm, and the callipers eased gently into the groove with the other hand, until the reducing diameter of the revolving wood permits their passage over the work. The callipers are used cautiously because cross fibres of wood in the groove may catch the tip of a leg and jerk them out of the hand. Should this happen, recheck their setting before using them again.

When parting down to expose a shoulder or other projection, allowance must be made for cleaning up the sides of it. This is because the parting tool initially enters the wood with a straight in scraping action, after which the tool handle is dropped sufficiently to bring the bevel to bear against the wood. However, the sides of the cut it makes are usually ragged to a greater or lesser degree, depending on the denseness of the wood, speed of the lathe, the sharpness of the tool and the amount of pressure applied, so some allowance of extra wood must be made for shearing off with the ragged fibres in a later slicing cut.

In this connection, a newly introduced parting tool of improved design largely overcomes the problem of roughness caused by the tearing of the wood fibres on the sides of the kerf. The new tool is grooved along one side, with a bevel of approximately 60° across the end. In use, it is brought to bear with the bevel uppermost, so that the projecting horns of the groove slice the fibres of the wood before the waste is lifted out. This ensures a clean cut requiring very little after treatment from the skew.

HOLLOWS AND CURVES

Some of the markings may be setting the positions for hollows (sometimes called coves) or curves, such as in a baluster or ornamental chair leg, in which case, if only shallow hollows are required, a sizing cut would not be needed. A shallow curve is usually shaped down from a large to a small diameter with a $\frac{5}{8}$in (15.875mm) or $\frac{3}{4}$in (19.05mm) square end shallow curve gouge, and then planed smooth with the 1$\frac{1}{2}$in (3.81cm) skew chisel.

Any tendency for the back edge of the bevel to bear into and leave a score mark on the wood can be obviated by swinging the tool handle closer to the work, so bringing the cutting edge more at right angles with the direction of travel, and by moving it up on the wood. By this means the offending part of the bevel is moved out of contact, a remedy less drastic than grinding away part of the bevel, as recommended in some manuals.

If preferred, and the curve is a shallow one, the skew chisel can be used for the entire paring down operation.

When a hollow is to be made, the lateral limits, having been laid out with the dividers or pencil, may be cut in with the skew chisel. Not deeply though. The intention is to form a small shoulder against which the bevel of the long nose gouge may bear as it starts cutting. If too deep a cut is made

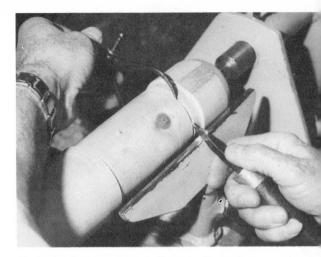
Parting in using spearpoint and callipers simultaneously

Shaping a curve using the $\frac{5}{8}$in (15.875mm) shallow gouge. Note the thumb assisting in control of the tool

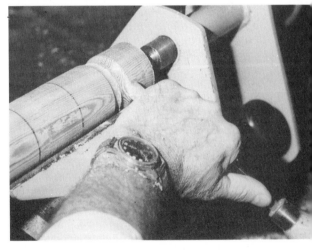
Shaping a hollow using the long nose gouge

with the skew, it means that the hollow will have to start at the bottom of these cuts, so it would have straight sides before the commencement of the curve.

As you acquire more skill with practice you will be able to make the first cut with the long nose without a preliminary skew cut. This is done by simulating with the gouge the angle at which the chisel is presented to the wood. The centre of the gouge cutting edge is brought to the wood in a vertical position, so causing the wood to bear with equal pressure on both sides of the blade. Thus there is no tendency for the tool to run in either direction. The slightest tilting of the edge to right or left would result, however, in the immediate movement of the cutting edge across the work, unless very firm control was maintained.

In turning a hollow the cut is started with the gouge on its side, handle to the left if starting the right hand side of the hollow first, and the bevel against the slight shoulder already prepared. By simultaneously raising the handle, moving it to the right and rotating it clockwise, the gouge slices a curving cut into the wood, so that when the bottom of the hollow is reached, the gouge is lying squarely on its back. The other side of the hollow is turned in the same way, care being taken not to run beyond the centre of the bottom. No attempt should be made to go beyond the centre as the cardinal rule always to cut downhill, or from larger to smaller diameter, still applies.

The depth and degree of curvature of the hollow are controlled entirely by how much the handle is raised and the gouge is twisted, and how well co-ordinated these movements are. Only experience will bring complete success, but provided the bevel and edge are always in contact, a hollow must result.

Any roughness at the bottom is smoothed out by careful gouge work, lying on its back with the bevel well up on the wood, and gently eased back until feathers of shavings appear, the gouge meanwhile being swung the smallest bit across the bottom of the hollow.

BEADS AND BALLS

Beads, or raised bands with rounded tops, often form part of the ornamentation on stool legs, banisters, chair rails, etc., usually in association with hollows and curves, so I will include them in this exercise.

The width of the bead is incised with the skew chisel, and the wood on either side reduced or V-cut until the resulting collar is the height required for the bead. A pencil is then held against the revolving wood at the centre of the collar, to guide in removing an equal amount of wood from either side in forming the bead. The corners of the collar may now be rounded down with either a gouge or skew chisel, according to the size of bead wanted.

For small beads the skew chisel is usually used, being presented with its corner a little to the left of the centre line for turning the left hand side of the bead, the handle angled slightly to the right, and the bevel rubbing. Now, by tilting the chisel a little on its left edge the corner is brought to the cutting position, and the handle is at the same time swung up and to the left, whilst the tool is simultaneously rotated anti-clockwise. If the first pass doesn't finish the curve down to the bottom, because the chisel wasn't swung upwards to the left enough, a second pass, starting at the point where the curve ran out, with the handle held a little more to the left, and the upward swing and rotary movement repeated as before, will complete the left side of the bead. The right

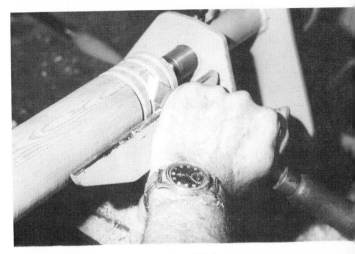

Preparing a bead. Cutting in with the skew chisel

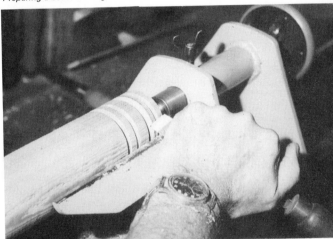

Shaping the bead down with the long point of the skew

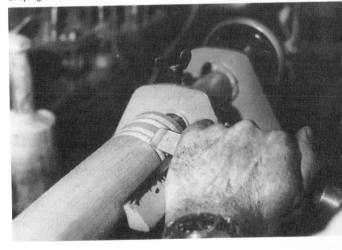

Finishing the bead with the long point of the skew

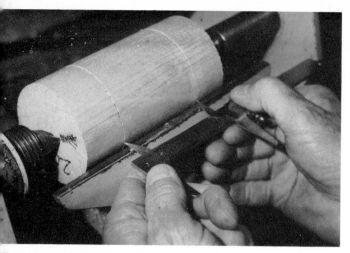

Laying off the diameter for a large ball, using a vernier calliper. Note the pencil mark on wood alongside the master fang of the driving centre

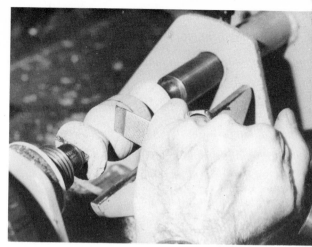

First cuts on a small ball using the ¾in (19.05mm) skew chisel. Note the tool rest too far from the wood

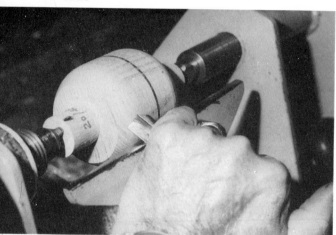

Shaping the ball, making first cuts with the ¾in (19.05mm) square end gouge

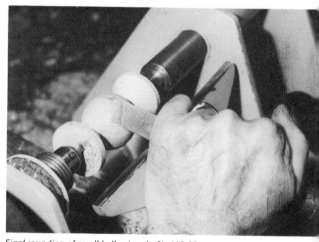

Final rounding of small ball using the ¾in (19.05mm) skew. Note vestiges of file teeth and hollow ground edge

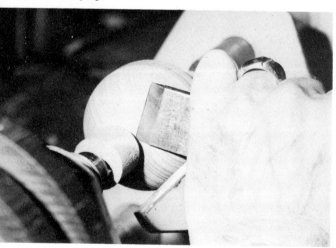

Finishing the ball using the skew chisel

hand side is shaped by using exactly the same movements reversed, care being taken to balance the curves.

The combination of movements just described maintains the bevel in contact with the wood, whilst only the corner is cutting. The instant the cutting action moves from the corner to the edge of the blade, it will climb back over the bead, incising a spiral which may well spoil it. Please don't let this warning deter you from practising beads at every opportunity. To cut a well rounded bead in two sweeps of the chisel is a very rewarding experience!

For shaping large beads or spherical forms including balls, the ⅜in (9.525mm) long nose gouge is usually used, whilst the ½in (12.7mm) square across gouge would be handier for balls say from golf to tennis ball size. Generally speaking, the larger the diameter in spindle work, the larger the gouge.

In turning balls, especially large ones, which have to *be* round before they *look* round, the cylindrical workpiece is marked off at two points equal to its diameter. The wood on either side is then reduced, so exposing a block of length equal to its thickness.

After that a pencil line is run around the centre of the block to assist in a balanced removal of the waste in forming curves.

The tool rest is at a comfortable height and just close enough to the workpiece not to impede the swing of the gouge, which is lying on its back with the bevel resting on the pencil line. The handle is then swung up and to the left, pivoting on the centre of the tool rest, whilst the tool is rotated anti-clockwise as it turns the left hand side of the ball. A fair amount of the wood has to be cut away, so three or four passes will probably be necessary for rounding each side, the right hand side being turned in exactly the same way except that of course the movements are reversed.

For in-between balls, say golf ball size, the ½in (12.7mm) square ended or ¾in(19.05mm) skew chisel is ideal. The dimensions having been marked out as described earlier and the workpiece parted down on either side, the chisel is laid flat on the rest with its bevel resting on top of the wood. A cut to the left is then started by tilting the corner slightly, simultaneously swinging the handle up and to the left as the tool is rotated in the direction of cut.

The corner of the chisel only is cutting, and the bevel is kept rubbing all the way. The degree of curvature is controlled by the amount of swing, lift and rotation of the tool, and as professional turners prefer not to make balls, you will not be too disappointed if your first efforts are not perfect spheres!

Any unevenness in the surface is taken out using the 1½in (3.81cm) skew chisel, very sharp, rested flat on the tool rest parallel with the bench top, and swung in a very light scraper action around the curve, the lathe speed being increased to suit. Such roughness as remains is then sanded away.

If circumstances demand it, a tool can easily be made from metal pipe which will simplify rounding balls, but it is not, strictly speaking, turning. (See Chapter 15). For parting off and final rounding of balls, which can best be done with the help of adaptors, see the section in the same chapter on centres for supporting balls during finishing operations.

CHAPTER TEN

Starting Operations: Faceplate Turning

Having dealt with the tools and techniques most used in spindle turning operations, I can go on to the more difficult, but in many ways more challenging and satisfying techniques of faceplate turning.

SETTING UP A BOWL

Let us suppose your first job is to be a bowl of 6in (15.24cm) diameter, 3–4in (7.62–10.16cm) deep. As it is the first attempt, use wood of average quality, because there is the possibility that however carefully you follow the instructions, the finished article will not come up to expectations. But don't let this prospect worry you. With the true artist, things never quite come up to expectations, which is why he goes on striving for perfection. And may it always be so.

A piece of offcut from a local builder will suit the purpose admirably, provided it has no knots or shakes, and is reasonably hard. Before it is set up, any projecting corners likely to unbalance the block and cause vibration are sawn off, bringing it to a roughly round shape, and as the first task is to turn the workpiece to a true disc, the lathe is set at a relatively low speed, say 500–750 r.p.m., for remember that the rule is, the larger the diameter, the lower the speed.

Mark out and set up the workpiece on the faceplate as described in Chapter 8, screw it to the headstock mandrel, and bring the tool rest into position. It should be slightly below the centre, and as close as possible to the edge of the wood. Now clamp up, and rotate the faceplate by hand to check that nothing is fouling. It sometimes happens that although the tool rest is clear of the wood, the saddle – where fitted – carrying the tool rest holder, is positioned too far forward, and a projecting corner of the workpiece strikes it. Or again, the wood is off centre so that the tool rest clears it in one position, but fouls it in another. It should therefore become normal routine always to rotate the job by hand, both in faceplate and spindle turning, after adjusting the tool rest, just to be sure.

THE GOUGE

Having assured yourself on these points stand in a comfortable position, square to the work, with the gouge, a ⅜in (9.525mm) square end, resting on the tool rest, the handle held low against the outside of the thigh by one hand, and the blade gripped fingers over the top with the thumb underneath, by the other. The meaty part of the hand should be resting on the tool rest, so that every movement of the cutting edge is fully controlled.

Withdraw the tool from contact with the wood, switch on, and advance the tool to make contact again with the lower edge of its bevel, i.e. not the cutting edge, at the centre of the workpiece. Now slightly lower the nose of the tool, still keeping the bevel rubbing, until shavings appear. At the same time rotate the tool on its side and incline it in

the direction of travel towards the edge of the disc, sliding it in an easy controlled movement across the face of the wood. It will be found that the tool moves towards the edge of the work of its own accord and control of its traverse is quite simple. For a heavier cut raise the handle a little, and for a lighter one, lower it.

Repeat the operation in alternate directions across the wood until a true cylinder is formed. When the disc is in balance, switch off, swing the tool rest round to the front of the workpiece, set close in as a fraction below centre height, and clamp up. Thereafter follow exactly the procedure as for the edge of the disc, but cutting from the centre to the edge only, and level off the face.

The reason the cut is started at the centre of the block is to allow for the possibility that the wood is of uneven thickness. At the centre there would be no undulation of the face of the disc, but towards the edge, where the peripheral speed is high, any undulation of the surface could cause the gouge to take an unexpectedly heavy cut on first contact.

METHODS OF CHUCKING

Having squared the face of the block, there is now the choice of shaping the outside and hollowing out the inside without removing it from the faceplate (it is taken for granted that the diameter of the faceplate is smaller than the intended diameter of the base of the bowl), or merely calling the fresh squared face the bottom, rounding the sides, and reversing the block to hollow out the inside.

The first choice has the obvious advantage of being quicker, and ensuring that the inside and outside surfaces would be turned concentrically with each other. Also, having decided to plane the base flat before mounting the block, it should require no finishing off apart from stopping the screw holes, that is, if you don't mind stopping screw holes and hiding them with baize. It also means that the bowl will have a plain, flat bottom with no recessing at the centre to give it more stability, just one more feature I don't much care for.

My preference then is for the second method, and as I use a screwchuck for the remounting, and cap its hole in the base of the bowl with an ornamental plug (all of which are described later in this chapter), I am not hampered by the normal procedures associated with remounting the workpiece by means of wood screws.

SHAPING THE OUTSIDE

Turn a 2in (5.08cm) wide by ⅛in (3.175mm) deep recess in what will now be its base, and surrounding this leave a raised rim 1in (25.4mm) wide and ¼in (6.35mm) high at its outer edge. As you are removing such a small amount of wood in forming the recess, a square end scraper supported

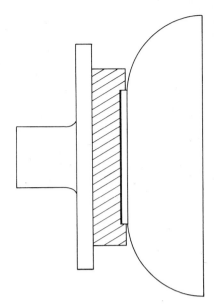

Shaping the rim on the base of the bowl for seating in scrap wood chuck. Note the top bevel of the tool at right angles to the wood

Section diagram of bowl in chuck, showing paper insert

close in by the tool rest, and presented squarely to the wood and parallel to the bench top, will do quite well.

This operation may be disapproved of in some quarters, as most manuals insist that the scraper be held in a trailing position, that is, inclined downwards at the cutting edge, to avoid a dig-in. In fact, the tool will risk digging in only if it is pointed upwards. Presented perfectly horizontally to the wood there is absolutely no chance of it doing so. Furthermore, by trailing the cutting edge downwards for safety's sake, it no longer contacts the wood at its most effective cutting angle, that is with the top surface of the scraper at 90° to the wood's surface. I can only suppose that the experts are so anxious to ensure the beginner doesn't point his scraper upwards that they advise him to point it downwards just to make sure, or perhaps it is because they advocate a scraper freshly ground with a burr at its edge which would cut best if inclined downwards?

Having cut the recess, reset the tool rest towards the edge of the base, and using a ⅜in (9.525mm) long and strong gouge or the nearest equivalent you have, commence rounding the corner of the bottom. The gouge should rest squarely on its back at the start of operations, with the bevel rubbing, and the tool rest angled slightly across the corner. Once the gouge comes into action it is rolled on its side and its handle swung outwards to set the arc of the curve right up to the top of the bowl. As the work progresses, the tool rest is repositioned from time to time to support the gouge as near as possible to the surface of the wood.

There will most likely be two rough areas where the tool has cut across the end grain, and perhaps a groove or two from the gouge. In fact, end grain can be particularly difficult to clean up in certain woods, and some turners attempt it by reversing the rotation of the lathe. This enables the fibres to be tackled from either direction, and greatly facilitates their removal. There is, however, one very serious disadvantage and possible danger involved in this method. The counter rotation of the headstock mandrel tends to unscrew the faceplate, so some precaution, such as a lock

washer behind it, has to be adopted for safety's sake. A less drastic and often quite effective way is to brush sealer thoroughly into the fibres and, when they are dry, to sand the then rigid fibres away.

Following the gouge work comes the round nose scraper, very sharp, to take care of the cross grain, whilst the corner where the side meets the base is cut in with the skew chisel, or scraped smooth with a sharp square ended scraper applied very lightly.

Before the bowl is removed from the lathe, the grain would be raised, sanded down and a stain, lacquer or carnauba wax finish applied as desired. (See Chapter 17.)

With the outside finished, the bowl is removed from the faceplate, in readiness for reassembly reverse way round for the hollowing out operation.

RECHUCKING FOR HOLLOWING OUT

The centering and remounting of the bowl must be very carefully done, otherwise the wall thickness will vary and the whole appearance of the bowl be spoilt. So secure the base of the bowl to the faceplate by means of a scrap wood chuck, thereby dispensing with the need to plug screw holes and hide them with baize.

The piece of scrap wood, large enough to take the base of the bowl, is screwed to the faceplate, its surface levelled with the gouge, and a ¼in (6.35mm) deep recess stepped in with the square ended scraper to make a snug fit on the base of the bowl. A piece of thick paper is now cut to the size of the recess in the chuck, coated on both sides with water soluble glue to just short of the outer edge of the paper (to prevent wood-to-wood adhesion at the side of the rim), and placed in the recess. The base of the bowl is next inserted and forced home by pressure of the tailstock mandrel, and the whole left to dry for 48 hours.

After this time, the paper will form a strong enough anchor to hold the bowl during the hollowing out process, but will permit the surfaces to be prised apart with a screw-driver when ready. To assist in this, a few slots cut through the side of the scrap chuck recess before glueing up, wide enough to pass the end of a screwdriver through, are an advantage. Alternatively, the workpiece is held in the hands and the chuck given several sharp blows on the edge of the bench.

Once the bowl is remounted, drill a ¼in (6.35mm) diameter hole at its centre to within ⅝in (15.875mm) of the bottom, thus making a simple but positive guide to the depth of hollow required. The next step is to form a shoulder with the skew chisel at ½in (12.7mm) to ⅝in (15.875mm) from the edge, against which the bevel of the ⅜in (9.525mm) long and strong or similar gouge can bear at the initial cut in.

The tool rest is adjusted to allow the gouge free movement across the face of the block, and as the cut progresses around the inside curvature, the tool rest is slewed round to keep it as near as possible to the face of the work. The gouge, bevel rubbing, is angled slightly in the direction of movement, and is rotated a little on its side, leading shoulder towards the wood.

A square end gouge is used for inside bowl work, so that all parts of its edge except the trailing point can be brought into use, whereas a long nose gouge, because its corners are rounded off, could use the centre of its edge only. This limits its effectiveness, so it is not recommended for bowl turning. The ⅜in (9.525mm) long and strong or its nearest available equivalent is preferred because it is robust enough to withstand the strain of cutting whilst projected well beyond the tool rest; its narrow deep section enables heavy cuts to be made, the shavings being thick but narrow, so offering less resistance to the tool and, for the same reason, generating less vibration.

During the past two or three years several very ingenious heavy duty chucks have been brought into use, obviating the need of screws, glue, etc. These have been designed primarily for the rapid mounting of blanks for bowl turning, although by using lathe turned adapters and similar simple

Hollowing a bowl with ⅜in (9.525mm) long and strong gouge. Note the peak of uncut wood at the centre of the bowl

fittings some can be readily adapted to spindle work or any chucking requirement.

One principle of operation is to expand segments of metal into a prepared undercut recess in the wood by tightening an outer screwed ring, or nuts set at the back of the chuck. Another method is by contracting a coil spring set in the face of the chuck on to a flange ready prepared on the workpiece, again by means of a screwed ring on the body of the chuck.

All these chucks have a positive self-centering action, support with safety maximum size blanks, and can be supplied to fit most lathes currently manufactured.

As the bulk of the waste wood is removed, the gouge moves further and further over the front of the tool rest, so that, because the bevel must be kept rubbing the wood, a conical shaped peak of uncut waste remains at the bottom of the bowl. This is dealt with by swinging the gouge handle horizontally out to the side and, with its bevel rubbing, by a series of passes across the top of the peak, cutting it clean away.

When the gouge work is finished, the surface may be rough in two areas where the end grain lies, but if the tool has been kept sharp, and the last cuts have been light ones, the roughness should be almost eliminated in cleaning up with the scraper. Certainly, the final grain raising and sanding will dispose of it.

BOWLS – ALTERNATIVE METHODS OF CHUCKING

Now to consider some alternative ways of chucking bowls. Having described one way of mounting the workpiece, which dispenses with the need to plug and hide screw holes in the base of the bowl, but entails remounting to hollow out the inside, let us consider some others.

A method not often used, because it restricts the choice of shape for the bowl, is to turn a short parallel section inside the lip of it. It can then be reversed as a drive fit on to a waste wood chuck to receive it, and the shaping of the outside completed. The mounting is extremely firm, as the pressure of the gouge in shaping the outside tends to force the bowl harder on to the chuck. A step must be formed on the chuck to control the depth of entry, and no excessive force used in mounting the workpiece, otherwise splitting may result when the wall thickness is approaching finished size.

The following method of mounting the block for turning both outside and inside without removal from the faceplate is used when the faceplate diameter is larger than the intended diameter of the base of the bowl.

First mount a piece of waste wood of say 1in (25.4mm) thickness on the faceplate, of larger size than the intended base of the bowl, using the outer ring of screw holes, and true its face. Now spot the centre of the wood in the lathe, and drive in a brad leaving the head protruding about ⅛in (3.175mm). Snip the head off and file the stump to a point. Remove the faceplate from the lathe, and drill right through the waste wood from behind, using the inner ring of screw holes. Now plane one face of the workpiece smooth and flat – especially flat – and carefully mark its centre with the centre punch.

The workpiece is now placed, centre punch mark upwards, on the bench, and the point of the brad married with the impression. When the block and waste wood chuck are accurately centered, long screws are passed through the prepared holes in the chuck, and driven into the back of

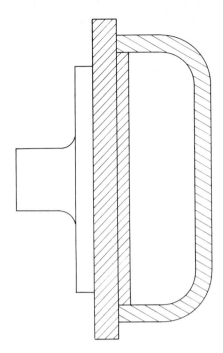

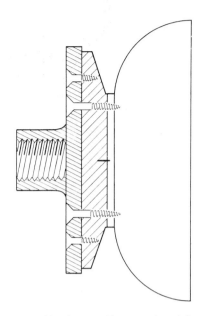

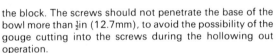

Section diagram of bowl mounted by the pressure of its lip on a waste wood chuck

Section diagram of bowl mounted by screws through faceplate and waste wood chuck

the block. The screws should not penetrate the base of the bowl more than $\frac{1}{2}$in (12.7mm), to avoid the possibility of the gouge cutting into the screws during the hollowing out operation.

This in fact is an aspect of faceplate *and* screwchuck work which should always be borne in mind: how far into the wood have the screws penetrated, and how deep can I go without fear of hitting them? The answer is to make a point of noting the length of that part of the screw which will enter the workpiece, and allowing at least $\frac{1}{8}$in (3.175mm) of clear wood between tool and screw tip in hollowing out.

CONCEALING SCREW HOLES

Having set up our bowl on the lathe, we can shape it down on the outside into the waste wood, and hollow it out, without it being removed from the faceplate. When it is finally finished and unscrewed, the holes are plugged with small dowels turned or filed to size, or stopped with filler, and the bottom covered with a glued on disc of felt, baize or leather.

The stopping is easily made by catching wood dust from sanding down on a sheet of paper placed under the work, and mixing it with glue to a paste consistency. But one word of warning. If you are using one of the popular press pack PVA type adhesives, add dust to the glue, and not vice versa. Otherwise the bellows action of the press pack will blow the dust from your mixing board long before the glue reaches it!

The shaping of the material to cover the bottom can be done in several different ways, although I must confess I use only one on the few occasions I do have screw holes to hide.

One method advocated is to place the material over the bottom of the bowl, and to run a pencil or chalk around the

Baize, sandwiched between discs, being cut by a skew chisel

edge to mark the size. The material is then cut free hand with scissors. Alternatively, the material is cut oversize and glued on. When dry the surplus is trimmed off, again with scissors. Well, these methods may be adequate, but they don't strike me as being particularly precise. I am working for perfection, not production, so I can afford the extra time and effort needed for really high class work. This, then, is how I prepare my material to ensure it is an exact fit on the bowl, and has a perfect, clean cut edge.

First mount on the faceplate a piece of waste wood larger than the diameter of the base, and face it flat and true. Now screw to it by one centre screw a piece of $\frac{3}{8}$in (9.525mm) ply or hardboard from which a disc of the exact size of the base of the bowl is cut, using the skew chisel to ensure a clean, smooth edge is obtained. Overcome any tendency for the workpiece to rotate on the screw by interposing a piece of double sided abrasive paper, cut to a disc of smaller size than the bowl bottom, to avoid damage to the point of the tool.

Now unscrew the ply or hardboard disc, interpose between it and the waste wood on the faceplate a square of the material selected, and bring the tailstock up until the dead centre engages in the hole in the disc. Clamp the tailstock, and tighten up the hand wheel to sandwich the material firmly between the waste wood and the disc.

Using a freshly sharpened skew chisel presented over the tool rest at the edge of the disc, and with increased speed on the lathe, cut the covering for the bottom of the bowl cleanly to exactly the right size. If it should be necessary, the double sided disc of abrasive paper can again be used to prevent any tendency for the material to slip.

When the faceplate is smaller in diameter than the proposed base of the bowl, it can be screwed directly to the wood without a waste wood spacer, and the bowl turned as described at the beginning of this chapter.

In this case one face of the block is planed off, centered, and on it a circle struck of slightly larger diameter than the faceplate. This can then be accurately located within the circle, and screwed on, so ensuring that the block is mounted centrally on the faceplate, ready for complete outside and inside turning.

A last method, and the one I have always used, improved by the refinements described in Chapter 16, is to reverse the bowl on to the screwchuck for hollowing out. This dispenses with the glued paper chuck, and the three hole faceplate, so eliminating the messy job of removing the glued paper from the base of the bowl, or the tedious – and to my mind unprofessional – chore of plugging screw holes and concealing them under a glued on disc of cloth or leather.

So proceed as follows. Centre one face of the block and secure it by screws to the faceplate; these screw holes will be removed during the later hollowing out routine.

Shape the outside and bottom of the bowl as previously described, and recess the centre of the base to a depth of $\frac{1}{8}$in (3.175mm), the recess being the same diameter as the face of the screwchuck. Use the square ended scraper for this, ensuring that the recess is flat bottomed, will allow snug entry of the face of the screwchuck, and has a small chamfer at its edge to facilitate connection.

At the centre of the recess drive a $\frac{1}{8}$in (3.175mm) hole to a depth of $\frac{3}{8}$in (9.525mm), and countersink its opening very slightly. This hole is for the screwchuck screw, and the countersink is to accommodate any lifting of the wood when the screw is driven home, which could otherwise unbalance the perfect seating of the screwchuck in the recess.

Recessing the base of the bowl for reversing on to the screwchuck

Ornamental plug being fitted to screw hole in concave base of dish, with spare plugs in foreground

Mounted in this way, the bowl will be accurately centered, and perfectly stable for normal hollowing out operations with gouge and scraper. To impart additional thrust to the block, and to reduce torsional strain on the screw, a disc of double sided abrasive paper is inserted between the chuck and the wood, whilst the rim of the recess resists the side pressure of the tool.

The screw should be no longer than $\frac{1}{2}$in (12.7mm), stout in diameter, and have a well defined thread. In fact, I always run a rat-tail file around the grooves of the thread of my screwchucks to increase the depth of thread and so give it more bite into the wood.

After the hollowing out is done, and the inside finished off, there remains only one screw hole to plug. I close this with a small mushroom shaped cap, with a head of $\frac{1}{4}$in (6.35mm) to $\frac{3}{8}$in (9.525mm) diameter by $\frac{1}{16}$in (1.587mm) thick, on a stem of $\frac{1}{8}$in (3.175mm) diameter by $\frac{1}{4}$in (6.35mm) long, usually made from boxwood, which I seal and polish before glueing into the base of the bowl. To my mind the yellow boxwood set against a dark walnut or mahogany background emphasises yet again the natural beauty of wood, inspiring the true craftsman to renewed effort in his search for perfection.

The plugs are made in batches of a dozen or so at a time, and are made in their entirety with the spearpoint tool described in Chapter 15. Details for making plugs are in Chapter 16.

CHAPTER ELEVEN

Some Projects Using Various Chucking Techniques

I will now consider other types of hollow ware and general turnery, and chucking and boring methods used in their production. (See illustrations on the following pages.)

POWDER JAR AND LID

For this, select a choice piece of dark wood, approximately 3 × 3 × 3in (7.62 × 7.62 × 7.62cm), and check it for shakes (splits) or other blemishes which may spoil the finished article.

Set it up between centres on the end grain, using the conical centre, and round it down, leaving it at its maximum diameter. Next square off the end, ensuring it is perfectly flat or slightly concave, drill a ⅛in (3.175mm) hole ⅜in (9.525mm) deep at the centre mark, and mount the blank on the screwchuck.

With a lathe speed of 1000 r.p.m. or so, spot in a centre hole with the point of the skew chisel, and bring up the dead centre to support the base. Now round the corners of the base with the ⅜in (9.525mm) or ½in (12.7mm) gouge, withdraw the tailstock, and deepen the centre hole to approximately ⅜in (9.525mm) by ⅛in (3.175mm) diameter.

Check that your screwchuck screw is no longer than ½in (12.7mm), and reverse the blank on to the screwchuck.

Reset the lathe speed at around 750 r.p.m., and with a modified 1in (25.4mm) Irwin bit chucked in the tailstock, drill down the centre of the blank to within 1in (25.4mm) of the bottom. Before proceeding to the next operation, however, remove the drill bit from the tailstock; the point can be a painful thing to jab your elbow on!

Now bring the tool rest up to the mouth of the hole, adjusted close in and just below centre height, and clamp up. Next, using the spearpoint or narrow ended chisel, open out the jar to bring it to a little over ¼in (6.35mm) wall thickness, and clean up the inside, bulging the sides slightly, and rounding the inside bottom corners, with the round end and side scraper.

Following this, and again using the square ended chisel, scrape down the outside edge of the mouth of the jar, leaving a projecting lip extending from the inside surface. This lip should be approximately ³⁄₁₆in (4.762mm) high, and ³⁄₁₆in (4.762mm) thick at its base, tapering in on its outside face to ⅛in (3.175mm) at the top. Now round the edge of the lip and sand, seal and wax polish the interior.

The next operation, to shape and finish the outside and bottom of the jar, will be done on a spigot chuck, prepared as follows. Secure to the faceplate a piece of softwood not less than 3 × 3 × 5in (7.62 × 7.62 × 12.7cm) long, and turn it down to make a spigot to fit the jar.

A shoulder is then formed on the spigot just beyond the point where it tightens in the jar, to make a bed for the mouth of it, and the shaft of the spigot extended well into the jar to increase its stability and to help dampen vibration.

Opening up the jar with a spearpoint after the initial bore with the 1in (25.4mm) modified Irwin bit

Forming the lip on the jar using the square ended chisel

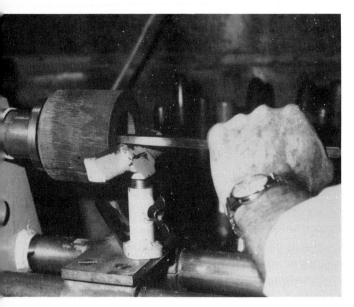

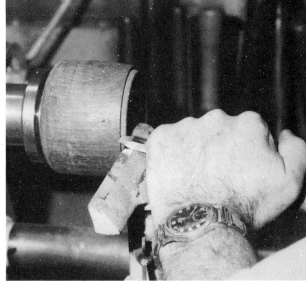

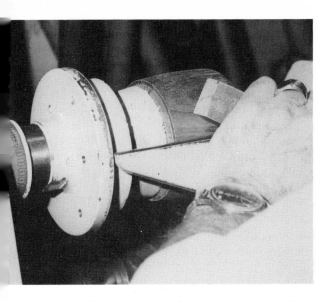

Jar mounted on the spigot chuck for shaping the outside; the base is supported by the dead centre. Note the shoulder formed on the chuck, and the absence of screws, the chuck being secured in the centre hole of the faceplate

Jar lid mounted on screwchuck for recessing of the underside and rounding of the outer edge

When the chuck is ready, mount the jar on it, making sure that it seats solidly against the shoulder, and bring the dead centre up to support its bottom. The jar should run absolutely true.

Now set the tool rest up to centre height position at the side of it, and using freshly sharpened gouge and skew chisel, bring the outside to its finished shape, maintaining a uniform wall thickness. When the outside form is to your liking, sand and seal the surface down to the base, and withdraw the tailstock. Reposition the tool rest at the base of the jar, with its top just below centre height, and clamp up.

Next, using the half-round scraper, turn out the centre of the bottom until the screw hole is erased, and blend the convex and concave curves of the base into each other. This operation leaves ample thickness in the bottom of the jar, whilst giving a pleasing appearance to it.

The bottom is now sanded and sealed, and a final waxing, polishing or lacquering applied overall, as desired.

The jar is now completed; next, the lid.

First select a nicely grained piece of ash, oak or similar light coloured stuff of ⅝in (15.875mm) thickness by not less than 3½in (8.89cm) square, mark its centre, drill to a depth of ⅜in (9.525mm) with a ⅛in (3.175mm) drill, and lightly countersink the hole.

Mount the workpiece on the screwchuck, and square off the face. Now, with dividers, strike a circle equal in diameter to the jar across its lip. Using a square ended scraper, recess the area within the circle to a depth of ¼in (6.35mm), opening up its diameter, and sloping its sides, to accept the mouth of the jar with about 1/32in (0.794mm) of side play. Round the edge and side of the lid to give a projection beyond the side of the jar of ¼in (6.35mm) all round, ensuring that the start of the lid curve coincides with the outer edge of the jar.

Next, sand, seal and finish the underside of the lid, centre it with a ⅛in (3.175mm) drill to a depth of ⅜in (9.525mm),

and reverse it on to the screwchuck. Now face off the lid lightly, strike a circle of 2½in (6.35cm) diameter on it and scrape in a flat bottomed recess of this size to a depth of ¼in (6.35mm). Following this, turn a disc from the same dark coloured wood as the jar, of 2½in (6.35cm) diameter by ½in (12.7mm) thick, and glue it into the recess of the lid with the grain at 90° to the grain of the lid.

When the glue is dry, turn the upper face of the lid to a slightly conical form, nicely rounded at the edge, and sand, seal and polish it. Lastly, blind bore the top centre to a depth of ⅜in (9.525mm) with a 5/16in (7.937mm) drill, in readiness for the knob.

The knob is ornamentally turned from the same dark wood, its base shaped to blend in profile with the top of the lid, and with a stem of 5/16in (7.937mm) diameter by ⅜in (9.525mm) long (less a fraction), to fit its hole. The knob is sanded, sealed and finished, and glued into position with its grain running with the dark wood surrounding it.

A minimum of glue is used to avoid oozing at the joint, and for added strength a screw may be driven into the shank of the knob from the underside of the lid, utilising the hole used in the last chucking operation. If the hole is first countersunk, and the head of the screw polished before fixing, whereafter it is given a touch of clear nail varnish, it will in no way detract from the quality appearance of the article. If a screw is considered unnecessary, then the screw hole can be capped with one of the plugs described in Chapter 16.

TOBACCO JAR AND LID

In this project the shaping and hollowing out operations require the same tools, but some variations in the chucking techniques are used.

First select a well seasoned piece of attractive wood, 5 × 5 × 6in (12.70 × 12.70 × 15.24cm) long, centre the ends,

Jar lid being blind bored for the knob after shaping the top, using a short screw in the screwchuck

A powder jar finished with carnauba wax polish. The wood is oak and Australian jarrah

and set up between centres. Round it down to its maximum diameter, square the end, measure in 1¼in (3.175cm) and part off the tail side of the mark. This disc will become the lid in due course.

Now remount the main section between centres, engaging the dead centre sufficiently to support the wood whilst side blows with the hand or mallet centralise it, before tightening the hand wheel. Following this, square the end true or slightly concave, lightly round the corners, and sand, seal and finish the base.

Drill out the centre with a ⅛in (3.175mm) drill to a depth of ⅜in (9.525mm), reverse the block on to the screwchuck using the sandpaper clutch, bring up the tailstock and engage the dead centre.

Now finish rounding the outside, shaping it to a slight barrel profile if preferred, but do not sand or seal it at this time. Withdraw the tailstock, exchange the dead centre for a 1in (25.4mm) or larger diameter modified Irwin bit, and reposition the tailstock to bore out the block to within 1in (25.4mm) of its bottom. Run the lathe at a slower speed for this operation, and use only light cutting pressure on the hand wheel, to avoid stripping the block from the screwchuck. When the depth limit has been reached, withdraw the tailstock and remove the bit.

Now position the tool rest across the end of the block at centre height, and commence opening up the hole with the spearpoint. Proceed with horizontal thrusting cuts penetrating to a depth of about an inch at each thrust, and moving progessively from the centre to within ⅜in (9.525mm) of the edge in each series of thrusts.

Hollow out to within ¾in (19.05mm) of the bottom, then change over to the round ended side scraper. Round the inside bottom corners, and bulge the sides to conform with the barrel shaped exterior, if that shape was chosen.

Reduce the walls to ⁵⁄₁₆in (7.937mm) thickness, but leaving the inside mouth of the jar parallel for the first

Workpiece being recentered after parting off lid portion (in foreground). The wood is New Zealand rimu. The mallet is made from plum wood

¾in (19.05mm). This will form a sealing surface for the lid in due course.

Finish off the interior with light scraping cuts using a freshly sharpened scraper and a higher speed on the lathe; sand and seal the surface. It sometimes happens that the hollowing out process relieves inner stresses in the wood, causing the exterior shape to change a little. It was for this reason that the outside was left unfinished.

If you now find that the jar exterior is running out of true, it will require to be supported at its open end before remedial action can be taken. Turn a disc on the screwchuck a little larger than the mouth of the jar, and taper it to fit the hole. Step a shoulder on the disc just above the point where the taper checked in the opening, and remove it from the screwchuck. Reassemble the jar on to the screwchuck, with the disc in position, its shoulder seated against the lip of the jar. Bring up the tailstock, and engage its centre in the screw

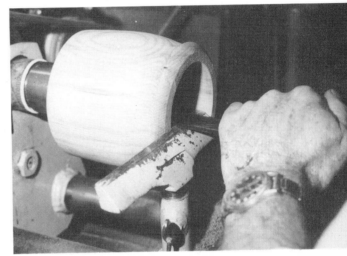

Smoothing the parallel mouth of the jar with round end side scraper to seat the sealing rings of the lid

Smoothing the outside of the jar after hollowing out, using a disc at the tailstock centre in support. Note the handgrip on the skew

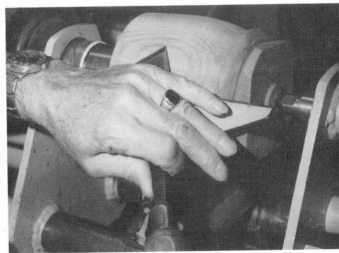

hole of the disc. Clamp the tailstock; take up the slack on the hand wheel, and clamp the dead centre. The workpiece is now fully supported, the outside can be trimmed up, and the final sanding, sealing and finishing done.

As this lid is required for a tobacco jar it must be airtight and made somewhat differently from the earlier one.

Set up on the screwchuck the disc parted off from the main block at the beginning, dress the face flat and smooth, and true the edge. Measure ¾in (19.05mm) back from the face of the disc, and cut in from the side with the skew chisel. Using the square ended scraper, reduce the diameter of the face back to the skew cut until the mouth of the jar will fit easily over it and the step on the lid sits flat on the mouth of the jar.

At this point a choice has to be made in the type of seal to be fitted to the spigot of the lid. Rubber rings, round in section, or flat flexible rings, are available, and either type properly fitted will make an airtight seal.

If you decide to use a rubber ring, scrape a groove around the spigot with a small round nose scraper. The groove is centered ⅜in (9.525mm) from the spigot face, and is wide and deep enough for the ring to enter freely, but protruding 1/16in (1.587mm) from the surface of the wood. The rubber should still be under tension when it is seated in its groove, the sides of which should be cut cleanly with the skew chisel before rounding the bottom with the scraper.

Should nylon or similar flat rings be chosen, two rings would be necessary, of an outside diameter about 1/16in (1.587mm) larger than the inside diameter of the mouth of the jar. Two grooves, equi-spaced ¼in (6.35mm) apart on the side of the spigot, of a width and depth to allow the rings a free fit into them, are sized in with the skew chisel, and scraped out with a file suitably ground to width.

This could be a 4in (10.16cm) HSE (hand safe edge), with its teeth ground off, and its end angled back to form a cutting edge across one corner. It would be used on its edge, cutting corner to the top, with the tool rest below centre height and the tool presented level with the bench top. The grooves are sized in with the skew chisel to cut through the fibres of the wood and so leave a clean entry for the scraper.

When the grooves are ready, assemble the rings and test the fit of the lid in the mouth of the jar. To assist easy entry of the lid, dust the inside of the jar mouth with french chalk or talcum powder. If the fit is right, it should be possible to lift the empty jar by its lid, but at the same time to remove it easily by holding the jar in the other hand.

If a rubber O-section ring has been used, and the lid is considered to be too tight, a slight deepening of the ring seating will suffice to ease it. Should nylon or similar flat rings have been fitted, however, the mouth of the jar must be opened up until an easier fit is obtained.

Once satisfied with the fit of the lid, remove the rings, and sand, seal and finish that part of it.

Following this, mount a piece of softwood on the faceplate, large enough to take the spigot of the lid. Level the face of the softwood chuck with the ⅝in (15.875mm) shallow gouge, and scrape in a ¼in (6.35mm) deep recess with the square ended scraper, to be a tight fit on the lid spigot, and tap it home into the chuck with the mallet or plastic faced hammer.

The top of the lid is now ready for shaping as desired, with the small gouge or scraper. The screw hole from the screwchuck provides a centre for boring in ⅜in (9.525mm) with a ⅜in (9.525mm) drill or bit, ready for fitting an ornamental knob of kindred wood, turned between centres, with

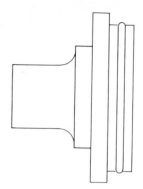

Diagram of lid grooved at the side for round section sealing rings

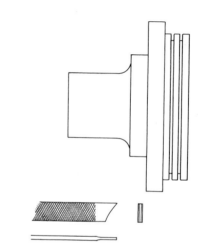

Diagram of the lid grooved at the side using a modified 4in (10.16cm) file, for flat section sealing rings. Note: A parting tool ground to this shape is used to part off eggcups (see Chapter 11)

a matching sized shank, and after complete finishing, glued into position with its grain in line with the lid.

As with the knob, the lid will be finished in all particulars before they are glued together.

Take especial care to wipe all surplus glue from view before it sets, as nothing looks worse on an otherwise well finished job than a heavy glue line, or blobs, and once dry it is almost impossible to remove without damage to the finish, or even the wood. At the point where sanding and sealing have been done, carnauba wax, friction or linseed oil polishing, or lacquering if preferred, would be carried out.

Finally, one last detail would require attention, the screw hole in the bottom of the jar. As the base is flat, it must be modified before the mushroom-shaped plug described in Chapter 16 can be used. However, this is easily done, requiring only that a flat bottomed recess approximately 1in (2.54cm) in diameter by 3/16in (4.762mm) deep be made over the screw hole position with the round nose scraper, after mounting on a spigot chuck. The area is then sanded, sealed and finished, and the plug glued in.

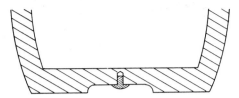

Section diagram of the recess cut in the base of the jar to seat the boxwood plug

These I consider are the touches which in a very real sense distinguish the unhurried amateur from the time- and cost-conscious professional. The amateur has infinite time and patience to indulge himself in pursuing perfection, while the professional, who has a living to make, cannot afford it.

TWO TONE VASE WITH TRIPOD LEGS

Wooden vases, in a variety of types and combinations of woods, with the inside tapered out to fit a small tumbler, present opportunities for using a number of different techniques and innovations. I shall start then with a simple two tone, tulip shaped vase, supported on three short legs.

Select a nicely grained piece of light coloured wood, oak, ash, elm or holly, about $4 \times 4 \times 6$in ($10.16 \times 10.16 \times 15.24$cm) long. Mount it between centres and square off one end. Centre and screw this end to the faceplate and bring up the tailstock to support the outer end of the workpiece on the dead centre. Square this end in turn, and round down the outside of the block to a tulip shape, with the top towards the tailstock, using the roughing out $\frac{3}{8}$in (9.525mm) deep U-gouge followed by the $\frac{5}{8}$in (15.875mm) or $\frac{3}{4}$in (19.05mm) shallow gouge.

Shape in the base of the vase to leave about 1in (2.54cm) of waste wood at the faceplate when parting off later, but without reducing the necked in area below $1\frac{1}{2}$in (3.81cm) diameter, for added stability during the boring and hollowing out about to follow.

Now bring up the 1in (2.54cm) or larger modified Irwin bit chucked in the tailstock, and bore down the centre of the vase to within 2in (5.08cm) of the faceplate. When the boring is done, withdraw the tailstock and remove the bit.

Then locate the tool rest across the mouth of the hole at centre height, and using the spearpoint tool as described for the tobacco jar, open up the body of the vase to fit the taper of a common $4\frac{1}{2}$oz glass, of size 2in (5.08cm) across the base, $2\frac{1}{2}$in (6.35cm) across the top and $3\frac{3}{4}$in (9.525cm) long, to enter its whole length into the wood.

Mark the lip of the vase $\frac{1}{4}$in (6.35mm) out of the hole, and scrape down outside the line $\frac{1}{4}$in (6.35mm), with a square ended chisel or scraper. This will leave a lip $\frac{1}{4}$in (6.35mm) wide and $\frac{1}{4}$in (6.35mm) high around the hole.

Remove the faceplate with the vase still assembled, from the headstock, and place to one side. Now select a rich coloured piece of $\frac{7}{8}$–1in (22.225–25.4mm) walnut, rosewood, mahogany or similar dark wood, 5in (12.7cm) square, and centre it. Strike a circle on its face the same diameter as the hole of the vase at its mouth, and mount the piece on the screwchuck with this circle towards the chuck. The purpose of the circle will be seen later.

Dress the face flat and smooth with the $\frac{5}{8}$in (15.875mm) shallow gouge, and with the dividers scribe a circle representing the outer diameter of the *lip* of the vase. Cut

The vase hollowed out and shaped, and the lip of the hole rebated for fitting the mouthpiece

Recessing the mouthpiece for fitting to the lip of the vase

The mouthpiece blank glued and held under pressure from the tailstock. A circle is marked on the face of the wood

in on the circle with the skew chisel and then, using the ½in (12.7mm) square ended chisel or scraper, remove wood on the inner side of the skew cut, that is towards the centre, to a depth of ¼in (6.35mm). Before this depth is reached, however, commence testing the fit of the lip of the vase in this groove. There should be no side play, and as soon as the shoulder of the jar makes solid contact with the face of the workpiece, cease scraping.

It will be seen that there is now complete wood to wood contact between the body of the vase and its lip-to-be: on the shoulder, up the side of the lip and across its top.

When satisfied with the fit, apply glue to both surfaces, bring them squarely together under pressure, and leave to dry. If this is done by removing the screwchuck with workpiece from the mandrel, and fitting the faceplate complete with vase in its place, the lip-to-be can be held in position on the vase by hand wheel pressure from the tailstock. By this means, when the glue is dry the assembly is ready in position for the next operation.

The circle scribed on the workpiece when it was first fitted to the screwchuck is now exposed to view, and indicates the width of the mouth of the vase. Before cutting out the mouth of the vase, however, first bring up the tailstock and engage the dead centre with the glued on blank.

Clamp the tailstock, adjust the dead centre with the hand wheel and secure it, then position the tool rest alongside the centre, close in at the centre height. Now cut the corners away with the spearpoint, leaving the blank a full ¾in (19.05mm) oversize. Reposition the tool rest alongside, and carefully blend the flared lip into the body of the vase with the ⅝in (15.875mm) shallow gouge. As the top of the vase is tulip shaped, or flared out, the cuts will move from the larger diameter at the lip to the smaller diameter just below it.

When you are satisfied with the blending of the curves, sand, seal and finish the outside of the vase down to the unshaped area by the faceplate. Now unclamp and withdraw the tailstock, and reset the tool rest across the mouth end of the vase, at centre height, and close in. Using the spearpoint or similar narrow ended chisel, cut in ⅛ or ³⁄₁₆in (3.175 or 4.762mm) on the inner side of the scribed circle, until the centre waste piece drops out. Take special care to ease pressure on the tool just before breaking through; the feel and sound of the tool will warn you when this is imminent.

When the waste disc has fallen away you will see there is sufficient wood left in the hole for aligning the inner wall and belling out the entrance, using the ½in (12.7mm) long nose gouge very sharp or, if you lack the confidence, the round end and side scraper.

Sand, seal and finish the inside and entrance, and move the tool rest into position by the base of the vase. Using the ½in (12.7mm) gouge and skew chisel, turn in the bottom curve, until the remaining spigot of waste is reduced to approximately ¾in (19.05mm), and saw it through.

The vase is now ready for remounting on a spigot chuck for the shaping of the bottom. Set up a piece of waste softwood 3 × 3 × 6in (7.62 × 7.62 × 15.24cm) long on the faceplate, using the screw-in method described in Chapter 16, and turn down the end to a taper fit into the vase. A really snug fit can be made of this if a broad chalk line is put down the length of the hole. This will transfer on to the high spots of the taper, indicating where wood has to be removed. With care and a sharp skew chisel there should be no sign of play when the taper is fully home in the vase.

In spigot chucking of hollow ware, whether by taper

Opening the mouth of the vase cutting on the marked circle with the spearpoint tool

fitting as here described, or a press fitting against a shoulder, as with the powder jar, it is essential that there is no rocking action, or the workpiece will move under pressure from the tool, and trouble will result. Where the operation allows it, extra stability is obtained by engaging the dead centre, capped if necessary by a suitably shaped insert between it and the base of the work. This means cannot be used here, though, because you are about to remove the waste from the bottom and round it into the sides of the vase. Set up the tool rest at an angle across the base of the vase chucked on the spigot, and with light cuts from the ⅝in (15.875mm) square ended gouge the sawn stump is cut away and the rounding of the bottom completed. As a variation, the bottom can be dimpled inwards at the centre with the round ended scraper. The turning is now done with, and the sanding, sealing and final finish may follow.

With the vase finished both inside and out, the next step is to prepare it for the fitting of the legs when these are made later. Take a pencil and, with the vase mounted on the spigot chuck, run a line around its base at a position where the legs are to be fitted. As these will protrude from the vase about 1in (2.54cm), and be set at an angle of approximately 45° to the vertical axis, it should not be difficult to gauge the right position for the pencil mark. For accuracy's sake, it would be applied whilst the lathe is running, of course.

The next operation is to plot the points around the pencil line, 120° apart, where holes for the legs are to be drilled, and to prepare a drilling jig to ensure that the leg holes are drilled all in the same plane with their axes radial to the centre of the vase.

Centering the leg hole jig ready for drilling its hole

This can be very accurately done if the following steps are taken. Turn a piece of 1½in (3.81cm) round or square material in hardwood, about 5in (12.7cm) long, down to a sliding fit in the tool rest holder of the banjo, leaving about 2in (5.08cm) at one end unturned.

Shorten the spigot, and cut down the underside of the head of the fitting to align the centre of the unturned end with a ⅜in (9.525mm) drill chucked in the headstock. Clamp the fitting in the tool rest, and drill it squarely through. This hole will now be on the centre line of the lathe when the drilling jig is seated fully home in the tool rest socket.

Mount the faceplate with the spigot chuck assembled, on the headstock, chuck the vase on to the spigot, and force it home on the taper.

The action which follows is to position accurately the faceplate and chucked vase for marking and drilling the holes for the legs. Take a length of ³⁄₁₆in (4.76mm) diameter wire, bend one end at right angles to engage a snug hole drilled in the front edge of the bench, and the other angled round to engage in a hole of the faceplate. When both ends of the wire are engaged, the workpiece is positively held, and a mark can be made on the pencil line using the tool rest as a guide. The faceplate is then rotated to repeat the operation for each of the remaining leg positions.

There will now be three equidistant markings around the base of the vase, so set these in with a centre punch or bradawl as a centre for the drilling operation to follow.

I have assumed that the faceplate is of the three hole variety, but should it be of the four hole type then the positions for the leg holes on the vase are marked around

the line with a folded strip of paper, as described later in this chapter.

With the hole positions now marked, realign the drilling jig to direct the drill into the vase at an angle of approximately 45° to the lathe's axis, and clamp up.

Fit the drill into the hand drill stock. A power drill is not recommended here; the depth of cut is too small, the fast cutting and weight of most power drills making them prone to overshoot the depth required. Gently insert the drill into the jig, and holding the hand stock as level and steady as possible, drill the first hole to a depth of ⅜in (9.525mm).

Rotate the faceplate and reclamp it for the drilling of the next hole, and repeat again for the third and last one. A mark made on the drill ⅜in (9.525mm) back from the point with a black felt tip pen will help in drilling to the correct depth.

If care has been taken, the holes should now be evenly spaced, and if the hand stock has been held level, so that the jig has not been strained out of true, they will be radially exact and all at a uniform angle.

Having made the holes, the next step is to select suitable wood and turn the legs between centres. For a balanced effect, the legs are best made from the same wood as the lip, or at least are of a similar colour. As the vase will be relatively light, even when loaded, and the stubs of the legs will be ⅜ × ⅜in (9.525 × 9.525mm), considerations of strength are not important, although it would be foolish to turn the legs across the grain.

A suitable piece having been selected, 6in (15.24cm) long by say 1in (2.54cm) square, turn down one end to fit the Morse taper of the headstock mandrel if so fitted, or to

Drilling jig and hand stock in position for drilling the leg hole in the vase

be a tight screw fit in the mandrel if it is threaded internally. Alternatively, utilise the internal thread of the faceplate after packing it forward on the mandrel by inserting a metal spacer behind it. (See the end of Chapter 16.)

The intention is to make the workpiece self supporting so that, although you use the dead centre for support as needed, when parting off or squaring the end up it will stay put without the dead centre.

Now turn the wood down overall, using the ⅜in (9.525mm) gouge followed by the skew chisel, to a smooth dowel of ⅝in (15.875mm) diameter. As only a 6in (15.24cm) length has been used, there should be relatively little vibration or whip, but for extra practice you could encircle the work with the fingers and control the end of the skew chisel with the thumb, as described in Chapter 9.

When satisfied with the finish of the dowel, square off the tail end, and using dividers mark lines on the revolving wood at ⅜in (9.525mm), 1⅜in (3.492cm) and 1⅞in (4.762cm) from the end. Cut in with the skew chisel on the lines and turn down the first ⅜in (9.525mm) to ⅜in (9.525mm) diameter. (See Chapter 15 for details of a sizing tool for repetition work.) Finally, slice a small chamfer on the end, and the stub of the first leg is formed.

Now take a ½in (12.7mm) square ended chisel, and apply it between the 1⅜in (3.492cm) and 1⅞in (4.762cm) skew cuts, with the bevel high on the wood, easing the edge back until shavings appear. By slightly tilting the chisel first on one edge and then the other, and raising the handle as the diameter reduces, the wood is rapidly cut

down to ⅜in (9.525mm) diameter, with the skew trimming the ends of the cut.

Next, using the same freshly sharpened chisel, and with the handle well round to the side in a skew cut position, with the bevel rubbing, taper down the leg diameter from ⅝in (15.875mm) at the first ⅜in (9.525mm) mark, to ⅜in (9.525mm) diameter at the 1⅜in (3.492cm) mark. Skew in at this point, round in the end of the taper, and also lightly round the corner at the ⅝in (15.875mm) end.

Lastly, move along ⅛in (3.175mm) from the small end of the taper and skew in at an angle back towards the tailstock to form a chamfer on the stub of the second leg. The area between the rounded end of the first leg and the chamfered end of the second leg is now sawn through close up to the stub end, and the first leg separated.

Repeat the marking out routine along the dowel, centering and supporting the end on the dead centre, and turn down the second and third legs. (An adapter fitted to the revolving centre, as described in Chapter 15, greatly simplifies re-centering.)

After the last leg has been parted off, square up the face of the remaining stub of dowel in the headstock, centre it, and drill in to a depth of ¼in (6.35mm) with the ⅜in (9.525mm) drill chucked in the tailstock. Insert a leg in the hole which, if the leg stubs have been accurately sized, should be a good fit. If it is not, stretch a piece of plastic wrapper over the hole and push it in with the leg.

Now check that the rounded end of the leg is running true before bringing up the tool rest to support a very sharp

Leg blank held in the Morse socket of the mandrel, marked out, and the first leg stub
finished. Note the ⅜in (9.525mm) ring centre used to set the diameter of the stub

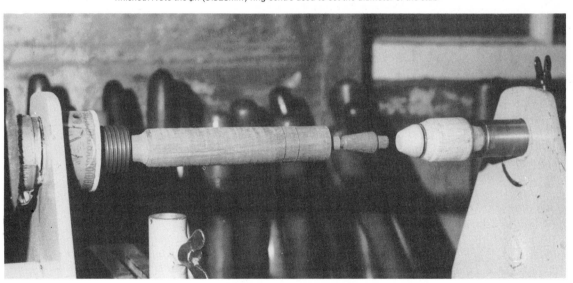

The first leg shaped using an adapter in the revolving centre, which
has been withdrawn to show the stub of the leg

square ended scraper or chisel in removing the small remaining stump left in sawing off, the tool being presented
at centre height, and swung scraper fashion around the
end.

Whilst the legs are chucked, sand, seal and finish them.

Finally check that each leg will push fit into its hole in the
vase, *and go fully home* before glueing up. In glueing up, to
avoid overloading the joint with glue and so having some
excess to wipe away which may harm your polished surface,
put a small dab of your adhesive, PVA or something similar,
from a feeder can, on the inside wall of the hole, and spread
it around with a toothpick or match. Then apply a similar
dab on the end of the stub of the leg, and again spread it
around the top with the match. This will be sufficient when

the two parts are brought together to ensure a well glued
joint, without exudation of surplus glue.

In making the foregoing articles we have used faceplate,
screw, spigot and hollow chucks, and between centre turning. There are, however, two other chucks often referred to
in books on woodturning, one of which can be useful in
situations where a clutching grip on the workpiece is required. The other, in my view, is very limited in scope, and
I have rarely used it. It consists of a hollow chuck with a
⅜in (9.525mm) hole drilled across the grain at the edge of
the main hole to carry a tapered wooden pin. In use, the
workpiece is inserted into the chuck, and the pin driven in
so that its taper binds on the side of the workpiece, and so
locks it in the hole.

Tripod base vases made of New Zealand kauri with mahogany tops and legs, carnauba wax polished. The screw hole is closed with a plug in the middle vase

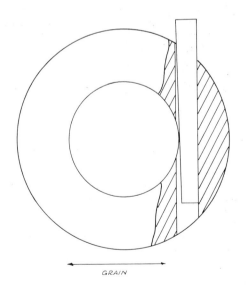

GRAIN

Diagram of the cotter pin hollow chuck. Note direction of taper and cotter fitted across the grain

To assist in retaining the workpiece, it is recommended that a shallow groove be turned on it to engage the pin, which is driven in against the direction of rotation. This ensures that any tendency, for the workpiece to turn will tighten the pin further into the hole. My objection to it is that unless the workpiece is almost exactly the size of the hole, the pressure of the pin forces the workpiece to one side, so throwing it out of centre.

The second chuck is called a split chuck and, as the name implies, is slotted or split into jaws to make it more flexible, so that by use of a sliding ring on its tapered exterior the jaws can be pressed in to hold the workpiece.

There is no set size for the jaw measurement, but I made mine at a time when I was chucking a large number of salt and pepper shakers, so it seems we make one at a time when it is needed, and of a size to take the job in hand. Whereas most designs embody a metal ring or turned hardwood square section ring to compress the jaws, I made use of the top of a tin.

The chuck is hollowed out of ash, beech or hickory to a diameter suited to the article to be held, and to a depth of at least 3in (7.62cm). The outside is then rounded down to give a uniform wall thickness of approximately $\frac{3}{8}$in (9.525mm), except for the mouth where for the first 1in (2.54cm) the wall thickness is left large enough to be tapered down for the metal fitting described later.

Following this, three longitudinal lines are marked along the outside, 120° apart, using the tool rest set at centre height as a guide for the pencil, and a base line scribed round the circumference, 3in (7.62cm) from the mouth. A groove $\frac{1}{4}$in (6.35mm) wide by $\frac{1}{8}$in (3.175mm) deep may be turned on the line to give greater flexibility to the jaws.

At each point of intersection of the peripheral line with the longitudinal lines a $\frac{3}{8}$in (9.525mm) diameter hole is bored radially through the wall. After this, longitudinal saw cuts are made radially down each of the three lines to connect with the ready drilled holes. The saw kerfs should be at least $\frac{1}{16}$in (1.587mm) wide, and to allow greater jaw movement may be opened out to $\frac{1}{8}$in (3.175mm). (Three coarse cut blades together in the hacksaw will make a simple job of this.)

The next step is to find a suitable sized tin with a body diameter approximate to the outside diameter of the chuck at its mouth. Having found a tin, cut the top 1in (2.54cm) from it, using a fine tooth metal fretsaw so as not to distort it unduly, and discard the rest. Then draw out the body part of the top of the tin, using a ball pein hammer on the inner surface, or by supporting it from the inside on the peak of an anvil or heavy round bar held in the vice, and hammering around the outside. By stretching the metal with a hammer in this way the body portion is flared out or tapered.

The outside surface of the mouth of the chuck is now tapered to conform with the taper of the metal fitting, sufficient wood being removed to allow the fitting to enter on the chuck about a quarter of the way before commencing closure of the jaws. Because the fitting encircles the mouth of the chuck, and has a rigid, flat face, being the original top of the can, it is easy to drive it squarely on to the jaws, so applying equal and simultaneous pressure on all three of them.

One major disadvantage of the ring type chuck is that the ring can only be tightened by a series of blows around its whole circumference, whilst care has to be taken to keep it square to the centre line of the chuck, otherwise uneven pressure is applied to the jaws and the workpiece is thrown out of centre.

SALT AND PEPPER SHAKERS

In making the salt and pepper shakers about to be described, the tail end support jig is essential. (See Chapter 15.) It supports the blank for hollowing out, and the formed, hollowed out shaker, whilst its top is being finished off and drilled and, if it has not been done at an earlier stage, whilst the decorative bruzz cuts are made around the body.

For the shakers any attractively grained, reasonably hard wood will serve, and if too light in colour, as say ash, elm or fruitwood, may be stained before final polishing. Take a piece of the selected wood 13in (33.02cm) long by 2$\frac{1}{4}$in (5.715cm) diameter, mount it between centres, square both ends back to an overall length of 12$\frac{3}{4}$in (32.385cm), and mark off at $\frac{1}{4}$in (6.35mm), 6$\frac{1}{4}$in (15.875cm) and 12$\frac{1}{2}$in (31.75cm) from the tail end.

Part in on the left hand side of the $\frac{1}{4}$in (6.35mm) mark, and the right hand side of the 12$\frac{1}{2}$in (31.75cm) mark to $\frac{3}{8}$in (9.525mm) diameter, and reduce from the $\frac{1}{4}$in (6.35mm) mark to the tailstock, and the 12$\frac{1}{2}$in (31.75cm) mark to the headstock to a smooth 1$\frac{3}{4}$in (4.445cm) diameter.

For a $\frac{1}{4}$in (6.35mm) along the main section adjacent to the parting cuts, reduce the diameter to a full 2in (5.08cm), and adjust to be a press fit in the bearing of the tail end jig.

Part off the discs at each end of the workpiece, marking them to their respective ends so that the grain pattern will match later, and mount the workpiece on the driving centre and tail end support jig, adjusted to maintain pressure of the workpiece against the driving centre.

With the wood now firmly supported, chuck a modified 1in (2.54cm) Irwin bit in the tailstock, and bore into the end of the workpiece through the hole of the jig to a depth of 3in (7.62cm) from the face of the jig abutting the wood. The

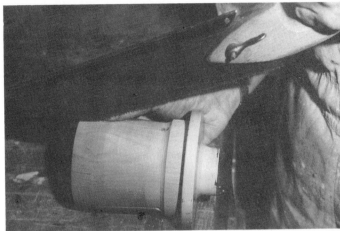

The slit jaw chuck hollowed out, radially drilled, and having jaws separated with the tenon saw. The wood is screwed into the hole of the faceplate, which can be firmly anchored in a vice for drilling and sawing operations

Shaping metal closure to a taper for fitting over the mouth of the chuck. A heavy round iron bar is used as an anvil

Closing ring in place on mouth of chuck

The base discs of shakers parted off and the workpiece mounted in the tail end jig with a 1in (25.4mm) modified Irwin bit ready to begin boring out

Shaker mounted in the tail end jig ready for reamering after graduated boring is completed

lathe speed should not exceed 750 r.p.m., and the bit must be withdrawn frequently to clear the waste.

At the set depth, change the bit to a size $\frac{3}{4}$in (19.05mm), and bore on to a depth of $4\frac{1}{4}$in (10.795cm). Again change the bit to a size $\frac{5}{8}$in (15.875mm) and continue boring to a depth of $4\frac{3}{4}$in (12.065cm). Change again at this depth to a $\frac{1}{2}$in (12.7mm) bit, and complete boring at the exact depth of $5\frac{1}{2}$in (13.97cm). Withdraw the bit and remove it from the tailstock.

Bring up the tool rest, and with it set at centre height, ease out the mouth of the hole with the round nose scraper to 1$\frac{1}{2}$in (3.81cm) to a depth of approximately 1$\frac{1}{4}$in (3.175cm). Remove the tool rest.

The shaker blank has now been hollowed out in a series of steps, which are smoothed into shape by means of the tapered boring tool or reamer described in Chapter 15. Fit the reamer into the tailstock, and feed it with a steady pressure of the hand wheel into the hole. Withdraw it frequently to clear the waste wood, and cease boring out when the tool has entered exactly 5$\frac{1}{2}$in (13.97cm) into the hole, measured from the face abutting the jig. The inside will now be of uniform shape, with a surface of shallow rings left by the saw teeth. No further finishing is necessary.

Then turn a flanged softwood plug to be a tight fit in the hole, reverse the workpiece end for end, remount in the jig as before, and repeat the boring and reamering operations. When the hollowing out is completed, turn a second flanged softwood plug, remount the workpiece between centres, and turn it to a smooth cylinder of 2$\frac{1}{8}$in (5.397cm) diameter. Now part in at its exact centre to a diameter of $\frac{7}{8}$in (22.225mm) and pencil mark 4$\frac{1}{4}$in (10.741cm) out from either side of the cut.

From the two marks back to the centre, taper down to the dimension cut, finishing smooth with the skew chisel to a very slight hollow curve, the two tapers being evenly matched. Following this, make a light secondary taper from the outer end of the workpiece to the pencilled mark, reducing the diameter there to 2in (5.08cm).

Sand and seal overall, taking care not to blur the corners, and cut a decorative line with the bruzz or skew at 3$\frac{3}{4}$in (9.525cm) up from each end. Now skew off the projecting ends used to locate in the jig, and part in at the centre to separate the two shakers, which at this time should be identical.

To finish the bases of the now separated shakers, prepare a softwood chuck with a tapered hole, and insert one in readiness for rebating its bottom for the base disc. Check that the shaker is running absolutely true in the chuck at a speed of 2000 r.p.m., tapping the rim as it revolves if necessary, and dress the lip of the hole true with the square ended scraper.

Cut a rebate in the mouth of the hole with the same tool, or a square ended chisel, to allow a press fit entry of the disc to a depth of $\frac{1}{8}$in (3.175mm) only. With the disc thus chucked, dress its surface smooth, in a slightly convex form. Reverse it, smooth the second face, and with a pencil mark a circle of 1$\frac{1}{2}$in (3.81cm) diameter on it. Using the round nose scraper, make a concave depression in the disc to the width of the circle, and a depth of $\frac{1}{8}$in (3.175mm) at the centre. Following this, penetrate the centre of the disc with the spearpoint tool, to make a hole of $\frac{3}{8}$in (9.525mm) diameter for the entry of a cork stopper.

Fine finish the surface of the wood, sand it smooth, lightly rounding the lip of the hole, and remove it from the shaker. Now deepen the $\frac{1}{8}$in (3.175mm) rebate to a depth of $\frac{1}{2}$in (12.7mm) below the mouth, and ease the fit of the hole to allow the disc to settle on to its seating. When an easy fit has been obtained, remove the disc. Round the inner corner of the base of the shaker, and sand it smooth.

Repeat all the foregoing operations on the second shaker and disc, ensuring that the finished thickness of the two discs is the same.

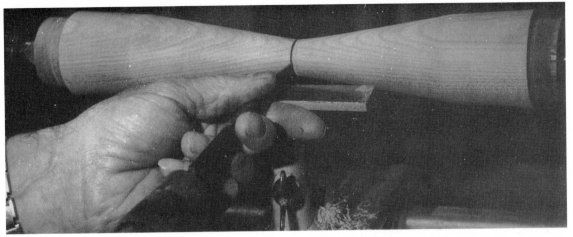

Parting in at the centre of the workpiece to separate the shakers after skewing off the jig locating ends. Plugs are used to remount the wood between the centres

Shaker chucked in the hollow chuck with the base disc chucked in the shaker for shaping the disc. The scraper has a long rake and fine edge

The shaker mounted on the driving chuck and open end jig for shaping and boring of the top

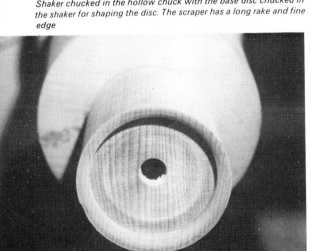

Close-up of the hollow chuck with the shaker base disc shaped and seated home

The tail end support jig was used earlier to support the bottom ends of the shakers whilst they were hollowed out. It will now be used to support the tops of them whilst they are shaped and the sprinkler holes drilled. Re-insert in the base of a shaker the softwood plug made earlier, and make a split collet as described in Chapter 15 to fit the top of the shaker, allowing a minimum projection of $\frac{1}{4}$in (6.35mm) through the back of the jig.

Mount the shaker with its base plug on the driving centre and its top seated in the tail end jig, clamped so as to maintain pressure of the workpiece against the driving centre. The tool rest may now be brought up against the top of the shaker, and with the lathe running at 2000 r.p.m., the top shaped and smoothed off.

The top may be flat, rounded or conical, whichever you prefer, a $\frac{1}{8}$in (3.175mm) diameter hole for the salt and a $\frac{1}{16}$in (1.587mm) diameter hole for the pepper being drilled after the shaping. For the pepper only, a circle of three spaced $\frac{1}{32}$in (0.794mm) diameter holes are drilled at the bench, after the sanding, sealing and polishing of the top, still mounted in the jig, is completed.

A pair of shakers finished in Australian jarrah and polished with carnauba wax. There is a boxwood cap on the cork stopper

The shakers are next given two liberal coats of sealer inside and, when dry, the discs, with the grain matched to their respective shakers, are glued in, using the barest amount of glue to ensure a good joint without exudation. Thereafter the shakers are mounted in the hollow taper chuck and the bases sealed, steel-wooled and polished.

Finally, a simple driving chuck is prepared, shaped to conform with the concave base of the shakers, with a centre pin to locate in the hole, and a thick cork washer interposed between chuck and shaker to act as a drive clutch. When all is ready, the shaker is set up between the chuck at its base, and the *revolving* dead centre in its sprinkler hole at the tailstock, and lightly steel-woolled and polished, the process being repeated for its partner.

If sufficient care has been taken at every stage, ensuring they are of identical height, and particularly in sanding and the use of steel wool around sharp edges, the shakers should have crisp lines, with quite distinct changes from curves to flats, and with only the outer edge of the bases actually in contact with the table surface, so ensuring maximum stability.

The corks are of the standard medical variety, fitted with boxwood caps ³⁄₁₆in (4.762mm) thick by ⅝in (15.875mm) diameter, undercut to provide a finger hold, and recessed ¹⁄₁₆in (1.587mm) deep by ⅜in (9.525mm) diameter to make a seating for glueing to the top of the cork. After glueing up, the cork is pressed home into a ⅜in (9.525mm) diameter hole drilled for it in a waste wood chuck, and its cap sanded, sealed and polished.

An interesting project which is both useful and an attractive piece of decorative turnery, involving both woodturning and some simple metal working, is made as follows.

A DEEP BODIED ASH RECEPTACLE WITH HAMMERED COPPER TRAY

Select a nicely grained piece of hardwood, 5in (12.7cm) long by 4½in (11.43cm) diameter, and set it up betweeen centres. Square the tail end, undercutting it slightly, sand, seal and finish the base, and after removing from the lathe drill out the centre to a depth of ⅜in (9.525mm) with a ⅛in (3.175mm) diameter drill. Chuck on the screwchuck, and bring up the dead centre in support.

Following this, square up the tail end, measure in 1½in (3.81cm) and part off on the line. This disc will become the cover or lid of the receptacle in due course. Reposition the dead centre to support the main block, and shape the outer end to allow a ½in (12.7mm) wall thickness around a mouth diameter of 2in (5.08cm), the lip of the hole being flared out to form a finger grip for lifting purposes, above a body bulged out to its full 4¼in (10.795cm) diameter.

The shaping of the outside is done with the ½in (12.7mm) or ⅝in (15.875mm) shallow gouge, followed by the ¾in (19.05mm) skew chisel to smooth out any gouge marks and to square the corner under the lip.

Sand, seal and finish the exterior, withdraw the tailstock, and position the tool rest ready for hollowing out the interior. With the tool rest at centre height, open out the mouth to 2in (5.08cm) diameter, to a depth of ⅜in (9.525mm), using the square ended scraper. Beyond this depth, open the mouth to only 1¾in (4.445cm) diameter, to form a step or shoulder in the hole, ⅛in (3.175mm) wide. This step will support the copper tray later.

Now commence clearing the waste wood from the interior of the workpiece, opening out the body of the jar below the shoulder to give a wall thickness of ½in (12.7mm), but leaving a pillar or spigot of wood standing centrally in the hole, with its upper end about ⅜in (9.525mm) diameter, widening out to about 1in (2.54cm) at the bottom, and blending into it.

Most of the waste will be taken out with the spearpoint, the final shaping of the inside wall, bottom and pillar being done with the side and round ended scraper. As the hole is deepened, the top of the pillar is also cut back until it is ½in (12.7mm) below the level of the step in the mouth, when its diameter should be no more than ⅜in (9.525mm) and well rounded.

Sand and seal the inside of the jar, taking care during the sanding not to trap the fingers between the pillar and the inside wall, and dismount from the screwchuck, replacing it with the disc originally parted off.

Making the lid

Now square the face of the disc, and reduce its diameter to 2in (5.08cm), offering the mouth of the jar to it until it is an easy fit.

Lightly chamfer the corner, and sand, seal and finish the face and edge of the disc, centering with a ⅛in (3.175mm) drill or spearpoint tool, ready for reversing on to the chuck.

Remount the lid, and turn it to your desired shape, endeavouring to flow the lines of the lid into the curvature of the jar. Now bore the lid's centre down ⅜in (9.525mm) with a ⅜in (9.525mm) drill for the spigot of the knob and, if the intended shape of the knob requires it, counterbore this hole out to ⅝in (15.875mm) or ¾in (19.05mm) diameter to a depth of ⅛in (3.175mm), using the ½in (12.7mm) square ended scraper or chisel.

Following this, mount a piece of the parent or similar coloured wood between centres, of 3in (7.62cm) length by ¾–1in (19.05–25.4mm) diameter, and turn it to an ornamental form flowing into the lid shape, with a ⅜in (9.525mm) diameter spigot ¼in (6.35mm) long, backed by a ⅝ or ¾in (15.875 or 19.05mm) collar ⅛in (3.175mm) thick, according to the size of the counterbored hole in the lid. So far as is possible, the joint between lid and knob should be invisible.

Leave enough waste at the driving centre end for parting off, the spigot having been formed at the dead centre end to facilitate testing its fit in the lid. Sand, seal and polish the knob up to the waste end.

After parting off the knob, which I envisage as being 2–2½in (5.08–6.35cm) high, of a graceful tapering shape, chuck it in the ⅜in (9.525mm) hole of a hollow chuck, round up the top end and sand, seal and finish. The knob may now be glued into the lid, with its grain in line, care being taken to ensure no excess glue exudes at the joint, and preparations begun for making the copper tray.

To make the copper tray

From a piece of 24 or 26 gauge copper sheet, cut a circle of 2in (5.08cm) diameter. The easiest way to do this is to scribe the circle close to one corner and cut the corner out. It is then a simple matter to trim round the line with tin snips, tidying up the edge with a smooth 6in (15.24cm) file.

When the disc is ready, scour one surface smooth with fine grade steel wool, and test it for a free fit in the jar. To allow for later variations in the wood due to atmospheric changes, the tray should have at least ¹⁄₁₆in (1.587mm) of side play.

After fitting, remove any burrs, repolish the metal, and prepare to hammer finish the surface.

Using a small ball pein hammer, with the copper disc rested on a flat end grain surface of hardwood, gently pein the entire surface. Move around the circumference, spiral fashion, until the centre is reached, and the whole surface has a hammered appearance. Re-check its free fit in the jar and adjust as necessary.

Following this, drill a ¼in (6.35mm) diameter hole at its centre, and open it up to ⅜in (9.525mm) diameter with either progressively larger drills (although these tend to snatch in the metal, and the copper may be marked by the vice in endeavours to hold it) or, better still, by a 4in (10.16cm) half-round file, or the end of a large round file rotated in the hole anticlockwise. Remove the burr, and flatten the disc.

The next operation is designed to shape the area around the hole into a funnel shape, so that when in use cigarette ash will find its way into the body of the jar.

The copper disc is formed in a simple punch and die set, turned from hardwood, the punch between centres and the die on the screwchuck.

Start with the die, turning a disc of 3in (7.62cm) diameter by 1½in (3.81cm) thick, squaring the face, and forming a shallow recess of 2in (5.08cm) diameter by ¹⁄₁₆in (1.587mm) deep, for locating the disc in the die, end grain to the top. Next, mark a circle of 1in (2.54cm) diameter on the recess face. Accurately centre the die and bore with a ⅜in (9.525mm) diameter drill to a depth of 1in (2.54cm) or as deep as the screw of the chuck will allow.

Following this, using the skew chisel scraper fashion, form a conical surface from the 1in (2.54cm) circle mark in to a depth at the centre of ½in (12.7mm). This surface must be smooth and flat in section.

Now remove the die from the screwchuck, and complete the drilling of the ⅜in (9.525mm) diameter hole through the bottom of the wood, held in the hand, and offered to the drill chucked in the headstock. The die is now ready.

For the punch, turn a cylinder of hardwood between centres, 5in (12.7cm) long by 1½in (3.81cm) diameter. Square one end, and mark in 1in (2.54cm) from it. Part down to ⅜in (9.525mm) diameter full on the tail side of the mark, and reduce the 1in (2.54cm) length to be a sliding fit in the ⅜in (9.525mm) hole of the die.

The last and most important operation is to angle the shoulder adjoining the spigot end, to conform exactly with the conical surface of the die.

Use the skew chisel, slicing down from the larger to the smaller diameter, and as the finished shape emerges, chalk the die surface and test the punch frequently to obtain a face to face fit between the die and the punch. When you are satisfied with it, check that the spigot of the punch does not protrude when fully home in the die, and slightly round the striking end of the punch.

In use, the die is placed on a solid surface, such as the corner of the bench, and the copper disc – the hole of which has been eased to a free fit on the punch – is laid in the recess of the die, hammered face upwards.

The punch is then passed through the hole of the disc, and seated in the hole of the die, when blows on the end of the punch (preferably with a mallet) set the disc into a conical form at its centre, the hole simultaneously opening out to about ½in (12.7mm) diameter.

After setting, the disc or tray is placed in the mouth of the jar, and the height of the central pillar in relation to the hole of the disc is checked. There should be sufficient space between the rounded top of the pillar and the lip of the hole of the tray to allow a cigarette butt to pass through into the jar. About ⅜in (9.525mm) should be ample, the distance being adjusted by further shortening and rounding of the pillar if necessary. The purpose of this pillar is two fold: the top serves as a surface for stubbing out cigarettes and, because it confines the opening of the jar to a relatively small area, it assists in extinguishing live butts which find their way into the jar. The replacement of the lid will of course ensure this anyway.

Having finished any adjustments which were found necessary, give the tray a rub with the fine steel wool to remove any finger marks, and apply a coat of heat resistant lacquer.

The final touch, as always, is to plug the screwchuck holes in lid and jar bottom with ornamental caps as described in Chapter 16.

Another both useful and decorative piece, in the style of a sombreroed figure pushing a two wheel container for flowers, offers some interesting exercises with all tools, and includes faceplate, flat and hollow turning, spigot and screwchuck details, jig drilling, and medium and small diameter spindle work.

A MEXICAN FLOWER CART VASE

This article is made up of eight separate parts, comprising: Pedro, his hat, the container, two wheels, two stub axles and a push bar, the axles and push bar being of identical diameter.

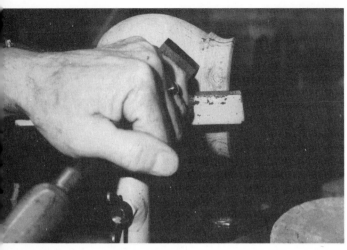

Workpiece on screwchuck having outside shaped with skew chisel

Hammer finishing surface of copper disc after cutting out with tin snips. A hardwood block is used as an anvil

Jar partially hollowed out showing the lip for the tray and central pillar being formed. The wood is New Zealand taraire

Hole in copper tray being opened up with the end of large file rotated anticlockwise, to prevent the file jamming in the hole

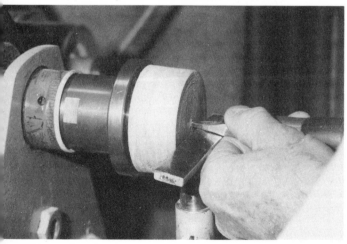

Lid rounded to diameter of jar mouth, being centre-bored with the spearpoint for reversing on to screwchuck

Die piece on screwchuck having face angled with skew chisel for shaping copper disc

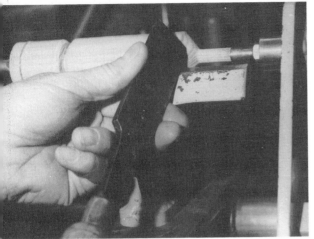

The die punch mounted between centres having its angled face formed with the skew chisel. Note the ⅜in (9.525mm) ring centre setting the diameter for the pin

A finished jar with lid lying in foreground, showing ornamental plug in screwchuck hole. Jar is of New Zealand pahutukawa, water stained

The punch and die with tray in position ready for shaping. Two formed trays in foreground. The hole in the tray has opened up

As the major part is our man Pedro, let's start with him.

Select a nice piece of well grained wood (of which you will require enough to complete the whole project) 7in (17.78cm) long by 3in (7.62cm) diameter. Free form a shape with a cylindrical head squared on top for the hat, rounded jaw and short thick neck, shoulders and chest swelling out over a low paunchy stomach and short legs belled out Mexican trouser fashion at the base. There are of course no arms, and the legs are formed as one cylindrical shape.

Most of the shaping will be done with a small gouge, with an equally small skew chisel smoothing off where it can be applied. The area around the chin and neck will require a narrow round ended scraper, similar to that described in Chapter 15. No waste need be left at the top or bottom, as the hat will cover the headstock end, and the base is cut off at an angle later, to simulate a man leaning into his load.

When you are satisfied with the overall shape, which is, of course, stylised, and should look humourous, sand the figure carefully, and seal and polish or coat with a clear lacquer as desired.

The hat or sombrero is turned next, and for this a piece 2½in (6.35cm) long by by 4in (10.16cm) diameter will be required, the grain running through the wood from top to bottom. Centre the wood on its short axis, round it down and square the tail end. Reverse it on to the smallest face-plate you have or, failing this, prepare a hollow chuck and force the squared end home into it.

Now dress the exposed face square with a very sharp round ended scraper (a gouge on the end grain may pull the workpiece from the hollow chuck), and strike a circle of the diameter of the top of the man's head.

Using the square ended scraper or chisel, recess within the circle to a depth of ¼in (6.35mm), offering the man's head to the recess from time to time to ensure a good fit.

Likewise, make sure that the bottom of the recess abuts the top of the head, to make certain of a good glue joint later.

When satisfied with the recess, round the surface between the hole and the edge very slightly, simulating the underside of a hat brim, and centre the recess to a depth of $\frac{3}{8}$in (9.525mm) with a $\frac{1}{8}$in (3.175mm) drill or bradawl, for reversing on to the screwchuck. Sand, seal and finish the underside, and reverse on to the screwchuck, increasing the length of the screw if necessary.

Now put a pencil mark around the circumference of the wood, 1in (2.54cm) out from the screwchuck, and reduce from this mark to the outer end of the wood on a taper of $1\frac{1}{4}$in (3.175mm) at the base to 1in (2.54cm) at the top of the hat.

Hollow out the inside of the brim with the round ended scraper, blending the crown into it, maintaining a wall thickness to the brim of approximately $\frac{5}{16}$in (7.937mm), and slightly bellying the outer surface of it at the same time. Dimple in the top of the crown, round the corners, and bring the top edge of the brim to a narrow rounded finish. Sand, seal and finish in the selected way, and put to one side for glueing on to the head later.

The next major component is the container, or cart, which will be in effect a vase with flowers when in use.

Set up a piece of your selected wood between centres, say 5in (12.7cm) long by 4in (10.16cm) diameter, round it down to a maximum size, and square the tail end, undercutting it slightly. Drill its centre to a depth of $\frac{3}{8}$in (9.525mm) with a $\frac{1}{8}$in (3.175cm) drill, and reverse it on to the screwchuck, using the sandpaper clutch insert previously described.

Now bring up the tailstock, chuck in a 1in (2.54cm) modified Irwin bit, and drill the centre down to within 1in (2.54cm) of the bottom.

After this, withdraw the tailstock, unchuck the bit to avoid damaging your elbow, and position the tool rest in readiness for opening up the hole with the spearpoint. Using the same procedure as described for the two tone vase earlier, prepare the hole for a tumbler of identical proportions, finishing with the side scraper to level and smooth the inner wall.

The tumbler should be about $\frac{1}{2}$in (12.7mm) below the lip of the hole, and an easy fit into it. Shape the lip to a slightly concave form, and smooth the corners.

Sand, seal and finish the inside and lip, and rechuck the piece on to a softwood spigot chuck.

At this point a choice can be made either to taper the outside to a uniform wall thickness of $\frac{1}{2}$in (12.7mm), or leave it parallel, and whether to round the bottom or to square it off. The decision having been made, proceed with gouge, skew chisel and round ended scraper if needed, to complete the outside. Sand, seal and finish as before.

The next major parts are the wheels which, when made, should be as near alike as possible. Prepare two pieces of the selected wood, of a minimum width of $3\frac{3}{4}$in (9.525cm) across by 1in (2.54cm) thick. Centre and drill in to $\frac{3}{8}$in (9.525mm) depth with a $\frac{1}{8}$in (3.175mm) drill, and mount one on the screwchuck. Square its face and strike a $3\frac{5}{8}$in (9.207cm) circle on it. Now, using the spearpoint, cut through on the waste side of the line to within $\frac{1}{16}$in (1.587mm) of the screwchuck, and break or saw off the corners. Centre in with the spearpoint, reverse it, and square the second face, reducing the thickness to $\frac{7}{8}$in (22.225mm).

Reposition the tool rest at mid-height to the side of the workpiece, and with a very sharp $\frac{1}{2}$in (12.7mm) shallow gouge dress the rim of the wheel square, check it for $3\frac{5}{8}$in (9.207cm) diameter, and strike a mark on it with a dividers $\frac{1}{8}$in (3.175mm) in from the front and back faces.

Now angle the front face from its centre back to the $\frac{1}{8}$in (3.175mm) mark at the edge, using the same gouge and taking care to leave no marks. Next scribe two circles on the face, of $1\frac{1}{4}$in (3.175cm) and $2\frac{1}{2}$in (6.35cm) diameter, making only the lightest impression, as these lines mark the limits of a $\frac{1}{8}$in (3.175mm) deep hollow curve to be scraped in with a sharp round nose scraper or scooped out with the $\frac{1}{2}$in (12.7mm) long nose gouge – preferably the gouge.

After the groove has been cut to width and depth there will be two areas of roughness where the end grain is exposed, so resharpen the scraper, increase the lathe speed, and skim a very light cut around the groove. This will remove most of the remaining roughness, but the last vestiges must be removed with abrasive paper, care being taken not to dub over or round the corner where the curve of the groove meets the flat face. This is the point at which a lot of otherwise attractive wood turnery is ruined. Careless use of abrasive paper will remove in an instant the sharp edge definition of a shoulder, or the crisp change of contour from a flat to a hollow curve. At least let the work look as if it has been turned with sharp steel tools, even if one must depend in some cases for the final finish on a discreet use of sandpaper.

I cut my 6in (15.24cm) wide garnet paper into 1in (2.54cm) strips with an old pair of tin snips, and roll the strip to a size which will comfortably fit the groove, changing the strip end for end as it wears. As a back-up for this I have a bottle cork about $\frac{1}{2}$in (12.7mm) diameter by 1in (2.54cm) long, and roll the strip over the face of this held in the groove, so presenting a fresh area of abrasive as the cork is rotated. By this means the groove is sanded smooth, and after sanding off the flat parts of the face, again using a flat cork or wood pad, all is ready for sealing and finishing later.

But do remember, in a situation where a hollow curve meets a flat, so forming a corner, always sand the groove first, the flat surface last. This ensures, if carefully done, that the corner between them remains square and sharp. See also the section on sanding in Chapter 17.

Before reversing the wheel on to the screwchuck and repeating the sequence of operations, chuck a piece of softwood of similar size to the wheel, and form its face to fit the turned face of the wheel. When the wheel beds firmly against the chuck, centre it and screw the wheel on to it. With the workpiece now rechucked, form its flat face identical with its other side.

Once the second face is finished and sanded, strike a light pencil mark on the front and back faces, $\frac{1}{8}$in (3.175mm) in from the edge, and round the rim of the wheel down to the mark on either side, using the round nose and square ended scrapers, to give it a convex tread.

Finally sand and seal as needed, and finish overall.

Repeat the whole sequence of operations for the second wheel, taking especial care to see that the diameters are the same, and the grooves, on one side at least of each wheel, match each other.

The last operation is to drill the centre hole out to $\frac{3}{8}$in (9.525mm) diameter, which may be done in any of several different ways. First, the Irwin $\frac{3}{8}$in (9.525mm) bit may be used in the hand brace, penetrating half-way from each side. Or, the wheel may be held between the dead centre and a $\frac{3}{8}$in (9.525mm) diameter jobbing drill chucked in the headstock, and fed on to the drill with the hand wheel, reversing the cut half-way through. Or again, the wheel is backed by the softwood male chuck used earlier, the screw-chuck hole in the chuck being centred on the dead centre and the wheel held against its face, whilst both are fed forward on to the drill with the hand wheel until penetration of the wheel is completed.

When both wheels are drilled there remains only the turning of the stub axles and push bar between centres before assembly gets under way.

A piece of the selected wood approximately ½in (12.7mm) square by 7½in (19.05cm) long is set up between centres, using the ⅜in (9.525mm) ring centre, as an easy check on the required diameter of ⅜in (9.525mm), and is turned down to a full ⅜in (9.525mm) with the ⅝in (15.875mm) shallow gouge, taking light cuts to reduce whip, and finishing smooth, fingers around the work, with a sharp skew chisel followed by fine sandpaper.

After this, square the end, and mark along 2¾in (6.985cm) for the push bar, 4½(11.43cm) for the first stub axle, and

The cart, after boring out, is rough hollowed with the spearpoint

The hat screwed to a small faceplate whilst the underside is shaped and recessed. Remember that the screw holes will be in the waste area around the crown of the hat when it is reversed

The cart mounted on the spigot chuck for shaping outside and bottom. Note the absence of screws, the spigot being screwed into the centre hole of the faceplate, which is set forward by a collar behind the boss

The hat reversed on to screwchuck for shaping the crown and brim. The round end scraper is dimpling in the top of the hat

Edge of wheel marked back for angling front and back faces, and circles scribed for groove on face. Note the contoured chuck in the foreground for mounting the wheel after it is shaped

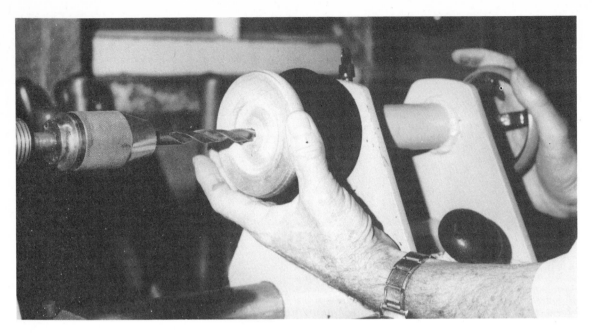

Axle hole being bored in the wheel supported on a shaped chuck at the tailstock. The wheel is being fed on to the drill with the hand wheel

6$\frac{1}{4}$in (15.24cm) for the second. Skew in at each mark, sufficient to enter a tenon saw blade, remove from the lathe and saw the sections apart.

Now mount a waste wood block on the screwchuck, and drill a blind hole of $\frac{11}{32}$in (8.731mm) diameter to a depth of $\frac{1}{2}$in (12.7mm). Drive the stub axle portions of the $\frac{3}{8}$in (9.525mm) dowel into the chuck, each in turn, and round one end. Whilst they are still chucked, check that the wheels are a twist fit on to them, and, if over-tight, ease the stub axle down with sandpaper. With the push bar – as both ends are hidden when assembled – a light chamfer at each end will suffice. Sand the rounded ends, and seal and finish all three parts.

The turning work is now done, and the final operations before assembly involve drilling holes for the axles and push bar, and sawing a wedge shaped slice from the base of Pedro.

To do this, first decide which part of the grain pattern is to be the front towards the container, and make a mark $\frac{3}{8}$in (9.525mm) up from Pedro's base on this side. Then, with the figure suitably protected with cork clams (or an offcut of carpet), clamp it in the vice and saw off a wedge shaped piece with the tenon saw, starting at the front mark and ending at the rear lower edge. Clean the sawn surface with the disc sander and seal it.

Mark a point on the centre front 2in (5.08cm) up from the new base and centre-punch it in readiness for drilling the push bar hole, and put Pedro to one side for the moment.

Take the container portion, and again choose the side which is to face towards the man. Mark a point 1$\frac{3}{4}$in (4.445cm) up from the base on this side as a centre for the push bar hole. Following this, at right angles to the mark, at either side and 1$\frac{1}{2}$in (3.81cm) up from the base, mark centres for the stub axle holes.

The hole positions having all been marked, drill them out to a depth of $\frac{3}{8}$in (9.525mm) with the $\frac{3}{8}$in (9.525mm) diameter jobbing drill, as follows:

The container is chucked on the spigot chuck, and the drilling jig positioned alongside at right angles to the axis of the work.

Taking care to keep the drill hand stock level and steady, as in earlier projects, drill the three holes out in turn, taking care not to overshoot the $\frac{3}{8}$in (9.525mm) depth for fear of penetrating the container wall.

When the holes are ready the two stub axles are glued in, round ends outwards, but not the push bar, as occasions arise when the assembly is dismantled for cleaning, polishing or other loving care.

I have left the trickiest job to last, which is drilling the push bar hole in the man at the correct angle to allow the bar to be level with the ground whilst Pedro leans towards

The cart mounted on the spigot chuck with the jig in position for drilling axle holes

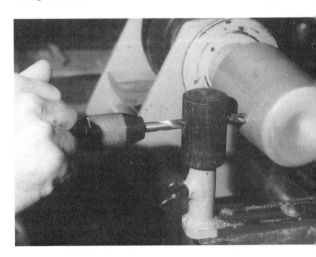

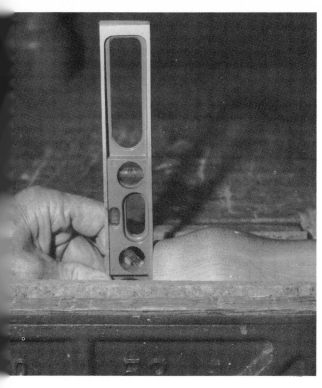

The completed Mexican flower vase, made from New Zealand kauri and finished in clear lacquer

Pedro gripped in cork clam vice and aligned with spirit level across base for drilling of push bar hole

Pedro having push bar hole drilled after aligning with the spirit level

it. It is in fact relatively simple, and follows the same procedure as that used in aligning the legs for boring rung holes when making stools.

Pedro is clamped by cork clams in the vice, with the centre punch mark on his front central and to the top. Then, with the spirit level laid vertically across his base, he is tilted to bring the bubble central. The ⅜in (9.525mm) drill chucked in the hand stock is next centred in the mark, and held perfectly upright whilst being bored in to a depth of ¾in (19.05mm).

After the push bar has been glued in all that remains is to check over the whole assembly, give it a rub with a soft cloth, insert the tumbler, water and flowers – in that order – and place it surreptitiously in a prominent position.

Your wife's surprise and pleasure will amply reward your labours.

AN ORIENTAL FLOWER CART VASE

The next project, also a decorative flower vase, but introducing off-centre turning, suggests an oriental man in a conical hat pushing a two wheeled cart with a lift out container. It comprises: the oriental man with hat, the container, two wheels, two axles, a push bar, a circular base for the container and a connector for the push bar.

The first requirement is to assemble enough wood of the one kind to complete the whole project. A variety of colours and grain patterns in one assembly detracts from the article, which should appear as an integrated, complete entity.

Starting with the man, select a piece 7½in (19.05cm) long by 3¼in (8.255cm) diameter, round it down and square one end. Centre it, preparing a hole for the screw, and reverse it on to the screwchuck. This will facilitate finishing the coolie hat later.

If you like, make a rough sketch to guide you in deciding how much to allow for his hat, head, neck, upper body, stomach and legs, and mark the position for dimensioning cuts with a pencil.

Once you have settled on the proportions, start free-forming the shape, with the hat towards the tailstock end, giving it a sharp edged brim and conical crown, the face round above an out-turned collar, full shoulders and chest, nipped in at the waist with a slightly out-turned rim suggesting a tunic, the form swelling out over the hips and sloping in at the feet.

Most of the shaping can be done with the narrow mouth ⅜in (9.525mm) gouge, backed by the ¼in (6.35mm) round ended scraper for working around the neck and collar, with the skew chisel smoothing off the underside of the hat, cutting in the corner between the neck and the collar, and the lip at the bottom of the tunic. The shallow curves on the hat, chest and lower portion of the body can also be finished with the skew.

When all the shaping operations are done, carefully sand and seal overall, trying not to flatten the edges of the tunic, collar or hat, and polish or lacquer finish as desired.

Withdraw the tailstock, skew the top of the hat to a point, and touch up. Finally, cut a wedge shaped piece from the base, as detailed in the previous project, measure 2¾in (6.985cm) up the centre front from the new base, and centre-punch on the mark. Apart from the hole for the push bar, which will be drilled later, the body is now finished.

As the container is made to hold a tumbler of similar size to that used in the previous project, the tools used and the sequences followed are the same, except for some small alterations in the design. Its base is squared off flat, and for 1in (2.54cm) up from the bottom is reduced to a parallel diameter of 2¹⁵⁄₁₆in (7.461cm).

Unlike the previous container, which had the wheels attached directly to it, this one is designed to sit in a hole formed in a circular base to which the wheels are fitted. The purpose of this is to allow the portion containing the tumbler and flowers to be lifted out and removed for changing the water as needed. Cut a chamfer on the bottom edge of the container to facilitate replacing it in its hole, and sand, seal and finish overall.

For the base, cut a piece of the selected wood, 5¼in (13.335cm) square by 1in (2.54cm) thick, centre one face and mount on the screwchuck. Level the exposed face with the ⅝in (15.875mm) shallow gouge, and on it strike a 5in (12.7cm) diameter circle with the dividers. Next, using the spearpoint parting tool, cut through on the waste side of the circle to within ¹⁄₁₆in (1.587mm) of the rear face (it is taken for granted that the workpiece is larger than the screwchuck) and remove the waste corners with a hacksaw blade, cutting in the kerf of the spearpoint. Alternatively, a piece of ply or hardboard may be sandwiched between the face of the screwchuck and the workpiece, and the parting tool taken right through into this.

The tool rest is now brought to the centre side position and, with a very sharp ⅜in (9.525mm) gouge, the edge of the disc is dressed and the corner chamfered.

Sand, seal and polish the face and edge of the disc, centre it to a depth of ⅜in (9.525mm) with a ⅛in (3.175mm) drill or bradawl, and reverse it. Repeat the finishing operations on the second face, and remove the disc from the chuck.

Now strike a new centre offset ¼in (6.35mm) from the original, along the grain, and drill a ⅛in (3.175mm) diameter hole squarely through the disc at this point.

Next, at right angles to the axis of the centres and running

The oriental man being turned between centres showing the ¼in (6.35mm) round end scraper shaping the collar

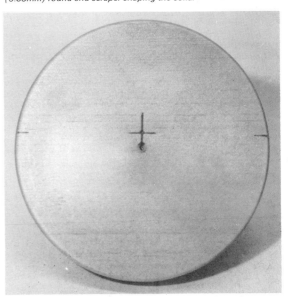

The baseplate marked out for position of off-centre pilot hole and axle holes at edge of disc

through the new centre, make a mark half-way down each side, to fix the positions for the wheel axles.

Remount the disc on the screwchuck, using the new centre, and from it scribe, with the dividers trailing over the edge of the tool rest, a circle of 3in (7.62cm) diameter.

As the hole for the container is next, set the tool rest at centre height, and with a square-to-the-face thrust of the spearpoint, cut into the wood on the inside of the line to half its thickness, keeping the edges of the cut as clean as possible. At the half-way depth withdraw the tool, turn its edge into the vertical position and smooth the left hand surface of the cut back to the line, maintaining the cut at right angles to the face of the disc.

After this reverse it, using the ready drilled ⅛in (3.175mm) hole as a centre, and again scribe a 3in (7.62cm) diameter circle on the face of the disc.

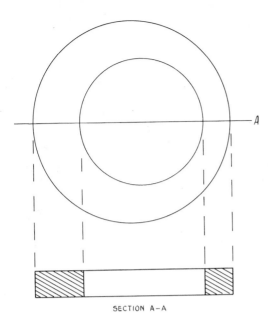

SECTION A—A

Plan and section view of baseplate

Baseplate mounted on offset centre on screwchuck being parted half-way in on the marked circle

Now reposition the tool rest and again cut in on the inside of the line to almost half thickness. Clean up the left hand side of the cut with the vertical edge of the spearpoint, as before, and then, with the tool freshly sharpened, gently cut through to separate the two parts, cutting in a V shape from the waste side to give free movement to the tool.

If by chance the two cuts don't quite line up, press fit the baseplate by its larger size hole on to a softwood chuck, limiting its entry to a depth of ⅛in (3.175mm) by a formed shoulder. This will ensure that the baseplate rotates square and true whilst the spearpoint, blade in the vertical plane, trims the smaller hole into line.

The baseplate can now be removed from the chuck and the surface of the hole sealed, after which there only remains the drilling of the axle and push bar connector holes – to be described later – and the base is finished.

The wheels are made next, following exactly the procedure for the previous project, except that they are reduced to 3in (7.62cm) diameter, with a corresponding scaling down of the groove width. The wheel axles and push bar are also made as before, except that the push bar length is 3in (7.62cm), and the stub axles 2¼in (5.175cm) each.

Last to be made is the push bar connector, which is simply a boss formed with a spigot or shank at one end for glueing into the base, and a transverse hole for the push bar at the other.

Take a piece of the selected wood, approximately 1in (2.54cm) square by 3–4in (7.62–10.16cm) long, and with the marking guage scribe a centre line along the two side grain faces and across the ends. Centre-punch on the line in the centre of each end, and 1½in (3.81cm) up from one end on both faces.

Now chuck a ⅜in (9.525mm) diameter drill in the head-stock, and with the workpiece held in the free hand, and supported on a wooden pad at the tailstock, centre either of the face marks on the drill, and feed forward with the hand wheel. If the blank is held perfectly square to the drill it may be taken right through, but to eliminate any doubt reverse the workpiece and complete the bore from the other side.

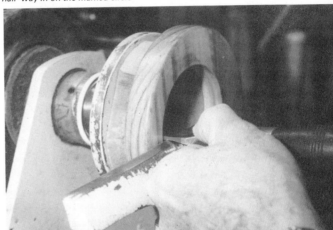

Baseplate mounted on softwood chuck for alignment of centre hole after cutting in from each side

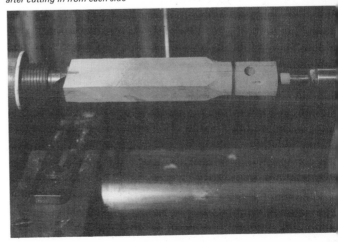

The push bar connector being shaped between centres after drilling of the transverse hole. The scribed centre line is for aligning hole and centres

Alternatively, the blank may be centred on the drill and tailstock dead centre, and the same procedure followed of reversing the bore half-way through, care being taken to avoid contact between drill and dead centre.

Once the hole is drilled the workpiece is set up on its centres, hole towards headstock, rounded down to a full ¾in (19.05mm) diameter, and marked off at ½in (12.7mm) and 2⅜in (6.032cm) from the tail end.

The top end is rounded in at the mark and the area from the ½in (12.7mm) mark back to the tailstock reduced to ⅜in (9.525mm) diameter, the shoulder being undercut very slightly to form a snug seating on to the baseplate.

After sanding smooth overall, part off the waste from the driving end, and chuck the workpiece by its spigot in a ⅜in (9.525mm) hole drilled in a waste wood chuck. The top of the boss can now be cleaned up, and the whole sealed and polished overall. This completes the push bar connector, and preparations for the assembly can begin.

Drilling the parts starts with the container base, the two marks previously made on the sides for the stub axles being first impressed with the centre punch.

Chuck the ⅜in (9.525mm) diameter drill in the headstock next, with the conical dead centre in the tailstock, and hold the base piece in position with the drill and dead centre each located in the impressions on the side of the base. Now feed the wood on to the revolving drill with the hand wheel, holding the base in the other hand, until a depth of ½in (12.7mm) is reached. Reverse the workpiece, and repeat the operation.

After this, test the fit of the axle dowels in the holes, easing them down with abrasive paper if necessary to ensure a push fit, and glue them in, round end outwards of course. Once they are glued in, make sure the dowels' pumping or hydraulic action on the glue doesn't cause the axles to creep back out of the holes by checking them once or twice.

Any tendency for dowels to creep out or even resist seating right home is easily overcome by filing a small flat the full length of the portion entering the hole. This forms an exit for the air/glue trapped within. As an extra precaution, measure the projection of the stub axles to ensure they are the same.

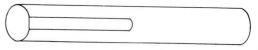

Diagram of axle dowel showing flat area for releasing trapped air and glue

Body having push bar hole drilled after aligning with the spirit level. Cork clams are used in the vice

The baseplate set up between drill and dead centre for boring of axle holes. The grain runs at right angles to the axis of the holes

The completed oriental flower vase, made from New Zealand kauri and finished in clear lacquer

When the stub axles have been fitted, mark the position for the push bar connector. Its centre should be on a line mid-way between and at right angles to, the axles, and be set ½in (12.7mm) back from the edge of the widest part of the wood surrounding the hole.

The position having been marked, drill a ⅜in (9.525mm) diameter hole square to the surface, to a depth of ½in (12.7mm). Test the fit of the connector spigot in the hole, and ensure that the shoulder sits on the base before the spigot bottoms in its hole. Now rotate the boss to bring the push bar hole at right angles to the axles, and glue the connector in.

When the glue is dry, assemble the wheels, then clamp the body by cork clams in the vice ready for drilling. Follow the procedure as for Pedro previously, taking the drill in to a depth of 1in (2.54cm).

Before glueing the push bar home, ease down its other end to be a free fit in the connector. This will allow the parts to re-align if any small error in the drilling occurs. Finally, polish overall with a soft cloth, add tumbler, water and flowers, and place in a prominent position: it will give much pleasure to all who see it, not excluding yourself.

TRIPOD BASED LAMPS

Table lamps with tripod bases offer opportunities to use up fairly small section materials – say under 2in (5cm) diameter – which can be formed into a variety of attractive shapes.

The lamp I shall describe was made of ash taken from a whaler oar, and after wet and dry sanding stained with a water base walnut stain and polished with carnauba wax. It stands approximately 18in (45.72cm) high, and has a leg spread of 10in (25.4cm) across.

To make, take a piece of 2in (5.08cm) diameter wood with a good grain pattern, 15in (38.1cm) long, centre it between fork and ring dead centres, square the end, and round down from a taper of 1¾in (4.445cm) at the tail end to 1¼in (3.175cm) at the driven end. Bring it to a smooth true taper, withdraw the dead centre and remount it on the hollow ring centre, using the impression already in the wood, and align with the conical dead centre from behind, as described for boring the floor standard lamp in Chapter 13.

Now take the ⅜in ((9.525mm) diameter long handled boring tool, and bore out the stem of the lamp to within 1in (2.54cm) of the driving centre.

Once bored out, remount the workpiece on the conical dead centre, mark off the wood from the squared end 1in (2.54cm), 6in (15.24cm), 10in (25.4cm), and 13in (33.02cm), and skew in on the lines, square to the axis of the work, to a depth of ⅛in (3.175mm), taking the angle cut from the right side of the mark.

After this, take dimensional cuts with the parting tool slightly to the right of the formed shoulder, to a ¼in (6.35mm) less diameter than the adjoining shoulder, with the exception of the first 1in (2.54cm), which is brought down to a full 1in (2.54cm) diameter to form the spigot for the base. Using the ½in (12.7mm) gouge, taper down from the full diameter at each shoulder to the dimensional cut to its left, starting from the spigot end. This will give a series of cones diminishing in length and diameter from base to top.

After the gouge work, use the skew chisel to level and smooth each taper, turning it on its edge to clean the underside of each shoulder back to the initial skew cut. Every corner must be clean cut, and only the minimum amount of wet and dry sanding should be necessary.

The last taper at the top is shaped in with the gouge to conform with the size of lamp socket being fitted, preferably the type secured by an adapter in the flex hole rather than one held by screws driven in the end grain of the wood. Before removing the stem from the lathe, skew off a ⅛in (3.175mm) chamfer from each shoulder, *after* sanding, so that the bevel is crisp and sharp.

The wood may now be water stained and left to dry, prior to sealing and carnauba wax polishing.

When the wood is dry, set it up between centres and seal and polish it, taking care to get the polish well into the corners of the tapers and not to burn the shoulder bevels by applying too much pressure. After polishing, remove the job from the lathe, position the stem with its top end centred on a ⅜in (9.525mm) jobbing drill chucked in the headstock and its base located on the conical centre at the tailstock. Hold the wood steady with the left hand, and feed it on to the drill with the hand wheel until the last inch of flex hole has been opened.

A No. 2 Taper ½in (12.7mm) BSB (British Standard Brass) tap should now be chucked in a ½in (12.7mm) Jacobs chuck in the headstock, the hole at the top of the lamp stem located on it, and the spigot end aligned by the conical dead centre at the tailstock. This will ensure that the tap cuts its thread dead square in the hole, the chuck being rotated by hand whilst the wood is held stationary, the slack being taken up on the hand wheel as the tapping proceeds. The thread is taken in far enough to allow the adapter to protrude from the wood ⅜in (9.525mm) when screwed fully home, but the lamp socket should be fitted to the assembled adapter (see Chapter 15 for assembly details) to confirm that the lamp socket sits on the wood.

After the stem, the next most important part to be made is the hub. As it is drilled in four places for the legs and stem, it needs to be about 3½in (8.89cm) diameter, free from defects, but may be made from any close grained wood which will take water staining. I used oak for this, as the grain pattern was not unlike the ash of the rest of the lamp.

Take a piece of selected wood a bit over 3½in (8.89cm) diameter and about 3in (7.62cm) long, and set it up on centres with the grain running lengthwise. Square both ends, chuck the 1in (2.54cm) modified Irwin bit in the tailstock, and drill to a depth of 1in (2.54cm) to form the socket for the spigot of the lamp stem.

Now change over to the ⅜in (9.525mm) modified Irwin bit and continue the hole down to within ½in (12.7mm) of the driving centre.

If pressure is maintained on the handwheel throughout the boring operations the fork centre will continue to drive the wood. Remember, however, to switch off the lathe before withdrawing the cutter. (See the discussion on long hole boring in Chapter 13.)

Drilling completed, remount the workpiece on the conical centre seated at the bottom of the socket or, if too deep, on a flanged plug turned to fit snugly in the hole. The outside of the hub may now be turned to any shape which pleases you, provided a wide angled surface is formed to make a seating for the three legs.

The hub of the lamp illustrated was shaped to match the contours of the stem, with the angle of the main bevel determining the degree of splay of the legs.

Mark off from the socket tail end, in pencil, ⅝in (15.875mm), 1⅛in (2.86cm), 1½in (3.81cm), 2⅛in (5.397 cm) and 2½in (6.35cm) positions. At the second 1⅛in (2.86cm) mark, skew in to a diameter of 2¾in (6.985cm), taking the V cut out to the two adjoining marks. At the fourth 2⅛in (5.397cm) mark, skew in to a diameter of 2½in (6.35cm), working in a V from the third and fifth marks, and reducing diameter at the fifth mark to 2¾in (6.985cm).

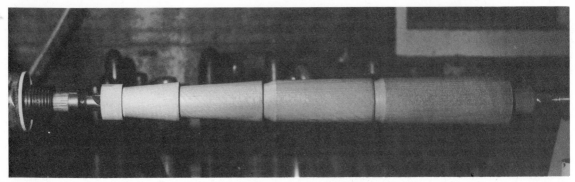

The stem marked off and individual tapers being cut. There is some ribbing which will require attention later

The stem mounted on tap and dead centre for true alignment of tap in cutting thread for lamp fitting adapter

From the fifth mark taper the end down to 1⅛in (2.86cm) diameter, and from the first mark taper off to 2¾in (6.985cm) at that end.

The face formed between the third and fourth marks will provide a long bevel into which the holes for the legs will be bored later, the axis of the holes being square to the face of the bevel.

Having skewed the hub to a very smooth finish, sand, seal and polish it, and lay out around the wide bevel the position for the three legs. This can easily be done with a curved strip of paper laid around the bevel, and cut to the exact length of the circumference. (See the illustrations for the floor standard lamp the the next section.) The paper is then accurately folded in three and the positions of the folds transferred to the bevel.

Following this, mount the hub between centres and drill small pilot holes at the leg positions half-way down the face of the bevel.

There is now the problem that the drilling jig (see p. 45) was designed for a ⅜in (9.525mm) drill, and the leg sockets are to be ½in (12.77mm), so it will be necessary to make a small modification to the jig. Take a tenon saw, and cut a ⅜in (9.525mm) wide slot from the top of the jig into the ⅜in (9.525mm) hole. This will allow the shank of the ½in (12.77mm) Irwin or Jennings bit, which is a fraction under ⅜in (9.525mm), to be laid level in the slot of the jig.

The jig can now be set up alongside the hub and the hub rotated to bring the first mark at the height of the horizontal point of the bit, when the headstock and workpiece are secured by wedging the drive pulley. The jig is then rotated to present the bit at right angles to the face of the bevel, and clamped.

With these preliminaries carefully completed, the bit is chucked in the carpenter's brace, and with continued care to preserve the angle and level of the tool the holes are bored out, each in turn, to a depth of 1in (2.54cm). Lastly, chuck the ⅜in (9.525mm) jobbing drill in the headstock, and hand feed the flex hole of the hub on to the drill to open the hole right through. The hub is now ready.

The legs are made next, a simple turning exercise, although accuracy in the dimensions of the spigots and length of leg is essential. Prepare three pieces of the selected wood, each 6in (15.24cm) long by approximately 1in (2.54cm) diameter; centre the first piece and square one end.

Mark with the pencil 5in (12.7cm) from the tailstock end, and taper from ⅞in (22.225mm) diameter at the mark to ⅝in (15.875mm) at the tailstock end, smoothing off with the skew. Now mark 1in (2.54cm) from the tail end, and reduce this last 1–½in (2.54cm–12.7mm) diameter, leaving it full size for fitting to the hub later.

Cut the shoulder clean with the skew, put a small chamfer on the end, and check the spigot for fit in a hole of the hub, easing it down to a nice fit as necessary.

Repeat these preliminaries for the remaining two legs, then start the next cycle of operations. Recentre a leg, and mark 2¾in (6.985cm) in from the tailstock end. Skew in on the line, taking angle cuts from the headstock side to reduce the diameter by ⅛in (3.175mm).

Now extend the taper to the full diameter of ⅞in (22.225mm) at the headstock end of the workpiece, smoothing off with the skew chisel, and part in on the 5in (12.7cm) mark with the spearpoint, clearing the cut on the waste side to allow the skew, or the spearpoint with its edge in the vertical plane, to clean up the end of the leg.

The blank for the hub rounded down, marked out and being bored for spigot of stem. The bit supports the blank whilst cutting the hole

A leg mounted between centres for final shaping during the second cycle of operations

Section view of ornamental fitting for flex hole in stem of lamp

The hub, with socket hole plugged, mounted on centres ready for turning to shape

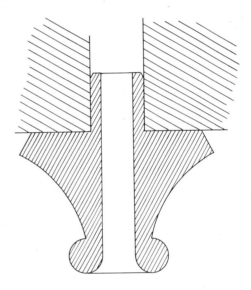

The hub secured between centres, having the leg holes bored using the modified jig

After this, take the parting tool in to leave a $\frac{1}{4}$in (6.35mm) diameter stub in the waste, and sand, seal and finish the leg overall. Next, make a small chamfer on the corners of the large end and middle shoulder, and saw off the waste taking care not to mark the workpiece.

Repeat the foregoing operations on the remaining two legs, and finally chuck a leg by its spigot in a waste wood chuck and carefully erase the waste stub from the end of the leg. Again repeat for the other legs, then sand, seal and polish the ends of all three.

As a final craftsman's touch before glueing up, turn an ornamental fitting for the flex opening at the bottom of the hub. It should have a nicely rounded bell mouth to prevent chafing of the flex, and be made of box, as was mine, or a similar dense, contrasting colour wood.

The finished lamp in stained ash, with oak hub and boxwood flex hole fitting

Display of lamps. From left to right: *Australian jarrah with elm base; New Zealand kauri; New Zealand kauri with oak base and jarrah insert*

It is drilled through the centre for the flex, with a flared, round-lipped mouth as illustrated, and is made to be a push fit into the hub. If felt necessary the ⅜in (9.525mm) flex hole in the hub can be opened up slightly, but I found that a ¼in (6.35mm) diameter hole in the fitting was ample for the passage of the flex and still allowed a wall thickness of ¹⁄₁₆in (1.587mm) on the fitting itself. When ready, sand, seal and polish the fitting, and secure it in the hub with a touch of glue.

Assemble the lamp dry initially, and check that the legs all go fully home, likewise the spigot of the stem, and that it stands upright. Make any necessary adjustments, and glue up the legs first. Last of all, carefully remove any surplus glue from sight, and connect up the flex and lamp holder.

A FLOOR STANDARD LAMP

A natural development of the table lamp just described is a floor standard lamp of matching design. The dimensions are expanded of course, and the stem is jointed, but otherwise the sequence of operations and the tools used are the same as before.

First select sufficient matching wood to cover the whole project. For the stem you will require one piece 21½in (54.61cm) long by 2¼in (5.715cm) diameter for the bottom half, and one piece 23½in (59.69cm) long by 2¼in (5.715cm) diameter for the top half. The three legs are 13¼in (33.655cm) long by 1¼in (3.175cm) diameter, and the hub, which, like the table lamp, may be of some similar wood in grain or colour provided it is close grained and free from defects, is 4¼ × 4¼in (10.795 × 10.795cm).

The top stem rough rounded, fitted with a plug in the socket hole and mounted on the hollow centre ready for boring out. The tailstock is swung clear of the long handled bit

Mount the 23½in (59.69cm) length between centres, round it down to a full 2in (5.08cm) diameter, and square both ends back to 23¼in (59.055cm). Next, using the 1in (2.54cm) modified Irwin bit as previously described in boring the table lamp hub, blind bore a 1in (2.54cm) diameter by 1in (2.54cm) deep hole at one end.

Now make and fit a tight, wide flanged plug in the hole, and mount this end on the hollow centre, using the impression made by the ring centre in turning the plug, and bore out the ⅜in (9.525mm) diameter hole for the flex, stopping short 1in (2.54cm) from the driving centre, as described earlier.

After the hole is bored, re-centre on the dead centre, and taper the workpiece down from 2in (5.08cm) diameter at the tailstock to 1¾in (4.445cm) at the headstock. Finish the surface smooth with the skew chisel, and mark off from the tailstock end 8½in (21.59cm) and 16¼in (41.275cm).

Skew in on the marks to a depth of ⅛in (3.175mm), taking angle cuts from the right hand side, and part in ¼in (6.35mm), cutting slightly to the right of the skew cut. Following this, using the ⅝in (15.875mm) shallow gouge, taper down from the full diameter at each shoulder to the dimensional cut on its left. This will give three cones diminishing in length and diameter from tailstock to headstock.

After the gouge work use the skew to level and smooth each taper and to clean up the corners, then finish in all details as for the table lamp. The top half of the stem is now completed.

Centre the 21½in (54.61cm) length next, using the ring dead centre, and round down to a full 2³⁄₁₆in (5.556cm) diameter. Square both ends back to 21¼in (53.975cm), and taper down from 2³⁄₁₆in (5.556cm) at the tailstock end to 2in (5.08cm) at the headstock.

The bottom stem tapered and marked out for shaping, showing dowel ends for assembly to top stem and to hub

Smooth off the taper with the skew chisel, remount the workpiece on the hollow centre as previously described, and bore out to within 1in (2.54cm) of the driving centre with the ⅜in (9.525mm) long handled bit.

After this, change back to the conical dead centre, and mark off the wood at 1in (2.54cm), 10in (25.4cm) and 20¼in (51.435cm). Skew in on the marks, and reduce the first 1in (2.54cm) to a full 1in (2.54cm) diameter for fitting into the socket of the base hub.

Next part in ¼in (6.35mm) to the right of the line at 10in (25.40cm) and left of the line at 20¼in (51.435cm), and from a square shoulder reduce the last 1in (2.54cm) to a full 1in (2.54cm) diameter, so making a spigot for joining to the upper half of the stem.

Now take the ⅝in (15.875mm) shallow gouge and taper down from the full diameter at each shoulder to the dimensional cut on its left. Follow this up with the skew chisel, to level and smooth each taper and to clean up the corners, after which finish in all details as for the table lamp. This completes the bottom part of the stem.

For the hub select a suitable piece 4¼ × 4¼in (10.795 × 10.795cm), free from defects, and set up on the driving and ring centres with the grain running lengthwise. Now follow in sequence all the operations as for the hub of the table lamp up to the marking out details, bringing the diameter down to a smooth 4in (10.16cm). The shape of the hub may be varied slightly from the style of the table lamp, but one long bevel for locating and setting the angle of the legs is still essential.

Mark off from the socket end at the tailstock: ½in (12.7mm) (first), 1½in (3.81cm) (second), 2¼in (5.715cm) (third), 3in (7.62cm) (fourth), 3¼in (8.225cm) (fifth) and 4in (10.16cm) (sixth).

From the first mark back to the tailstock taper down to 2⅝in (6.667cm) to give a smooth concave surface. When finally polished this curved face will reflect the light beautifully.

At the second mark skew in to 3¼in (8.225cm) diameter, extending the sides of the skew cut out to the first and third marks in a V form. Again at the fourth mark skew in to 2½in (6.35cm) diameter, extending the sides of the skew cut out to the third mark at one side and the fifth mark at the other, having first reduced the diameter at the fifth mark to 2¾in (6.985cm).

From the fifth mark taper on a shallow curve down to an end diameter of 1¼in (3.175cm), using the gouge and smoothing off finally with the skew.

The surface formed between the third and fourth marks will provide a long bevel into which the ¾in (19.05mm) diameter holes for the legs will be bored, the axis of the hole being square to the face of the bevel, and radial to the centre.

Now slice off the tops of the corners formed at the first and third marks to a width of ⅛in (3.175mm), and sand, seal and polish the hub overall. Next, using the paper strip method described earlier, lay out around the wide bevel the position for the three leg socket holes.

Follow the procedure as already described, using the modified drilling jig; although the bit is larger in cutting diameter, the shank portion which fits in the jig will be the same size as for the ½in (12.7mm) bit.

When the socket holes for the legs have been drilled, the hub is ready. The legs are made up last, and are a simple spindle turning exercise, although accuracy in the fit of the spigots and length of the legs is essential.

Prepare three selected pieces, each 13½in (34.29cm) long by about 1¼in (3.175cm) diameter, centre the first piece, and

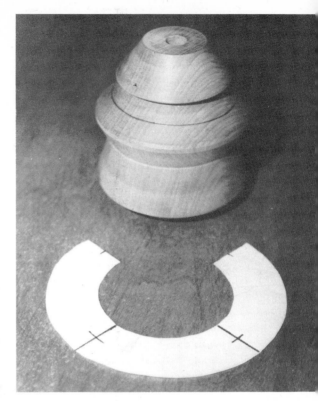

The shaped hub with centre line marked on wide bevel and paper strip ready for use

The leg hole positions ready for marking on to the wide bevel by means of the paper template

round it down to 1⅛in (2.875mm) diameter, smoothing off and squaring the tail end with the skew.

Now mark off at 1in (2.54cm), 6½in (16.51cm), and 13in (33.02cm), and skew in on the marks.

Reduce the first 1in (2.54cm) to a full ¾in (19.05mm) diameter, to form the spigot of the leg, and chamfer the end. Test its fit in a hole of the hub, easing it down to a nice fit as necessary.

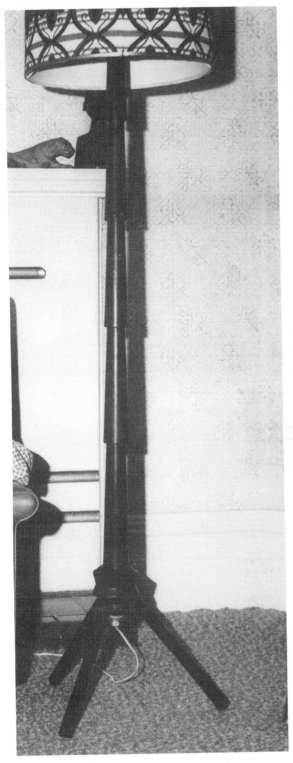

A completed floor standard lamp. In the lamp described in the text the splay of the legs has been increased

Next part in to a full ⅞in (22.225mm) diameter to the left of the 6½in (16.51cm) mark, and taper down from the 1⅛in (2.857cm) diameter at the 13in (33.02cm) mark to the dimensional cut at the centre of the leg. Skew the taper smooth and true and clean the shoulder back to the 6½in (16.51cm) mark. Now reduce the diameter of the shoulder at the centre of the leg to 1in (2.54cm), and taper down from there to a full ⅞in (22.225mm) diameter at the spigot end, smoothing off with the skew chisel as before.

Part in on the left of the 13in (33.02cm) mark, clearing the cut on the waste side to allow the skew chisel room to clean up the end of the leg, and leaving about ¼in (6.35mm) diameter connected to the waste. Sand, seal and finish overall.

Next cut a small chamfer on the corner of the 1⅛in (2.857cm) diameter end, and saw off the waste, taking care not to mark the leg. Repeat all the foregoing operations on the remaining two legs.

Finally chuck a leg in a waste wood chuck by its spigot, and carefully remove the waste stub from its end. Repeat for the other legs, then sand, seal and polish the ends of all three.

Test all the legs for entering fully into the hub, and dry assemble the whole lamp standard to check the upright attitude of the stem. Make any necessary adjustments by easing a leg slightly out of its socket during the glueing up operations, although if due care has been taken at all stages in forming the legs and boring the hub no adjustment should be needed. As a last finishing touch, turn an ornamental fitting for the flex opening in the base of the hub, as described for the table lamp, and connect the wiring.

A NEST OF EGG CUPS

Egg cups always make a useful addition to the home, and if they stack vertically and take up little space, are that much more acceptable. These I shall describe can be made in any attractive wood, and are best finished off without lacquer or polish, but wet sanded, sealed when dry, given a light rubbing of liquid paraffin or teak oil, and then burnished dry with shavings or a soft cloth. They are designed so that the base of one will nest in the top of another; they are then all bored through from top to bottom and will slide down onto a dowel set vertically in a baseplate.

Take a piece of the selected wood 2¼in (5.715cm) square by 12in (30.48cm) long, and round down to a smooth cylinder of 2in (5.08cm) diameter between centres.

Square both ends and turn a short spigot ⅜in (9.525mm) long to be a tight screw-in fit in the mandrel hole of the faceplate, as described in Chapter 16, slightly undercutting the face abutting the faceplate to ensure a solid contact between them at the outer edge of the wood. If the fit is made tight enough to require the use of the strap wrench to turn the workpiece fully home, then all risk of 'chatter' is eliminated when hollowing out the unsupported end of the workpiece.

As the next step, to maintain uniformity in both the inside and outside shapes of the cups, two profile gauges or templates will be required. These can be cut from metal (aluminium sheet is ideal), or three-ply, hardboard or stiff card. I always make my templates in ply or metal, and take pains over them in the belief that, inscribed with their purpose and carefully put away, they will always serve again.

Use a standard egg cup hollow as a guide to shaping the inside gauge, and form it with a shoulder to rest across

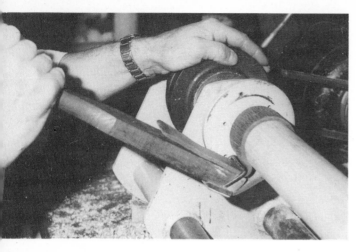

The egg cup blank being screwed into the faceplate hole using the strap wrench

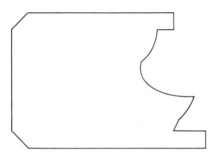

Diagram of plywood gauge for the outer shape of the egg cups

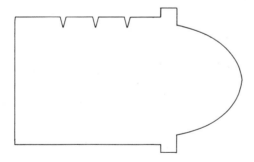

Diagram of a combined profile and marking out gauge for the hollow of the egg cup and the position of dimensional cuts

the lip of the cup when the gauge is fully home – say 1in (2.54cm).

The profile gauge for the outside shape of the cup is made from the same material, the desired section profile being drawn full size on paper, and then stuck to the gauge material. When the glue is dry, the outline on the paper is cut around with fretsaw and file and a shoulder formed to control the gauge from the mouth end of the cup, as with the inside gauge. A suggested shape is shown at the end of this section, with dimensions which give a stacked height of only 6½in (16.71cm) for six cups.

When the templates are ready the 1in (2.54cm) modified

Irwin bit is chucked in the tailstock and, revolving at 750 r.p.m. fed into the end of the workpiece to a depth of ⅝in (15.875mm). The bit is then exchanged for a ½in (12.7mm) Irwin, or a jobbing drill, and the hole counter-bored to a depth of 1¾in (4.445cm) from the top of the cup. After this, the tailstock is withdrawn and the drill removed.

The tool rest is brought up across the end of the workpiece next, and with the lathe now running at 2000 r.p.m. the inside of the hole is roughed out to shape, working from the centre outwards, starting with the spearpoint to remove most of the waste, followed by the round nose scraper, taking very light cuts towards the headstock.

Any pressure exerted against the side of the hole, unless very light, may cause chatter, especially if a broad area of the tool's edge is in contact with the wood or the tool is in the slightest degree blunt. For this reason it is always preferable to use a narrow ended tool cutting more towards the headstock than a wide edged tool cutting into the side of the hole.

Make frequent checks with the gauge, and when the shoulders contact the lip of the hole it is ready for wet sanding. Take care not to bell out the mouth of the cup, using a narrow strip of wet and dry paper over the end of the finger, and when the inside is smooth enough polish it dry with an absorbent rag and seal it. Finally, rub over with liquid paraffin, and burnish it dry with shavings or a soft cloth in the lathe.

For the shaping of the outside which follows, the tail end of the workpiece can be supported by the tailstock, using a half-egg shaped adapter inserted in the cup and centered on the ring centre impression made when the adapter was turned. If, however, you have by this time made yourself a revolving centre as described in Chapter 15, then the adapter is turned with a pin to fit the revolving centre, which is a much better arrangement.

With the adapter in position supporting the end of the workpiece, and the lathe turning at 2000 r.p.m. lay off the position for the dimensional cuts, using the template as a guide, and start shaping the outside.

Simple, clean lines are best suited to this project, and all finishing cuts where possible should be done with the skew chisel to reduce the amount of wet sanding to follow. The burning in of decorative lines around the top half, using the wire method described in Chapter 15, may be considered, or the burning of the lip by pressure from a piece of waste hardwood, but neither would be suitable on a dark wood.

After oiling and burnishing as for the inside, the first cup is parted off the length, using the skew chisel for the base trimming and parting cuts to ensure a smooth, undercut bottom to the cup. There will be a fairly wide separation and loss of wood of course, so if you prefer, the parting off can be done with the parting tool, and the cup bases all cleaned up in one operation, as described later. After parting off, the tailstock mounting the conical dead centre is brought up to engage the impression in the end of the workpiece, and the end squared off.

The tool rest is then brought close in to the end after the tailstock has been withdrawn, and the spearpoint used to form a 1in (2.54cm) diameter recess about ⅛in (3.175mm) deep in the end of the wood for locating the Irwin bit.

Following this, the tailstock dead centre is replaced by the Jacobs chuck carrying the 1in (2.54cm) modified Irwin bit, and the end of the workpiece bored in to a depth of ⅝in (15.875mm). From there the sequence of operations as for the first cup is repeated, until the set of six is done.

There now only remains the levelling, smoothing and finishing of the bases if this wasn't done at the time of parting off. For this purpose turn a chuck shaped to locate on the outside of the lip of the cup, with a central pin of ½in (12.7mm) full diameter, long enough to engage fully in the bottom hole as a twist tight fit. With the cup aligned by its lip and the pin it will run perfectly true whilst the skew takes a fine undercut slice from the bottom. This will not only smooth it, but also ensure that it sits steady when in use.

An alternative method of supporting and driving the cup is to build, from thick cork glued to a wood base, an egg shaped driving chuck. This locates in the hollow of the cup, bearing on the lower sides and bottom, whilst the base hole of the cup is supported on the conical dead centre. Cork gives a positive drive without marking the wood, and similar chucks made for other applications will be found extremely useful.

First cup on blank being hollowed with round end scraper after initial boring and drilling

Parting off the first egg cup supported by the egg shaped adapter in the revolving centre. The base of the egg cup will be smoothed off on a special chuck later

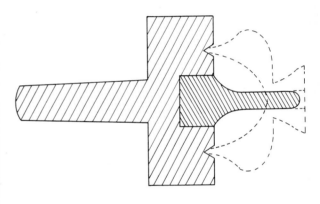

Sectioned diagram of the special chuck to support the egg cup on a true axis whilst the base is smoothed and slightly undercut

Recessing the outer end of the blank to centre the bit for hollowing out after the first cup has been parted off

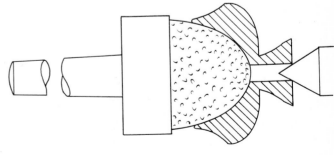

Section diagram of an alternative method and chuck for supporting the cup whilst its base is smoothed and undercut

Display of cork clutches, with sample cork sheet used as vice clams, and chucks which can be used to drive or as drill or pressure pads in the tailstock

The finished nest of egg cups. The wood is ash, water stained. The stand has been carnauba wax polished, the egg cups paraffin waxed and burnished

THE EGG CUP STAND

This consists of a straight length of ½in (12.7mm) diameter dowelling in the parent wood, stepped and glued into a circular base of 3in (7.62cm) diameter.

The dowel is made long enough to extend about 1½in (3.81cm) above the stacked cups, the dowel top and base disc being incised to match any ornamentation on the cups.

As, unlike the egg cups, it will not be immersed in water from time to time, the stand is wet sanded, sealed and carnauba wax polished, after which the finished masterpiece can be presented with pride to the lady of the house.

A SERVING OF SERVIETTE RINGS

Although all serviette or napkin rings are made identical in one respect – with the hole through the middle – the finishing of the outside offers a wide range of choice in decorative effects. Full play can be given to one's skill with the skew chisel and long nose gouge in producing ogees, curves, beads and coves in a variety of combinations, some sample shapes being pictured at the end of this section. Sets of rings may comprise four or six pieces, each approximately 1½in (3.81cm) long by 2in (5.08cm) outside diameter, with a 1½in (3.81cm) hole, but it is suggested that you provide enough of the chosen wood for an extra one, just in case.

The wood is preferably a dense, close grained variety for strength, and if making six, cut two 6 × 2¼in (15.24cm × 5.715cm) diameter lengths, and centre and set one up in the lathe. Square one end, and turn a ⅜in (9.525mm) long pin or spigot oversize to the diameter of the faceplate mandrel hole. Undercut the shoulder slightly, and assemble the workpiece to the faceplate in the way described in Chapter

16. (Using this screw-in method of chucking my lathe takes 12in (30.48cm) lengths with no suggestion of chatter, but until you have mastered the technique I suggest you stick to using a shorter workpiece.)

Chuck your largest bit up to 1¼in (3.175cm) diameter in the tailstock next, and bore into the end of the wood to a depth of 2in (5.08cm), with a lathe speed of 750 r.p.m. When the correct depth is reached (determined by adhesive tape or a black felt tip pen mark on the shank of the bit), withdraw the tailstock and un-chuck the bit. Now position the tool rest across the end of the wood at centre height, and using the spearpoint with horizontal thrusts along the axis of the work, open up the hole, working from the centre outwards to a hole diameter of 1½in (3.81cm), finishing with very light cuts from a round nose scraper, and belling out the mouth to a rounded taper.

Sand the inside beyond half-way in, prepare a taper plug for the open end, and bring up the tailstock dead centre in support whilst the ring is parted off a full 1½in (3.81cm) from its end, easing back on the dead centre before cutting through to avoid jamming the tool.

Following this, turn a softwood chuck (softwood is used for all chucks of this type because a really tight press-in fit is achieved without risk of damage to the workpiece), about 3in (7.62cm) long by 2in (5.08cm) diameter, and form one end to suit the method of drive chosen: a taper or screw-in pin to fit the mandrel hole, or a larger pin for screwing into the faceplate, as done for the original workpiece.

Once you have firmly mounted it in the headstock, taper the end of the chuck to accept the bell mouth of the ring to almost half-way, ensuring it is a tight fit and runs absolutely true. (If a pencil mark is then struck around the chuck by the end of the ring the chuck can be used as a plug gauge for the openings, so they can be made all alike.) One way of ensuring this is to make an internal sanding tool as follows.

Take a piece of straight grained 1¾in (4.445cm) diameter wood, 5in (12.7cm) long plus enough extra for driving or screwing into the headstock mandrel or screwing into the centre hole of the faceplate.

Turn between centres to 1⁷⁄₁₆in (3.65cm) diameter for 5in (12.7cm), shaping the rest to suit your intended method of mounting when the tool is in use. Shape the 5in (12.7cm) section to a smooth parallel cylinder, slightly tapering 1½in (3.81cm) from the outer end to a diameter of 1¼in (3.175cm) at the end.

Next, taking care to cut straight down the centre, saw a slot 4in (10.16cm) deep from the end, and round the lips of the slot for its full length. The tool is now ready for fitting with abrasive paper. This is cut to a width of 4in (10.16cm), and a length to encircle the tool with an extra 1in (2.54cm), (½in, 12.7mm, at each end), to tuck into the slot. Fitted with a fine grade of paper, the tool is used after each ring has been hollowed out to 1½in (3.81cm) diameter, the rings being fed on to the tool to bring all the holes to a standard size.

The serviette ring is now mounted on the freshly made tapered spigot chuck. Using the round nose scraper newly sharpened, form a rounded taper in the mouth of the hole to match its other end, and finish with fine grade wet and dry paper. After this, reassemble in the mouth of the hole the taper plug used in the parting off operation, and bring up the tailstock in support. Now set up the tool rest at mid-height on the side of the ring, and with it thus fully supported shape it with skew and gouge to your chosen design. A word of warning, however: remember that you have a further five to make, all exactly alike, so the more intricate the design, the more difficult it will be to reproduce.

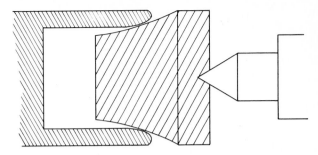

Section diagram of the shaped and sanded end of a ring supported on an adapter at the tailstock ready for parting off

The ring in position on a tapered drive chuck, ready for shaping and finishing the outer end of the hole using the round end scraper

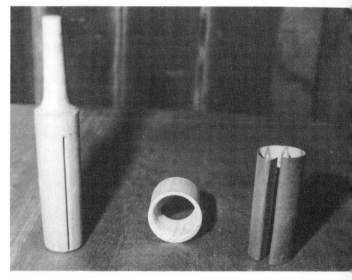

The internal sanding tool showing sandpaper sleeve and sanded ring

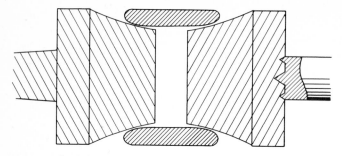

Section diagram of a ring mounted between a tapered driving chuck and plug for shaping outside

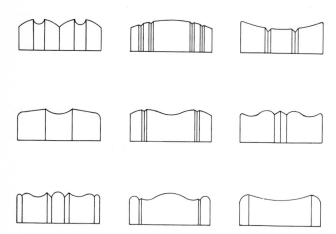

Diagram of a selection of shapes for serviette rings

When the outsides are finished and ends nicely rounded back to a true 1½in (3.81cm) length, carefully sand overall, seal inside and out, and finish with wax polish or lacquer.

Repeat the whole sequence for each ring in turn, ensuring that all are exactly the same length and diameter, with the hole size standard, as any discrepancy here will show up badly when they are stacked on the stand.

Although I have followed the full sequence of operations required to make one ring from start to finish, it would of course be done differently in practice. One operation would be completed on all the rings in succession, before changing over to the next sequence requiring perhaps different tools, lathe speeds or accessories. This line system, as it is called, used throughout industry, saves considerable time and helps achieve a uniform result at each stage of production.

THE STAND

As with the egg cups, a vertical stand to keep the rings together when not in use sets the rings off really well. The centre pillar is made long enough to allow a turned knob to protrude at the top, with a diameter just under the hole size of the rings so that they rest squarely on each other.

The base is a simple one, 4in (10.16cm) in diameter, turned on the screwchuck and ornamented to match the coves, hollows and beads on the rings, with a

¾in (19.05mm) diameter socket cut to a depth of ½in (12.7mm) to match a spigot ready turned on the pillar.

The two parts are best finished independently of each other, including wax polishing, before glueing up, but if lacquering is intended this should be done afterwards.

When glueing dowels to baseplates it pays to have the base set up on the screwchuck with the dowel held in by pressure from a pad in the tailstock poppet. It is then easy to rotate the job by hand to check that the dowel is perfectly upright in relation to the base, and bring the grain in line.

A variation of the two foregoing projects would be a combined stand for both egg cups and serviette rings. The centre pillar could take the rings as before, with six short pegs arranged around the base to take the egg cups. Alternatively, the centre dowel could be ornamented and be purely for lifting purposes, the base being set with short pegs for the egg cups. These are then assembled on their pegs upside down, with their bottoms, suitably reshaped, forming a location for the rings nested on them.

This would be a logical arrangement as napkin rings are required at every meal, whereas egg cups are usually needed only at breakfast time, and then not every day (unless you keep chickens!).

The completed serviette rings on their stand. The wood is water stained ash, polished with carnauba wax

A STAND OF STOOLS

Although strictly speaking the chucking methods used in this group of projects are routine, they do have some interesting aspects relating to boring, which merit their inclusion. Stools come in a variety of shapes, so making them adds just that little extra to the sum of one's experience. Besides which, it is amazing how useful they become in the home or the workshop. No family should be without one! Their tops may be round, oval, square or oblong; the number of legs three or four, which may be braced by no rungs, two rungs, three rungs, four rungs, or two rungs joined by one or maybe two cross rails. There is a wide choice! I propose we deal first with the common round top, three leg, no rung variety – the type one imagines as having been used by dairy maids.

Three leg, round top, no rung stool

Select a piece of 1½in (3.81cm) thick by 10½in (27.94cm) square elm, deal or similar wood, plane one face flat and smooth, scribe a 10in (25.4cm) diameter circle on this face, and saw off the corners. Mount it on the screwchuck, using the double faced sandpaper clutch described elsewhere, and dress the unplaned face flat and smooth with the shallow gouge.

Strike a circle of 10in (25.4cm) diameter once more, and part in on the waste side of the line with the spearpoint. Turn a generous chamfer on the front corner, and lightly round off the back corner as well. Bring the outer edge to a smooth finish with the ⅝in (15.875mm) shallow gouge, really sharp, then sand smooth the front and side faces and remove from the lathe.

Now place the disc planed side up on the bench, and strike an 8in (20.32cm) diameter circle in pencil on it, marking six radial positions around it. Three intermediate marks are centre-punched next, and will be used for drilling the leg holes, whilst the marks opposite them will align the gauge for setting the angle at which they will be drilled. As this gauge will be essential to get the correct angle in all leg hole boring, some pains to achieve accuracy and durability in its construction are justified.

Take a piece of prime board, 1in (2.54cm) thick by 2in (5.08cm) wide by 12in (30.48cm) long, and plane it flat and square on all sides. With a coping saw cut a semi-circular piece of ¾in (19.05mm) radius from a 1in (2.54cm) face, with its centre 2in (5.08cm) from the end. Exactly opposite the recess thus formed, on the other 1in (2.54cm) face, screw a piece of ⅜in (9.525mm) thick by 1½in (3.81cm) wide by 7in (17.78cm) long batten, inclined outwards towards the adjoining end at an angle of 105°. Apply glue to the joint and check the angle again before finally screwing the batten in position.

When the gauge is ready the seat top is laid on a flat piece of waste wood on the bench top, centre punch marks upwards, and the gauge positioned on it with the recessed edge aligned with two diametrically opposite marks, the recess straddling the centre punch mark nearest the operator.

The gauge, seat and waste wood are next clamped to the bench top, and the 1in (2.54cm) boring bit chucked in the carpenter's brace and centered in the mark encircled by the recess of the gauge. The brace is now inclined to align it with the gauge batten, the brace chuck being positioned to bring the bit parallel to it and at the same angle.

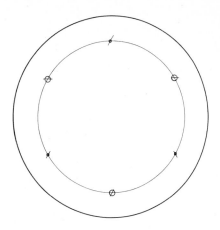

Diagram of the seat top marked out ready for boring leg holes

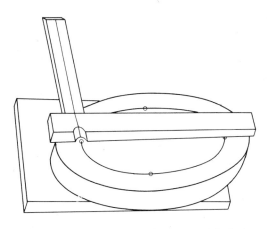

Diagram of the hole boring gauge and seat top ready for boring

With care being taken to maintain the angle in both planes, the hole is bored clean into the waste wood, after which the whole operation is repeated for the remaining holes.

Be sure to bring a fresh area of the waste wood under the bit position for each new hole, otherwise part of the seat top may be torn away if the bit exits on to a hole already in the waste.

Once the holes are bored they are opened up very slightly on the top side with a half-round file, to help the legs grip when the wedges are driven home during final assembly.

After the leg holes have been bored, the seat top is slotted to form a hand hold for lifting, so with it still bottom up on the bench, mark the position at its centre, along the grain, for three 1in (2.54cm) diameter holes spaced 1in (2.54cm) between centres, the centre mark being offset ⅛in (3.175mm) from the line.

Interpose the waste wood as before, and bore vertically right through the disc with the 1in (2.54cm) bit chucked in the hand brace. Once bored, join up the three holes with chisel, rasp and file, bevel the edges of the slot thus formed, and sand smooth overall.

A leg marked out and partially shaped

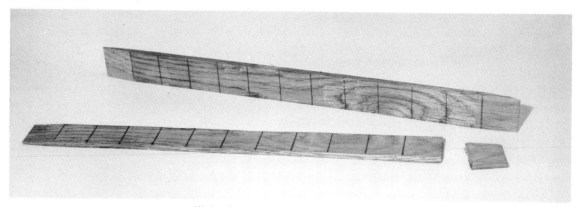

Wedges for legs in strip form. The wood is oak

The legs, which come next, are turned from long grained pieces of ash, beech or deal, each 14¼in (36.195cm) long by 2in (5.08cm) square, and are centered and the first leg set up between the ring and driving centres. Rough round down the wood, smooth it to a uniform cylinder of 1½in (3.81cm) diameter, square one end and mark off at 4in (10.16cm), 6in (15.24cm) and 12in (30.48cm) from the tailstock.

From the 4in (10.16cm) mark taper down to 1in (2.54cm) at the tail end, on a concave curve, and repeat between the 6in (15.24cm) and 12in (30.48cm) marks, except that the diameter there is 1¼in (3.175cm), forming a stop for the spigot entering the seat top.

Cut in with the long nose gouge from the 12in (30.42cm) mark to the end, and turn to a full smooth 1in (2.54cm) diameter, easing down to a good fit in a hole of the seat and marking each spigot to its hole as you go.

Smooth the leg overall with the skew, but leaving the parallel section between the 4in (10.16cm) and 6in (15.24cm) marks distinct from the adjoining curves. This area can then be incised with some simple decoration which suits your fancy.

Use the skew again to turn a round chamfer on the bottom corner of the leg, and smooth overall. Finally, before assembly, cut a saw kerf to a depth of 1in (2.54cm) in the top of each leg, along the grain, and make wedges in oak or beech to match. The easiest way to make wedges, which may otherwise become a fiddly job, is to cut first a strip of oak or beech 1in (2.54cm) wide by $\frac{3}{16}$in (4.762mm) thick by 4in (10.16cm) long. Mark it off into four sections, and taper the two outer ends to a wedge shape on the sanding disc, taking the taper up to the mark. Next saw off one of the end wedges, and shape the freshly sawn end of the remaining 3in (7.62cm) piece in the same way as before. This wedge is cut off in turn, and the freshly cut end of the remaining length shaped like the rest. The last two wedges are then cut apart and the job is done. When the wedges are ready,

The tin shield in position when cutting back the ends of legs.
(These wedges are in fact longer than those described.) The
hacksaw teeth point towards the operator, cutting on the pull
stroke

glue and assemble the legs, bringing the saw kerfs in line
with the outer edge of the seat, add a touch of glue and
drive the wedges home.

Allow 24 hours for the glue to dry, then cut the leg ends
back flush with the seat top, and sand the area smooth,
using a sanding block along the grain. To avoid marking the
seat during the cutting back operation use a fair sized piece
of tin with a 1in (2.54cm) hole towards one edge, placed
over the stub of the leg. A hacksaw blade can then be used
to remove the waste close up, with a plane to finish off (after
removing the tin guard of course!).

After sealing overall, give the whole stool a light rub over
with steel wool, dust off, and finish with clear lacquer,
suspending the stool from a screw hook in the bottom of
one leg so that any dust settling on the surface will not be
seen.

Three leg, round top, three rung stool

First of all, to make it easier to grip the legs whilst being
bored and to avoid marring them in the vice, do not shape
them, apart from the spigot ends, until *after* the holes are all
done.

To set the position for the rungs, run a pencil mark round
each leg whilst still in the lathe, 5in (12.7cm) up from the
bottom. On this line, in the same grain area of each leg, a
centre punch mark is made, and a leg clamped in the vice
with this mark central and uppermost.

The seat top, with one other leg assembled, is now fitted
on the spigot of the leg in the vice, and a spirit level laid
against the two legs at the point where they enter the underside of the seat.

The seat top is next rotated on the clamped leg until the
spirit level is in the vertical position, and its cross bubble is
central. At this point a location mark is made with the pencil,
partly on the spigot of the clamped leg and partly on the
underside of the adjoining seat.

The spirit level is next laid, still in the vertical position,
against the underside of the seat, and the clamped leg tilted
in the vice to bring the cross bubble central. Check that the
centre punch mark is still in the centre top position between
the jaws of the vice, and the location marks are still joined
when the cross bubble is central, and then securely clamp
the leg.

Now chuck a ½in (12.7mm) diameter boring bit in the
carpenter's brace, remove the top leg to clear it, centre the
bit in the punch mark, and with the brace held perfectly
upright bore into the leg to a depth of ⅝in (15.875mm).
Repeat the procedure for the remaining two legs, following
a left or right hand sequence, until each leg has one hole
done, and each leg has been numbered to its socket in the
seat.

At this point assemble the legs in the seat top and measure
the distance from inner face to inner face at the rung position, and add twice ⅝in (15.875mm) for the length of the
rungs.

Aligning the first leg for rung hole boring using the spirit level

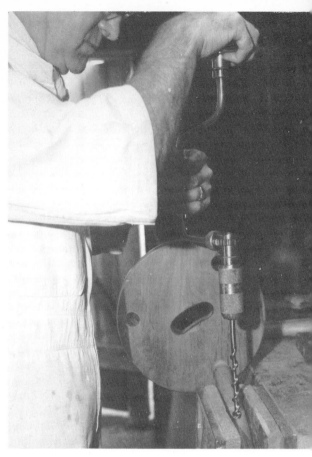

A leg being bored for rung after vertical alignment with the spirit level

These are now made to suit your fancy, but should match the style of the legs, with of course $\frac{5}{8}$in (15.875mm) long by $\frac{1}{2}$in (12.7mm) diameter ends on each, fitting snugly into their own numbered holes, when the second sequence of these has been drilled.

When the rungs are ready assemble two legs joined by a rung into the seat top, and grip one in the vice with the other off to one side.

Assemble the third leg in its hole above the clamped leg and lie the spirit level against them, close to the underside of the seat, in a vertical position. Rotate the clamped leg to bring the cross bubble central, then transfer the spirit level, still vertical, to the underside of the seat. Now tilt the clamped leg in the vice to bring the cross bubble level, and when the bubbles are central in both positions clamp the leg and centre punch on the 5in (12.7cm) mark at its top centre.

Following this, chuck a $\frac{1}{2}$in (12.7mm) boring bit in the brace, removing the top leg to make way for it, centre the bit in the punch mark, and with the brace held perfectly upright bore into the leg to a depth of $\frac{5}{8}$in (15.875mm).

When the first leg is finished, it is unclamped and the leg to which it is connected by the rung is in turn gripped in the vice. Once again, the third leg is inserted in the hole above it, and the spirit levelling and boring procedures carried out as before.

After the second leg has been bored, its place in the vice is taken by the third leg, connected by its rung to an adjoining leg, and the full sequence of operations as for legs one and two repeated.

When the last leg has been bored, assemble the rungs to their respective legs, (the rung ends having been marked to their related holes when turned), and fit the legs into the seat top. Check that the stool stands level, making any necessary adjustments by easing a leg into or out of its hole slightly, then glue up, wedge and finish overall as already described.

A leg being aligned by spirit level before boring its second rung hole. A split adapter is holding the shaped leg in the vice

Four leg, round top, two rung stool

If you decide on a four leg design, place the seat top planed face upwards on the bench and scribe a pencilled circle of 8in (20.32cm) diameter on it. Around the circle lay out four equidistant points, and mark them with the centre punch.

If the wood has a distinct grain pattern running across it, try to balance the leg positions to the grain, so that when two legs are square to the front the grain lies with them. It is purely a matter of appearances, but it shows attention to detail, an important element of high class work.

As the legs will be splayed outwards to provide stability, the simple 125° angle gauge, already described, will again be essential. The gauge in this case is laid along two diagonally opposite centre punch marks, but in every other respect the boring and finishing of the seat top follows the same pattern as before. The same applies to the making and fitting of the legs, except of course that an extra one is required!

In the next operation – the drilling of the legs for the rungs – the usual high standard in marking out and hole boring is essential. As two rungs only are to be fitted they will ob-

viously run diagonally from leg to leg across the centre, and so cross over in the middle. If preferred, they may be made fairly light, say of ½in (12.7mm) diameter, in ash or beech, in which case they can be sprung around each other, and the holes in the legs for them all drilled at the same height. If heavier rungs are decided on, however, the hole positions in each pair of diagonally opposite legs would have to be offset to allow the rungs to clear each other at the centre crossover position.

So, assuming two ½in (12.7mm) diameter ash or beech rungs are chosen, mark each leg 5in (12.7cm) up from the bottom, on the same grain area, with the centre punch, and assemble two of them in diagonally opposite holes of the seat top, marking them to their respective holes. Grip one of them in the vice with its punch mark to the top, and the other directly above it.

Now lie the spirit level vertically against the two legs, close to the underside of the seat, and rotate the seat on the spigot of the clamped leg to bring the cross bubble central. Once adjusted transfer the level, still in the vertical position, to the underside of the seat, and tilt the leg clamped in the vice to bring the cross bubble central.

So, by rotary movement of the seat and vertical adjustment of the clamped leg, both spirit level readings are centralised, and the leg brought to a position where a hole drilled at the mark will be at the correct angle in both planes provided the brace is held perfectly upright.

The finished stool, with radiata pine seat and New Zealand tawa legs and rungs. Finished in clear lacquer

After the top leg has been removed to make way for the brace, the ½in (12.7mm) diameter boring bit is chucked in it, centered in the mark and the hole bored down to ¾in (19.05mm) depth, every care being taken to maintain the bit in a truly upright position.

Once the hole is bored, the opposite leg is replaced in its socket, and in its turn gripped in the vice mark upwards, with the drilled leg positioned above it. The complete levelling routine is again carried out and the second leg drilled. Thereafter, both drilled legs are removed from the seat top, the other pair fitted in their respective sockets, and the full sequence of operations repeated.

When all have been bored for the rungs assemble them in the seat top and measure the distance diagonally between the legs, inner face to inner face at the rung hole. Add 1½in (3.81cm) and cut two ½in (12.7mm) diameter dowels accordingly.

Now remove the legs, fit a dowel between an opposed pair, marking the ends to their respective sockets, and re-insert the legs into the seat top. Repeat this for the second pair of legs, and check that they will go fully home into the seat despite the resistance of the rungs. Once satisfied on this point, disassemble the parts and cut a saw kerf in the top of each leg to a depth of 1in (2.54cm) with the grain. Prepare four wedges for them, in oak, beech or ash, glue all the joints and reassemble the stool.

Ensure that each leg is fully home in its socket and that the stool stands steady on all four legs before driving each wedge, faced with glue, fully home in its slot. Should there be any rocking of the stool when stood on a level surface the simplest remedy is to tap back out of its hole a short leg until the stool stands firm.

When the glue is dry, cut the leg ends back to the top of the seat, using the metal guard and hacksaw blade, and sand smooth overall. Finish with a sealer and clear lacquer as described earlier.

If turned rungs larger than ½in (12.7mm) diameter are chosen, then one pair of holes in opposite legs must be raised or lowered to clear the rungs at the centre crossover position, the ends of them remaining at 1in (2.54cm) length by ⅝in (15.875mm) diameter as before. The amount of the offset of the holes will depend on the diameter of the rungs at their centres, but it is easily calculated.

Suppose that each rung is 1in (2.54cm) diameter at its centre, then the sum of half their diameters, viz. ½in plus ½in (12.7mm plus 12.7mm), equals 1in (2.54cm), would be the offset between the holes to ensure the rungs just cleared each other where they crossed over. The rung hole mark for one pair would be moved up ½in (12.7mm) from the 5in (12.7cm) mark, and ½in (12.7mm) down for the other pair. Apart from this requirement, the legs are drilled and the rungs fitted and assembled exactly as before, the legs with the high rung being assembled first of course.

Four leg, round top, four rung stool

When four rungs are fitted, the first step after turning the legs (using a template as described in Chapter 9) is to number them to their respective sockets in the seat top, and to centre-punch a mark on the same grain area of each, 5in (12.7cm) from the bottom.

Setting out dimensions on the leg using template. The template is notched for the pencil and marked with diameters at the notches

Adjusting the position for the leg when boring the second rung hole, using the spirit level. The legs have not been shaped at this stage, in order to assist holding in vice

As the rung holes will only be drilled to a depth of $\frac{5}{8}$in (15.875mm) in a 1$\frac{1}{2}$in (3.81cm) diameter area of the leg, they can be drilled at the same height without seriously weakening them.

The important thing, as before, is to ensure that the rung holes are all accurately drilled at the same angle in both planes; i.e. the rung enters the leg parallel with the ground – the vertical plane – and on a line with its neighbouring leg – the horizontal plane. As described earlier, the simplest way I have found for drilling this compound angle accurately is by careful use of the spirit level and accurate alignment of the brace and bit.

The finished stool. The top is of New Zealand radiata pine, the remaining wood of Indian origin, species unknown. The stool has been clear lacquered. The hand hole lies along the grain

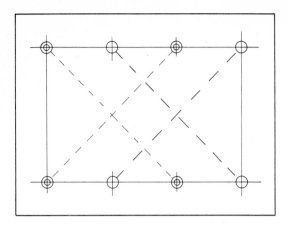

Diagram of the oblong seat top marked out for leg hole boring

*A group of stools finished in various woods and styles.
All have been clear lacquered*

Assemble two neighbouring legs in the seat top, and with the empty leg holes to the top grip the leg to be drilled at about the point where the hole is to be made, with its centre punch mark to the top and central in the vice jaws. The spirit level is now laid horizontally across the legs close to the underside of the seat and the seat top rotated on the clamped leg until the bubble is central. A reference mark is then made on the leg spigot and adjoining seat top.

The spirit level is next transferred to a vertical position against the underside of the seat top, and the leg tilted in the vice to bring the cross bubble central. Again, by rotating the seat top and vertically adjusting the clamped leg to bring the spirit level readings true, the leg is brought to a position where a hole drilled at the mark will be at the correct angle in both planes provided the brace is held perfectly upright.

As before, the $\frac{5}{8}$in (15.875mm) diameter boring bit is chucked in the carpenter's brace, centered in the mark, and the hole bored down to a depth of $\frac{5}{8}$in (15.875mm), constant care being taken to keep the bit upright the whole way in. The second set of rung holes is bored in exactly the same way as the first, except that the clamped leg is joined horizontally by its rung to a neighbouring leg throughout the aligning and boring operations.

Four leg, square top, two rungs and rail stool

In this arrangement the rungs each join an independent pair of legs, and a central rail joins the two rungs in turn. The seat portion of a square top stool is cut to shape and finished ready for boring as a simple carpentry exercise. In this case, the marking out is done with the try square, the position for the legs being pricked at the corners of a square drawn 1in (2.54cm) in from the edge of the wood. The angle gauge is aligned diagonally with opposite marks and the procedure followed as before. Thereafter, all operations up to the fitting of the two rungs follow the sequences already described, the rungs being made with a heavier central boss to anchor the cross rail, and all three made to a matching design.

The rungs are centre-punched in the same grain area at their centres, and drilled square in with the $\frac{1}{2}$in (12.7mm) diameter boring bit to a depth of $\frac{1}{2}$in (12.7mm). They are then assembled to their legs and the legs fitted to the seat.

The distance between the inner face of the rungs at the rail hole is measured next, and the rail turned to this length plus 1in (2.54cm), the ends being turned parallel for $\frac{1}{2}$in (12.7mm) to $\frac{1}{2}$in (12.7mm) diameter.

When ready, the legs are removed from the seat, the rail fitted between the rungs, and the whole reassembled. Any small adjustments are made, and then the whole article is glued up and finished as already described.

Four leg, oblong top, two rung, two rail stool

As with the square top the oblong seat is prepared for boring as a hand tool exercise at the bench. When ready, the marking out is done in the form of two overlapping squares, with their three outer sides drawn 1in (2.54cm) in from the edge of the wood, the hole positions being pricked in at each outer corner. The gauge is then aligned diagonally from each corner to the opposite mark on its respective square, clamped up, and the holes bored as described earlier.

Laying out the leg positions in this way ensures that each leg has an equal amount of projection both to the front and side of the seat top. If a diagonal across the full length of seat top is taken, it will have the effect of increasing the splay of the legs to the side, at the expense of the front and rear – the very places where it is needed! After the holes are bored in the seat, the procedure as for the square top is followed up to the rung making.

The rungs joining each end pair of legs will both be formed with two bosses, 2–3in (5.08–7.62cm) apart, to take the two rails, the whole being turned to a matching design. As before, the rungs are marked off and centre-punched on the same grain area for the rail sockets, and drilled straight in to a depth of $\frac{1}{2}$in (12.7mm) with the $\frac{1}{2}$in (12.7mm) boring bit.

They are then assembled to their legs, the legs fitted to the seat, and the inner distance between the rungs at the rail holes measured off. The rails are then made to this length plus 1in (2.54cm), the ends being turned to $\frac{1}{2}$in (12.7mm) diameter for the last $\frac{1}{2}$in (12.7mm). Thereafter the assembly and finishing off is completed as for the square top.

CHAPTER TWELVE

Offset Turning

From time to time a need arises for offset turnings, such as in making oval handles for hammers, or offset feet for furniture, the baseplates on floor lamps often having three or four feet arranged around the edge to widen the base and so provide more stability. The secret of offset turnery lies in the marking out, as the actual turning follows the usual pattern of gouge work, although some skill with the skew may also be required.

OVAL HANDLES

To make an oval handle, take a piece of beech, ash or hickory, 1½in × 1¼in (3.81cm × 3.175cm) by the required length plus ½in (12.7mm) and strike centres at each end.

Through these centres draw lines to connect pencilled lines running centrally along the length of the narrow faces. Next draw a line through each centre at right angles to this, and on this cross line mark a false or offset centre on either side of the true centre, ¼in (6.35mm) from it.

Following this, using the ring centre for extra support, mount the workpiece on a corresponding pair of false centres. With the lathe set at 1000 r.p.m. and using the ⅜in (9.525mm) deep U gouge, turn down until the turned surface almost breaks the line running the length of the wood. At this point remount the workpiece on the opposed pair of false centres, and again turn down to the longitudinal line.

There will be a certain amount of vibration in all offset turning, naturally, so it behoves you to ensure that the centres are secure, the tool rest clear of the flying corners of wood, that all is clamped up firmly and that you present the gouge or skew with caution until the initial cut is taken.

Adjust the tool rest to the wood as the rounding down proceeds, to give maximum support to the tool, and finish with the skew, taking extra care with your angle of presentation and the position of the bevel.

After the offset turning is done, remount the workpiece on the true centres and skim off the peak of the curves along the pencilled lines, reducing to 1⅜in (3.49cm) on this dimension, and again finishing with the skew chisel.

Finish blending the curves into each other by means of the abrasive paper cut into 2in (5.08cm) wide strips and held by its ends against the revolving wood. Complete the sanding with a finer grade, and seal the surface. This will prevent the handle from rapidly becoming impregnated with grime from dirty hands. Finally, shape down one end for fitting into the hammer head, round in the bottom end with the skew chisel, and part off.

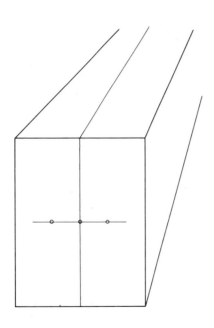

Diagram of false centres marked out on workpiece

One side of handle turned on false centres. There is a pencil line through the true centre and along the length of the wood

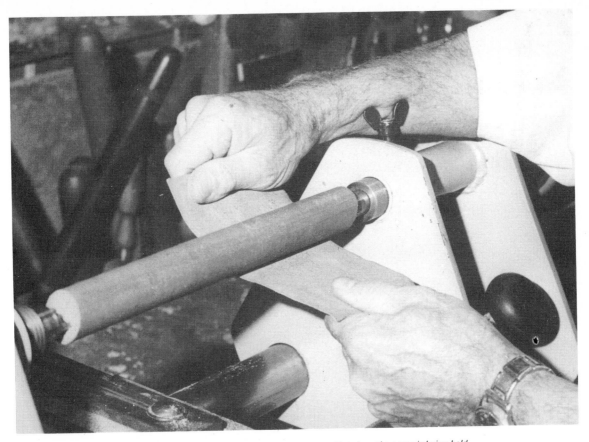

Blending the curves together using garnet paper. Note how the paper is being held

Handle being turned on true centres

OFFSET FEET

The major difficulty in making a set of three or four offset feet is attaining uniformity of size and shape, so marking out is of paramount importance. To begin, take three (or four) pieces of the selected wood, $2\frac{1}{2} \times 2\frac{1}{2}$in (6.35 × 6.35cm) × $2\frac{1}{2}$in (6.35cm) long, and centre on the end grain. Set up the first piece, and round down to its maximum diameter, squaring the end and marking off at $\frac{3}{4}$in (19.05mm) and $1\frac{3}{4}$in (4.445cm).

Skew in on the lines, and reduce the area from the $\frac{3}{4}$in (19.05mm) mark to the headstock to 2in (5.08cm) diameter and round the corner at the $\frac{3}{4}$in (19.05mm) mark. Now mark at both ends of the workpiece, in the same plane, false centres offset $\frac{1}{2}$in (12.7mm) from the true centres and, using the ring centre, remount the workpiece on these.

Reset the tool rest to clear the off centre wood, and turn down the end between the $\frac{3}{4}$in (19.05mm) mark and the tailstock to $\frac{3}{4}$in (19.05mm) diameter, taking great care in skewing in against the shoulder, which of course continues to fly round out of centre, and chamfer the end of the spigot.

Now check the fit of this in its prepared hole in the lamp base and, when satisfactory, sand and seal the top of the foot portion.

With the top side of the foot finished, remount it in the lathe, spigot towards the tailstock. At the $1\frac{3}{4}$in (4.445cm)

Turning the spigot of the foot using the offset or false centres. The tool rest is well back to clear the eccentric rotation of the workpiece

Chuck for smoothing underside of foot, showing hole to clear spigot. A completed foot is in the foreground

mark part in gently with the spearpoint to $\frac{1}{4}$in (6.35mm) diameter, at the same time rounding the corner, then remove the workpiece from the lathe and saw off the waste. The bottom of the foot will be somewhat rough from the parting tool, so I propose to smooth it off in a chuck made as follows.

Set up a waste wood block on the faceplate, about 3in (7.62cm) diameter by 2in (5.08cm) thick, face it flat, centre it and scribe a circle of the same diameter as the foot. Offset $\frac{1}{2}$in (12.7mm) from the centre of the block, mark a second centre, and bore in to a depth of $1\frac{1}{2}$in (3.81cm) with a 1in (2.54cm) bit at this mark. Now turn a recess approximately $\frac{1}{2}$in (12.7mm) deep to the size of the circle, testing the foot, its spigot in the hole, for fit. When a good press fit is obtained in the chuck, smooth off the bottom of the foot with the shallow gouge, finishing with sandpaper and sealer.

This completes one foot, but each of the foregoing operations would be repeated for the remaining feet at points where operations in the sequence change, so avoiding needless duplication of effort.

A different design of foot, requiring less skill with the skew chisel, can be made as follows, the toe in this case appearing some distance below the lamp's base, and not flush with it, as in that just described.

Select three or four pieces of suitable wood 2$\frac{1}{2}$in (6.35cm) square by 2$\frac{1}{2}$in (6.35cm) long, centre on the end grain and round down to 2$\frac{1}{4}$in (5.715cm) diameter. Square the tail end, and mark in 1$\frac{1}{4}$in (3.175cm) with the pencil. From this mark, back to the end, round down with the skew chisel on a convex curve to 1$\frac{1}{4}$in (3.175cm) diameter. Finally, with a pencil, strike a mark around the workpiece $\frac{1}{2}$in (12.7mm) in from the tailstock.

Now mark a pair of false centres, in the same plane, $\frac{5}{16}$in (7.937mm) out from the centre at each end. Set up the

Chuck holding foot whilst its bottom is smoothed off. Soft poplar is used to make the chuck

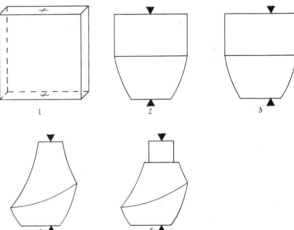

Diagram showing sequence of operations in making the second type of foot

The second type of foot mounted on false centres whilst the top is shaped down to ¾in (19.05mm) diameter. The pencil mark was made when the foot was on true centres

workpiece on the false centres, and having repositioned the tool rest to clear it, turn down from the ½in (12.7mm) mark to a diameter of ¾in (19.05mm) at the headstock in a nice hollow curve using the ⅝in (15.875mm) shallow gouge.

Mark in ⅝in (15.875mm) from the headstock end this time, and skew a square shoulder at the mark. From the skew cut, back to the headstock, reduce the workpiece to a parallel spigot of ¾in (19.05mm) diameter, keeping the shoulder square and chamfering the end ready for entry into the hole prepared in the base of the lamp.

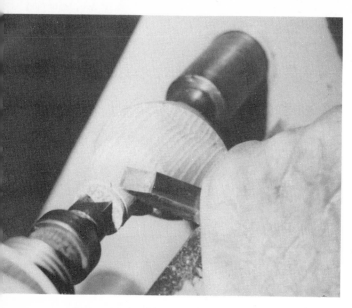

Sand, seal and polish overall, except the spigot, and repeat the complete procedure for the remaining feet, finishing one cycle of operations on all before going on to the next.

The holes in the lamp base are deep enough to allow the spigot to enter up to the shoulder, and after the feet have been glued in, but before it has set, they are checked to ensure that they all project radially from the centre of the base.

WOODEN SPOONS

Although only a minimum amount of offset is required in their making, wooden spoons may be considered under this heading. They offer a quick and easy project, are always useful in the kitchen, and make a small though acceptable gift to friends. Beech is the preferred wood, but any stable variety, without odour or taste, will be suitable.

Cut a strip 2in (5.08cm) wide by 10in (25.4cm) long from a ¾in (19.05mm) board, plane one wide face flat, and mount between ring and driving centres, the tailstock centre being offset ⅛in (3.175mm) towards the planed face.

Square the tail end and mark off at ¼in (6.35mm) and 2½in (3.81cm) from it with the pencil. Then, using the ⅝in (15.875mm) long nose gouge, turn down between the marks to a flattened oval shape approximately 1¾in (4.445cm) across, like the bowl of a spoon, rounding in the corner to a handle diameter of ⅝in (15.875mm) but leaving the rest of the handle unturned.

Foot mounted on false centres for turning of spigot. The ½in (12.7mm) square end chisel is being used in a skewing position

The spoon head turned from blank and marked out ready for shaping, with finished spoons alongside. Wood is New Zealand kauri

The spoon bowl being hollowed out with the ⅜in (9.525mm) carpenter's gouge

Next, with the pencil checked by the finger against the side of the bowl, scribe a line ¼in (6.35mm) in from the edge on the plane face, and a second line ¼in (6.35mm) down from that face on the side of the bowl. As the handle portion was left in its original square shape it can now be gripped in the vice or clamped to the bench whilst the hollow of the bowl is gouged out and the back rounded off. A ⅜in (9.525mm) carpenter's gouge, or a long nose turning gouge of similar size, will serve to remove most of the waste from the bowl, working from the line towards the middle.

Avoid making the bowl too deep. Make it about ¼in (6.35mm) at the centre, and when a uniform curvature has been achieved with the gouge scrape the tool marks out with the newly ground round end of a power hacksaw blade, working along the grain. After the tool marks have all been erased, finish with narrow strips of graded paper lapped over the rounded end of a cork.

The spoon is now turned over and the back of the bowl shaped down to the second pencil line by means of a Surform rasp and smoothed with file, scraper and graded paper, maintaining a rounded form, but leaving the end stub for re-mounting in the lathe.

With the bowl finished inside and out, the workpiece is recentred and the handle tapered from ⅝in (15.875mm) diameter at the headstock to ½in (12.7mm) by the bowl. Smooth off with the ¾in (19.05mm) skew chisel, and blend the handle into the bowl using the long nose gouge.

After this, part in close to the driving centre, round the end with the skew, and after reducing the waste at each end to ³⁄₁₆in (4.762mm), saw it off.

The stub ends can now be dressed down with file and sandpaper, the spoon wetted overall to raise the grain and, when dry, sanded lightly along the grain using a fine grade paper. Finally, give the wood a thorough rubbing all over with salad oil, and burnish dry with shavings or a soft cloth. Putting a hole through the handle, or skewing ornamental lines around it, is not advised, as any recesses inevitably fill with flour or other cooking substances. The corner between the handle and bowl is rounded out for the same reason.

CHAPTER THIRTEEN

Long Hole Boring in Lamps and Boring in General

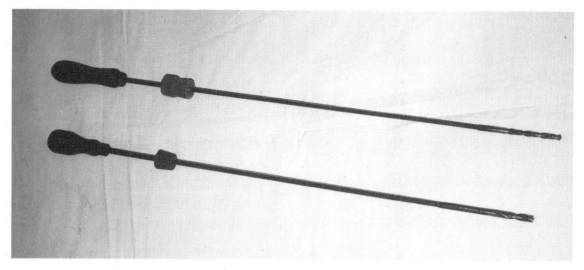

Long holeboring tools made from jobbing drills welded to steel rods. The corks are used as depth indicators

One of the problems associated with turning table and, particularly, floor standard lamps is boring the hole lengthwise through the stem for the flex.

If you are contemplating making just a few of either of these, and over the course of time you surely will, it is worth your while to purchase or have made a long handled drill or bit, ⅜in (9.525mm) diameter by about 30in (76.20cm) long.

If you are buying it I would recommend a shell or spoon bit, which has a hollow half-round shank for clearing the waste. The spoon bit has its forward edge sharpened, as it might be the tip of a spoon, whilst the shell bit has a sharpened transverse lip formed half-way across its end. Both bits keep on centre very well, and are preferred for this reason.

Should you be having your long handled bit made up, however, a common ⅜in (9.525mm) jobbing drill welded squarely on the end of a steel rod will serve the purpose, provided the rod is of slightly smaller diameter than the drill, which should be sharpened as described later in this chapter.

Under no circumstances use soft iron reinforcing rod or similar metal for your tool, and if you can obtain an old rifle cleaning rod, so much the better.

It is good practice to drill the hole through the lamp half-way from each end, whilst still in the rough. In this way any tendency for the drill to run off centre is checked before it becomes irremediable, and should the worst happen, hours of work spent finishing the lamp are not wasted.

Floor standard lamps are usually made in two sections, which simplifies boring and reduces whip during the turning operations. An ornamental detail at the connecting dowel

and socket joint effectively hides it, but unless the lamp is to be painted the grain of the wood should also be matched up at the joint if possible.

The workpiece is supported during the boring operation by a hollow ring centre set in a post and mounted in the tool rest holder. The ring locates in the impression left by the ring centre used during the earlier roughing down, and the drill is entered into the wood through the hollow centre.

The sequence is as follows. After roughing down, the workpiece is mounted on the driving centre and the tool rest banjo with the hollow centre fitted in the tool rest socket is brought up to engage the centre in the impression on the end of the wood.

Simultaneously the tailstock with its conical dead centre is brought up to enter it in the rear of the hollow centre. This sets it at the correct height and lateral position for boring, whereupon the banjo and hollow centre mount are clamped and the tailstock withdrawn.

Any slack at the driving centre end is taken up by screwing the hollow centre forward in its mount, so forcing the wood home, when the centre is itself clamped. With the lathe running at a low speed of say 700 r.p.m. the drill is fed through the hollow centre and the bore started. Steady pressure is maintained on the handle of the drill, and it is withdrawn frequently to clear the chips from the hole.

When the drill has penetrated half-way the workpiece is reversed, and the driving centre replaced by the threaded shank of a ⁷⁄₁₆in (11.112mm) coach bolt, with its head cut off, chucked in the Jacobs ½in (12.7mm) chuck. The coach bolt enters the hole and screws in, screw chuck fashion, to drive the wood.

To provide an impression at the tailstock end for the hollow centre the wood is supported initially on the conical centre, the tool rest positioned alongside, and the skew or parting chisel used to cut a groove for the hollow centre. Thereafter it is set up and adjusted as before, and the drilling is recommenced.

Should it be preferred to drill through from one end only of a shorter stem, care must be taken to measure the depth of penetration of the drill so that it doesn't chew into the driving centre. Leave about ½in (12.7mm) of wood to be drilled through after removing the workpiece from the lathe.

When preparing the dowel and socket joints for floor lamps, the following procedure should be adopted.

DRILLING THE SOCKET

Before drilling the ⅜in (9.525mm) hole in the socket end of the bottom half of the stem, chuck a ¾in (19.05mm) or 1in (2.54cm) modified Irwin bit (depending on the outside diameter of the stem at the joint) in the tailstock. With the job mounted on the fork centre support its tail end on the point of the bit, and as the lathe is switched on start feeding the bit into the wood, boring to a depth of 1in (2.54cm). The pressure maintained on the hand wheel will keep the wood in engagement with the fork centre, and the tail end will be supported by the bit cutting the hole.

When 1in (2.54cm) depth is reached switch off, and when the wood has ceased to rotate, withdraw the tailstock. For obvious reasons do not ease up pressure on the hand wheel until the motor is stopped.

Next turn a short plug to fit the socket, with a wide flange to sit on the outer end of the hole. Use the ring centre in turning the plug, so that its impression can be used in locating the hollow centre at the end of the workpiece. Now set up and align the hollow centre as described earlier, and

Aligning the hollow centre by means of the conical centre in the tailstock

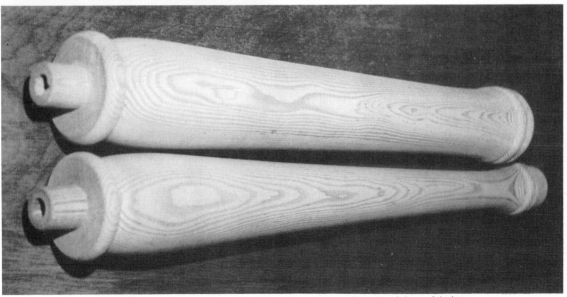

Finished stems with a spigot on each, as is usual, except when the external shape of the lamp precludes it. (See the lamp described at the end of Chapter 11.) The wood is Canadian pine

bore through the plug and on into the wood. When the desired depth is reached withdraw the drill and remove the plug from the socket by gripping the wide flange provided for this purpose.

TURNING THE SPIGOT

The spigot or pin for the joint, on the upper lamp portion, can be turned at any stage of the operation, but only after the socket has been bored out. The reason is of course that we want the joint to be a good fit, and as the Irwin bit will bore a hole of an arbitrary size the spigot can be turned to fit it. But not the other way round.

If the spigot is turned before boring out the ⅜in (9.525mm) hole then the ring centre is used at the tailstock end. However, should you decide to turn the pin after boring out the hole, then the ring centre must be exchanged for a conical dead centre, which will sit in the ⅜in (9.525mm) hole quite happily.

Having turned the spigot to a snug fit in the socket, the callipers are set at the diameter of the spigot and a second 1in (2.54cm) long spigot turned at the bottom end of the lower stem. This will fit into the hole of the baseplate when this is turned as a separate faceplate operation later, or the yoke/hub of a three legged base if this style is used.

Cut small chamfers on the pins to ease them into their holes and ensure the contact faces of the two lamp sections are dead square to ensure wood to wood contact when glueing up. Always be sure in any dowelling work that the dowel is a fraction shorter than the depth of the hole.

FITTING THE FLEX

The first difficulty you are likely to meet in wiring lamps is getting the wire to feed through the hole. Pushed from behind the flex will almost certainly buckle and jam in the hole, unless it is a really loose fit, so I suggest that you have a long piece of reasonably thick copper or steel wire with the end looped over. Push this through the hole, pinch the end of your flex in the loop and draw it back through the hole. Simple!

Another problem which arises is how to lead the flex out from the bottom of the lamp. In fact, the difficulty is really in deciding which of several alternative methods to use. The flex can be brought straight through the bottom and then recessed into a groove running to the edge of the base, the bottom being then covered with baize to hide it. Another way is to bore a hole radially through the circular base, to align with a slot opened in the side of the spigot standard. In assembly, the wire is fed down the inside of the standard before the base is fitted, and threaded via the slot into the radially drilled hole of the base. The base and standard are then glued together. Yet another method, suitable for any type of base, is to fit three small feet, sufficiently long to make enough clearance for the flex between the base and the ground.

If the foregoing procedures appear too difficult or involved for aspiring turners, and I must say the actual operations are far less complicated than they appear from the description, then an easier but far less interesting way is to use what is known as a split turnery technique.

In this method the lamp standard is made up of two identical halves, each with a groove formed down the centre of one side, but stopped short of one end to provide a location for the driving centre.

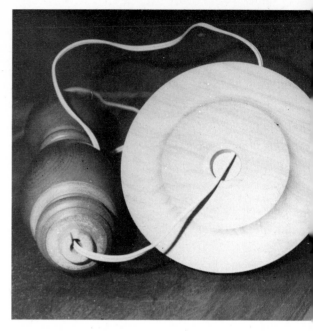

Fitting the flex in a lamp with a radially drilled base. Note the slot in the side of the spigot to clear the flex

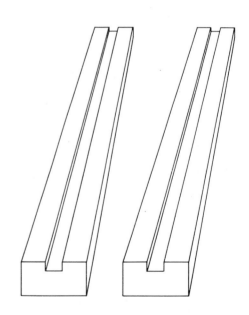

Diagram of a split stem showing the groove for the flex cut in before glueing up

The grooves are made ¼in (6.35mm) wide by ⅛in (3.175mm) deep, so that when the two halves are glued together they form a channel ¼in (6.35mm) square for the wire flex. Needless to say, the abutting surfaces must be flat and true, and well clamped up to eliminate the glue line as much as possible.

The tailstock and poppet adjusted to register depth of bore

For those who aren't happy making grooves (and a simple means of cutting them is described in Chapter 15) I suggest a split turned standard made up of four parts. This is prepared from four equal-sized pieces, with a bevel along one corner of each, the bevelled corners being brought together at the centre of the standard in glueing up and so forming the channel for the flex.

BORING IN GENERAL

Whilst on the subject of boring holes, let us discuss some problems which arise, and ways of dealing with them. It often happens, when boring out an article such as a small jar, a trinket box or a mustard pot on the screwchuck, that when the bit point is brought into contact with the wood the centre is slightly off line, causing the bit to 'orbit' around the end of the work. On other occasions there may be no wood at the centre of the workpiece into which the bit point can locate. When this happens there are two alternatives open to you.

The centre in the first case can be recut with the point of the skew or spearpoint chisel, or in either case a recess cut into the end of the workpiece, the diameter of the cutting end of the bit. The wings of the bit will centre inside the recess, and a true boring result.

When a hole of a certain depth has to be bored, it is good practice to wind the tailstock poppet back in its housing until its front face is flush with the face of the casting. The tailstock with the bit chucked in position is then slid forward until the point of the bit has penetrated the centre hole of the wood far enough to allow the cutting edge of the bit to contact the face of it when the tailstock is clamped. As the hand wheel is used to bore the hole, the projection of the poppet from the tailstock casting registers the exact depth of cut.

Should the depth to be bored be greater than the length of the fully extended poppet then stop the bore at a predetermined depth, say 3 or 4in (7.62 or 10.16cm), and wind the poppet back until it is again flush with the face of the tailstock. Unclamp the tailstock and slide it bodily forward until the bit contacts the bottom of the hole, and re-clamp. Thereafter add the original 3 or 4in (7.62 or 10.16cm) to all subsequent measurements to get the exact depth of the hole.

THE IRWIN BIT

The Irwin bit figures quite often in these hole boring operations, so I will consider some aspects of it.

Always bear in mind its point when approaching the bottom of a bore. It projects forward of the cutters about $\frac{3}{8}$in (9.525mm), so must be allowed for.

It is taken for granted that you have already filed the screw tip down to a four sided pyramid point at the time the square shank was cut off for chucking in the lathe. This point will need to be refiled from time to time to keep the corners sharp; take care to remove a balanced amount from each flat so as to keep the point central.

You may also notice when winding the bit forward with the hand wheel that it rotates out of true. This is usually because the shank of the bit, although polished after forging, is not necessarily exactly round; it isn't essential for its original role.

So when you find the bit point orbiting as you wind it forward, loosen the chuck, rotate the bit slightly, re-clamp it, and test it again. It will usually find an accurately centred position after two or three tries.

The bit, as with any cutting tool, needs to be kept sharp, but certain points have to be watched. Always sharpen the inside surfaces of the spurs only, using a smooth file and

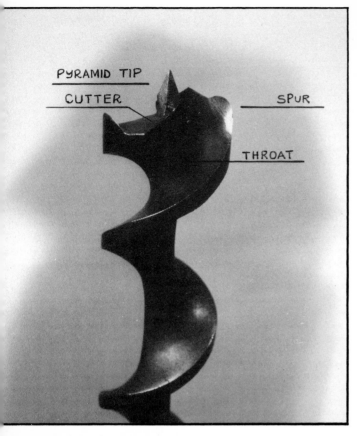

The Irwin bit modified for the lathe, with names of parts

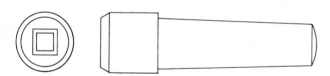

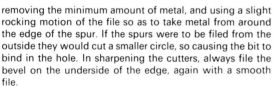

Diagram of an adapter/chuck for holding the square shanked bit

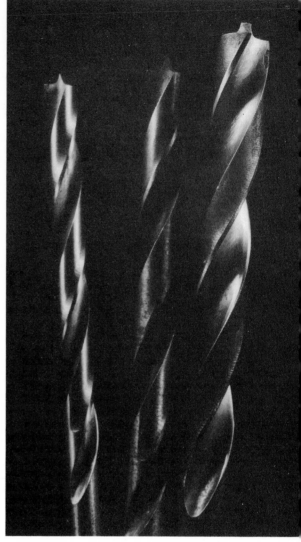

The jobbing drill reground for use in the lathe

removing the minimum amount of metal, and using a slight rocking motion of the file so as to take metal from around the edge of the spur. If the spurs were to be filed from the outside they would cut a smaller circle, so causing the bit to bind in the hole. In sharpening the cutters, always file the bevel on the underside of the edge, again with a smooth file.

I find a 4in (10.16cm) smooth half-round is best for sizes up to 1in (2.54cm), but care must be taken not to undercut with the edge of the file. With all filing jobs try to maintain the original angle of bevel, avoiding the temptation to finish the job quickly by removing the metal from the edge rather than the whole area of the bevel. By altering the angle of the bevel in this way the cutting action of the bit is impaired and the edge is lost more quickly.

If you are not happy at the prospect of sawing the square shanks from your bits, wishing to use them for carpentry as well, I suggest you do the following. Turn a piece of beech, ash or hickory to fit the Morse taper of your tailstock poppet, leaving the forward end parallel for an inch or so, of the diameter of a suitable iron or brass ferrule or sleeve, which you now drive on the adapter/chuck supported on the bench. Bore this end accurately to a depth of 1¼in (3.175cm) with a 5/16in (7.937mm) drill. With a ¼in (6.35mm) chisel ease out the hole as a taper square to fit the shank of the bit. If you make it a good fit it will withstand constant use and make a useful addition to your collection of hand made lathe accessories. (See Chapter 15.) There is still the snag that the screw point must be filed square for use in the lathe, which is going to make hard work of boring holes with the carpenter's brace, but a lot of the effort will be taken out of it if a pilot hole of ⅛in (3.175mm) diameter is drilled for the point of the bit before commencing to bore by hand.

THE JOBBING DRILL

Ordinary engineer's or jobbing drills are an essential part of the woodturner's kit, being in regular demand for drilling screw holes, blind boring small diameter spigot holes for knobs, and the like. If the bevels are reground in the following manner for cutting wood they will hold the drill on centre as it cuts, eliminate snatching of the drill into the wood when drilling in the lathe, and when blind boring the hole will have a flat bottom to match the spigot fitting into it. To achieve this result, the two bevels are ground to a very flat angle with minimum rake, and with the cutting edges square to the axis of the drill. At the centre where the opposed bevels meet, the thin web of metal joining the flutes is ground to a short tapered point about $\frac{1}{16}$in (1.587mm) high, with a chisel edge. This serves to hold the drill on course, and eases the cutting action.

CHAPTER FOURTEEN

Decorative Turnery

At some stage in pursuing his new hobby the aspiring woodturner will want to experiment in making vari-coloured built up articles, and some writers devote considerable space to the subject of polychromatic or decorative turnery. I will be frank at the outset, and admit I am not much smitten by it, and will always prefer the integrated beauty of grain, colour and texture of clear polished, whole wood.

A large part of the making of built up woodware involves the outlay of considerable time, and great accuracy in marking out, angle cutting and glueing up; in fact, a high level of skill in the handling of basic carpentry tools generally. Much time can be saved if one is the happy owner of power equipment, but I question whether even a minority of us have more than perhaps a power hand drill. So I shall proceed on the assumption that you want to know how it is done, and are prepared to take especial pains with hand tools to complete your first projects. After that you will decide whether to make suitable jigs to facilitate your hand tool work, or to install bandsaw, thicknesser, planer and radial saw, as the professional does, or just go back to what is in my mind the most satisfying turning of all: turning solid wood.

At the very beginning you should be warned that unless your angles and surfaces are accurately cut to give solid contact at all glued joints there will be an inherent danger of the article collapsing whilst being turned, not to mention that heavy glue lines in the finished piece will certainly spoil its appearance.

When building up bowls in alternating coloured woods, brick wall fashion, it is absolutely essential that the bricks on any one level be of uniform thickness, to ensure close union between each tier of bricks. It is also important that the various woods used together in any one project be equally well seasoned, and that the adhesives are of high quality. There will be variations in the density or hardness of the different woods used in the same article, so it is important always to have sharp tools, firm control, and no inhibitions about using scrapers when the need arises.

One advantage in turning bowls or hollow ware built up brick fashion (checkered, as it is called) is that there is no end grain to present a rough surface on opposite sides of the work, the grain running continuously around it. Another advantage is the opportunity to use up oddments of wood which might otherwise be wasted.

Care must be taken not to overheat the wood in prolonged sanding operations – something which should never arise anyway – as some glues become plastic when heated and so may be weakened. Because modern glues set very hard, tools lose their edge very quickly in turning glued up timber, so you must be prepared to spend more time at the oilstone in this work. This applies particularly with plywoods. If you can manage without using it for your bowl bottoms so much the better.

Lidded jar capped at both ends with contrasting coloured wood rebated on. Body is of New Zealand manuka, caps of Australian jarrah. Buffed oil finish on body, carnauba wax polished caps and lid

LAMINATED WORK

First there is the build-up of parallel alternating coloured strips of wood for bowls, lamp bases and the like. This form can be varied by having one coloured strip wider or narrower than the other, or by alternating the angles so that the strips, instead of being parallel, are slightly tapered and placed wide end to narrow end, alternately.

There are no particular problems in the building up process, except to ensure that all contact faces are flat and true, and to balance the colours in centering the work for turning.

A further variation on this theme is to make lamp bases, dishes and so on from wedge shaped sectors of various coloured woods, put together like the slices of a cake, after being cut to angle in a mitre box as illustrated. Select an even number of pieces and calculate the angle of the sides from the formula given below.

If the tip of each sector is cut off before asembly there will be a ready made hole for the flex if a lamp base is intended. Use several large Jubilee clips joined together to make the cramp for drawing the pieces together in glueing up, or if you intend making a quantity, invest in a Flexicramp of the size required.

An alternative effect can be got by inserting parallel strips of a distinctive coloured wood between sectors of the same colour. In this case the angles remain the same, but the centre is opened up and, unless required for the spigot of a lamp stand, would need to be plugged. This should be done with a plug turned across the grain, so as to present side grain to the surface, otherwise an ordinary dowel type plug showing end grain would spoil the appearance of the article.

CHECKERED WORK

Another common form of building is the bowl made up of rings, each ring comprising alternating coloured woods. To minimise wastage the rings are made of progressively larger diameters from the base upwards, the bricks in the base ring being cut wider to permit of blending them into the baseplate, which is usually a piece of thick ply, less likely to shrink or warp in use.

The mitre box with tenon saw in position and sawn sectors in foreground

Sectored disc clamped in a Flexicramp after glueing up

The sectored disc with inserts opening up the centre for the lamp flex

The sectored disc mounted on the faceplate ready for facing off

Sketch plan and elevation for making up bricks for the checkered bowl

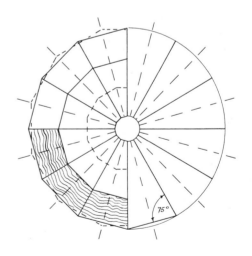

The size, i.e. length, width and thickness, of the bricks, the angle of their ends, and the number required in any one tier or ring can only be determined by making a full scale plan and sectional elevation of the bowl. For easy calculation in one method I shall describe an even number of bricks to a row is preferable, and as the bricks in any one row straddle the bricks in adjacent rows it will be seen that there are the same number of bricks or blocks in each row.

The first move then is to draw a full size plan, or top view, of the bowl. After that, draw a sectional elevation or side view of the bowl cut through the middle. As there are 360° in a circle, the included angles, that is, the angles at which the ends of the bricks are cut, are easily calculated.

Let us say you have sufficient variety of coloured woods to permit six changes of brick. Twelve bricks to a row would allow the whole range of coloured bricks to be viewed from any one side. A circle of 360° divided into 12 parts would produce 12 triangular sectors, each sector having an angle of 30° at its inner end ($360 \div 12 = 30$). As the sum of the angles of any triangle must equal 180° it follows that the outer angles of the sectors must each be 75°, viz. $30 + 75 + 75 = 180$. So 75° would be the angle at which each end of each brick would be cut. The full size plan is thus divided into 12 sectors, each of 30° at the centre and 75° at each outer corner.

Reverting now to the sectional elevation, superimpose on the section of the bowl a tier of bricks, each say ¾in (19.05mm) thick, and of a width sufficient to take the full depth and curvature of the wall of the bowl. Each brick should allow at least ½in (12.7mm) of waste on either side

The improvised sanding disc and table. The disc has a multi-ply back, for screwing on to the mandrel, and the pipe is used as a spigot on the table

of the bowl profile. The bottom layer of bricks will be much wider than the others as the bottom of the bowl will be turned in from it. An alternative is to reduce the width of the bottom row and to insert a base disc of thick plywood or stable, well seasoned wood.

The bricks, each representing one ring or tier in the make-up of the bowl, are now plotted from the sectional elevation on to the sectors of the full size plan. The exact length of bricks in each row can be measured from the plan; the included angles are already known, so the next step is to prepare a mitre box, unless of course you do have a tilting saw table.

Make sure your angles are exactly right, and if sawing from the strip have a stop at the correct distance from the saw kerf, with its face angled to match the end of the strip *after* it has been turned over for the second cut on each brick. If short lengths are being utilised, the same mitre box can be used except that the first angled cut is made as near as possible to the end of the oddment before it is reversed against the stop for the second cut. If the stop is fixed with a screw it can be readily repositioned for shorter or longer bricks from other rows, as the angles remain constant.

With care, and a fine tooth tenon saw for cutting, the brick joints should require no dressing with a plane or sander. However, a sanding disc screwed to the faceplate is very easily made, and a sanding table soon improvised from a square of heavy ply screwed to a thick piece of beech or oak, bored for a tightly fitted spigot of metal the diameter of the tool rest holder. With an angled block of wood accurately clamped to the table the ends of the bricks could be sanded flat and true in a jiffy.

When glueing up take pains to have everything methodically arranged beforehand. Remove from the bench all unwanted gear, especially those bricks for the rings not yet

being worked on. Lay out the bricks for the ring being made in the sequence of assembly on a dead flat working area, metal for preference, but otherwise covered with plastic sheet to prevent work adhering to the table. Use a good quality glue, rubbing the bricks well together, and glue up a half ring at a time.

When each half ring is dry it can be planed across its exposed ends, or presented to the new sanding disc if it will accommodate both ends simultaneously (but make sure you hold down the end in contact with the upturning side of the sanding disc!).

This method ensures a dead true join of the two halves, eliminating any small errors which have developed in the assembly of the half rings.

Allow at least 24 hours for the glue to set and, when all the rings are ready, plane or sand their top and bottom surfaces lightly to ensure a good flat joint, and glue together. Take care to position each tier correctly, brick wall fashion, and prevent any tendency for the rings to move out of concentricity by driving a few nails around the outside edges. Cramp firm overall, and leave to dry.

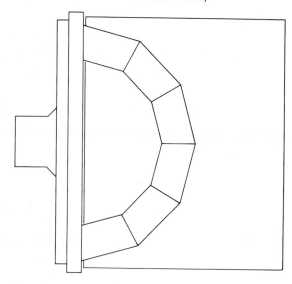

Diagram of half ring being squared up on sanding disc

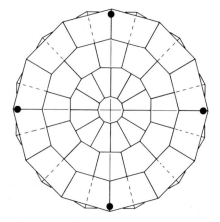

Diagram of the glued up bowl with the centering threads in position

When ready, the bowl is secured to the faceplate with screws driven into the waste wood on the inside, great care being taken to centralise the faceplate as accurately as possible. A simple way to do this is to drive a tack into opposite corners on four sides, and stretch a fine thread between each opposite pair of tacks. The threads will intersect at the centre of the workpiece, providing an accurate point on which to locate the faceplate without impeding the placement and screwing on of it in any way.

Mounted in this way the base hole is rounded out, and a close fitting plug long enough to surface on the inside is fitted. Alternatively, the bottom is trued up, a $\frac{1}{2}$in (12.7mm) rebate turned in, and a disc of ply or well seasoned, stable timber glued in to form the base.

The outside is turned to shape using a narrow mouthed gouge, working from the base to the top, taking light cuts. Keep the gouge very sharp as the glue will rapidly blunt it. Remember the tool is meeting a succession of corners, so positive control and care are needed and no shame attaches to reverting to the scraper.

Prepare the base in your preferred way for reversing on to the faceplate, although if the bottom has been plugged a screw chuck may not hold too well if it is a dowel type plug, presenting end grain to the screw. Sand, seal and polish the outside of the bowl and reverse it for turning out the inside. Once again, use your narrow mouthed gouge, very sharp, and keep the tool rest as near as possible to the cutting edge. Change over to the side and end cutting scrapers when the gouge is too far in for comfort, and finish with freshly sharpened tools, light cuts and a faster pulley.

Sand, seal and polish, and cap the screw holes with buttons as described in Chapter 16. Do bear in mind with glued up work that, unless it is *not* a water soluble glue, it is not wise to overdo the wet and dry method of sanding, although after initial dry sanding to bring it to near perfection, wet and dry sanding can finish it.

INLAID WORK

Another form of decorative turnery entails insetting various coloured plugs in different arrangements around the periphery of otherwise ordinary bowls or containers, often with lids decorated in a similar way. These can look very attractive if carefully done, the points to watch being:

1. that the marking of positions for the plug holes is accurately laid around the article. This is done by encircling it with a strip of paper and carefully folding it to equal the number of plugs to be fitted. The paper is then again laid around the article and the position of the folds transferred to the wood.
2. that the cutter used is centered accurately on its mark, square to the face of the work, and the article is securely held either in the lathe or bench vice whilst the boring, if done by hand, is under way.

The cutter must have sharp spurs and maintain accurate alignment to ensure the mouth of the plug hole is not deformed in any way. If a screwpoint cutter is used consideration must be given to the possibility of the point breaking through the wall before the plug hole has reached full depth, which is usually $\frac{1}{4}$in (6.35mm) and certainly not less than $\frac{1}{8}$in (3.175mm). In practice, the plug holes are cut when less than $\frac{1}{16}$in (1.587mm) of wood remains to be removed in the

A bowl finished in the inlaid style. (By courtesy of Evans Brothers (Books) Ltd)

Cutting the rings on the faceplate with a hardboard backing to protect the point of the tool. Note how the tool is gripped

turning operation, so that plug and workpiece are brought down together. The plugs themselves can be cut with a plug cutter, if you own one, in which case your hole cutter must exactly match it.

Alternatively, strips of wood of a width and thickness a little over the finished diameter of the plug are cut *across* the grain, and the strips centred up and turned down to plug size. The parting tool is used to separate them, leaving each about ⅜in (9.525mm) long, with a small chamfer for entering the hole.

They should be a nice sliding fit in the hole, and all glued in with their grain running in the same direction. If dowelling or similar cylindrical material were used it would show end grain at the surface and appear most uninteresting.

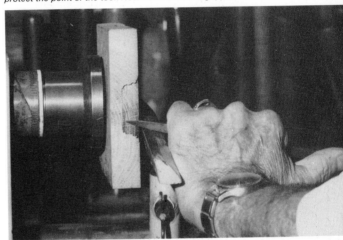

Cutting the rings on the screwchuck, which is of smaller diameter than the ring hole

TIERED RING WORK

Yet another form of decorating is done by turning rings of different coloured woods out of boards. Glued one on top of another, with the grain of each layer at 90° to the next, hollow ware for such things as humidors, vases, biscuit barrels and tea caddies can be built to any reasonable height or diameter with a minimum wastage of wood. The rings are cut on the faceplate from squares of wood, using the spear-point tool thrust straight in as described in Chapter 16, a waste wood backing being first secured to the faceplate to save the tool from striking it. An alternative method is to use the screwchuck, taking the tool almost through, then reversing the workpiece and cutting in from the other side. Needless to say, the corners are cut away first, before freeing the ring from the centre waste piece. These centre discs come in handy later as inserts in lids, bottoms on smaller diameter hollow ware, or to build up yet smaller pots or jars.

In glueing up the rings the grain of each should alternate so that as far as possible stresses in the wood are balanced and the grain pattern distributed around the article.

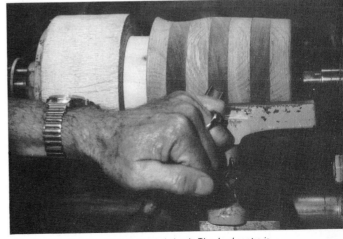

Shaping the glued-up jar on a tapered chuck. The dead centre is being used to support the base

COOPERED WORK

One other way of constructing hollow ware is by building up with staves running lengthwise, in the way beer and wine barrels are coopered, except of course that in this instance the staves are glued together, and so require no bands to keep them tight. Here again the staves can be made in various coloured woods, whilst turning presents no problems as the grain runs lengthways, with no cross grain at all.

The length of the staves will be the height plus ¼in (6.35mm) of the finished article, and their thickness will be the wall thickness plus ¼in (6.35mm). If you plan to bulge the sides barrel fashion they will need to be proportionately thicker. Determine next the width and included angles of the sides of each stave, so fall back on the full size plan similar to that used in the checkered bowl project earlier in this chapter.

Lay out a full size circle to represent the outer diameter of the article; in this case it could be 6in (15.24cm). Divide it into sectors equal in number to the intended number of staves making up the item (preferably an even number, say 10 or 12), and plot their positions on the plan, the diameter of the inner circle being determined by the selected thickness of the staves. Using the formula as with the checkered bowl, calculate the degree of angle of the outer corners of the staves, and prepare a shooting or planing box to reproduce this angle, the width of the staves being taken from the plan.

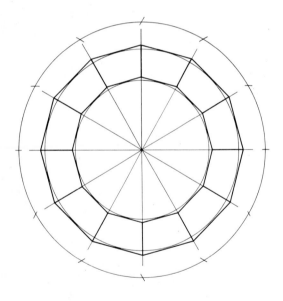

Sketch plan of barrel showing size and angle of staves

If the height of the article is to be 6in (15.24cm), cut lengths of about 25in (63.5cm) long by 1¾in (4.445cm) wide by ¾in (19.05mm) thick, each length providing four staves with about ¼in (6.35mm) of waste per stave. These can now be planed to accurate width and angle in a shooting box made as follows.

Shooting box for staves

Take a piece of 3in (7.62cm) wide flat material about 28in (71.12cm) long by 1in (2.54cm) thick, and reduce it to a parallel width of 2½in (6.35cm). Next cut two similar 28in (71.12cm) lengths, one of 2in (5.08cm) plus the base thickness 1in (2.54cm) = 3in (7.62cm) wide, and the other 1½in (3.81cm) plus the base thickness 1in (2.54cm) = 2½in (6.35cm) wide, and screw them lengthwise to the sides of the base, thus forming an open ended trough.

Now prepare two 28in (71.12cm) lengths of ¼in (6.35mm) hardboard or ply, one 1⅝in (4.127cm) wide and the other 1⅛in (2.857cm) wide, and secure the narrow one to the inside of the narrow side, and the wider one to the wider side, their edges touching the bottom of the box. Use tacks for this, so they can be prised off if any adjustment is found necessary.

It is taken for granted that you have a standard iron jack or smoothing plane with a 2in (5.08cm) iron, with the sole of the plane enclosing both edges of the iron, as in use the outer edges of the sole will bear on the hardboard inserts in the box, so controlling the angle of cut on the stave lengths.

These lengths, one at a time, on edge, are laid in the box, at the end of which a stop has been fixed, and are gripped with a wedge at each end and a double wedge at the centre to keep them against the widest hardboard batten. Obviously, if they are held against the narrower or lower batten they will be planed that much more and be too narrow to produce a 6in (15.24cm) diameter barrel. So plane one edge to angle, that is, until the plane is resting on the battens and is no longer cutting, then reverse the stave end for end and angle its opposite edge.

It would be wise before proceeding to check the angles of the first stave with an angle gauge and to make any necessary adjustments to the box before continuing. When all the stave lengths are prepared cut each into four and select the number and colour of pieces required for the first article, removing the remainder to a separate place.

It should be made clear that the foregoing calculations are all based on a 12 stave barrel of 6in (15.24cm) outside diameter, so any departure from these figures would require a complete revision of the dimensions of the shooting box.

After the staves have been cut to length and are ready for assembly, the operation can be greatly simplified by the use of a jig designed as follows.

Assembly jig for staves

Take two pieces of 1in (2.54cm) flat material big enough to turn a ½in (12.7mm) deep square sided groove in one surface of each, the groove being the dimensions of the circles as laid out on the earlier plan.

Bore a ⅜in (9.525mm) diameter hole through the centre of each disc, and obtain a suitable ¼ or ⅜in (6.35 or 9.525mm) bolt long enough to screw the two discs together when the staves are positioned in the grooves. If one disc is placed on the bench, groove and bolt upwards, with the stave edges faced with glue and stood on end in the groove they can, when all are assembled, be capped with the second disc and bolted up with a fly nut.

Once the staves are held steady it is a simple matter to encircle them with circlips one at each end, joining two or three Jubilee clips together if necessary, to give the required

The shooting box for staves in use. The wedges lock the stave in position

The assembly jig for barrel in use. Short Jubilee clips have been utilised by riveting to a metal strap

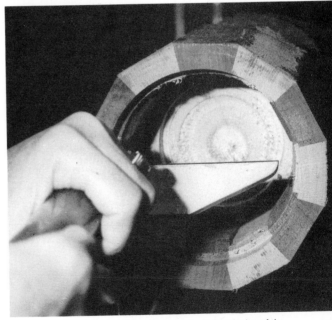

The glued-up barrel mounted on the spigot chuck for rebating of the bottom end

length for going round the job. With the clips screwed up tight the stave joints are closed completely and the discs can be removed.

Thereafter take care to clean out any glue from the grooves of the jig and surplus from the inside and outside of the article. As mentioned already, modern glues can really take the edge off your tools, however good their quality.

Give the glue at least 24 hours to dry before mounting the blank on a tapered softwood chuck. This should have a

shallow taper so as to make a good friction fit for supporting and driving the blank. If one end of the blank is squared up on the sander, and a stop shoulder formed on the taper, these two faces can be brought into contact so as to give greater stability to the blank during the first turning operation. This involves the round nose scraper, used very carefully to square off the outer end of the blank, prior to cutting in a rebate with the narrow ended chisel for the bottom disc.

Should you prefer it, the spigot chuck can be made long enough to be supported on the dead centre at its outer end during the squaring and rebating operation, but do not use excessive force in driving the blank on to the spigot chuck, for obvious reasons.

After the rebate is turned prepare a disc of matching or contrasting coloured wood; step it into the bottom and glue up. Thereafter, having allowed a full 24 hours' drying time, bring up the tailstock and support the base during the outside turning operation. If the blank is going to be bulged out in the middle like a barrel, start the narrow mouth gouge cutting from the centre outwards towards each end in turn.

The bottom will also be dressed flat at this point, with the centre area recessed so as to give stability if it is intended to stand on end, and a centre hole for reversing on to the

screwchuck would be cut with the spearpoint or bradawl.

A wide shallow gouge, say ⅝ or ¾in (15.875 or 19.05mm), is used for the final light cuts on the outside, freshly sharpened and with the lathe running at about 1000 r.p.m., followed by the 1½in (3.81cm) skew. Sand, seal and polish the outside and bottom, and reverse on to the screwchuck.

So far only the outside of the barrel has been finished on the assumption that it was not intended to do any work on the inside; in a barrel capped at both ends the inside would be hidden anyway. However, if it is intended to round out the inside a different procedure must be followed.

After the bottom has been finished, and before touching the outside, reverse the blank on the screwchuck. Next, using the internal tool rest described in Chapter 15, set it at centre height close to the inside wall, checking it for clear-

A selection of coopered articles in New Zealand kauri and puriri, Australian jarrah, oak and mahogany of uncertain origin, and beech fillets dyed and plain. All have been carnauba wax polished

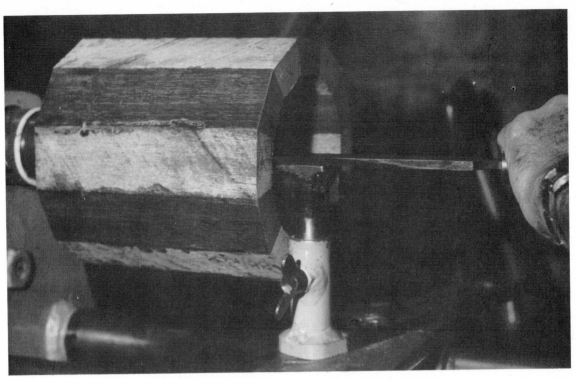

Barrel mounted on screwchuck having inside shaped using internal tool rest and round end side scraper. The scraper lies flat on full length of tool rest

Shaping the outside of barrel using a disc at the tailstock in support

The finished barrel and lid. The body and lid are in alternating
mahogany and oak, carnauba wax polished

ance by rotating the workpiece manually before clamping up.

Now work in gently from the mouth with the round nose scraper, very sharp, and firmly held, taking light cuts along the length of the inner wall, but leaving the bottom untouched as this was faced and sanded before glueing up. The aim is to have only a small part of the edge of the tool actually cutting, so as to reduce vibration to the minimum. When most of the flat parts of the staves have been cut away the side cutting scraper can be utilised to remove any grooves or ridges left by the previous tool.

Finish with abrasive paper, taking care that your hand has free movement within the workpiece by testing with the lathe stopped and inserting the hand holding the paper and then rotating the barrel by hand.

With the inside sealed, turn a waste wood disc to fit the mouth of the hole and bring up the tailstock dead centre to support the job. The outside can now be turned to shape and sanded, sealed and polished as described earlier.

The last operation, if you intend fitting a lid, would be to step a rebate inside the lip of the hole. Do this with a narrow ended chisel used scraper style, and presented horizontally towards the headstock. (For details of lid making see the beginning of Chapter 11.)

POST BLOCKING

Yet another form of decorative work is known as post blocking and consists of overlaying contrasting coloured woods on a central core or block. The core must be flat and square on all sides and, most important of all, accurately centred. If the core should be the slightest fraction out of centre the overlays in the finished job will be unbalanced, and the whole effect ruined.

Mount the core between centres, and check its concentricity by nicking the corners with the skew chisel at the tailstock end. Correct any eccentricity by knocking the core across the dead centre with the butt of the chisel handle and tighten the hand wheel to set the centre when the core is running true.

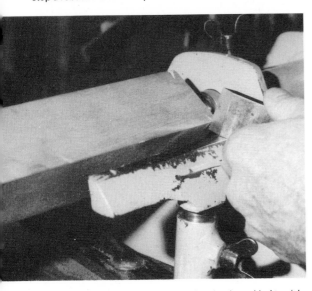

Centering the core for post blocking using the skew chisel to nick the corners

Centering the core using the turned end and plane method. The surface towards the camera will need to be planed down

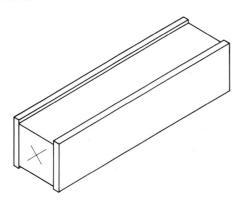

Diagram of the first pair of blanks glued on to the core. Note the slight overhang

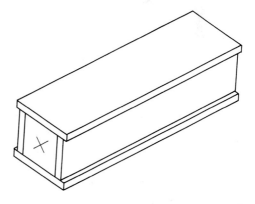

The second pair of blanks glued on after dressing back the edges of the first pair

An alternative method is first to centre the core as accurately as possible, then, taking the narrow ended chisel, to cut in at each end until a complete circle has been formed on the end surfaces. Any face of the blank which is proud of the turned circle can now be planed down to it. Thereafter the faces of the core must be absolutely true to the centres.

When the core is ready glue two blanks of selected wood to opposite sides of it, leaving the edges slightly proud of the surface. After the glue has set, carefully plane the edges of the blanks flush with the core, and glue on the remaining two blanks. When the glue has again set, the workpiece is ready for turning.

Because centering is so important in this type of job, it is essential to have one fang of the driving centre marked and to pencil a corresponding mark on the wood to ensure correct reassembly (as described in Chapter 5). If it is intended to build up more than one lamination on the core, you will see that it is essential to have each blank in the first lamination exactly the same thickness. And so with every additional lamination except the last.

A beautiful example of post blocking using a variety of New Zealand woods, and incorporating a sample of sectored work. (By courtesy of Sovereign Woodworkers (NZ) Ltd, Wanganui, New Zealand)

A pestle and mortar in New Zealand taraire, oil finished, and gavel in ash and mahogany, carnauba wax polished

An assortment of hollow ware comprising (from left to right): *lidded pot in water stained New Zealand pohutukawa; dry flower stand in Australian blue gum; trinket jar and lid in Australian blue gum; cigarette ash jar in New Zealand pohutukawa with copper tray, aluminium lining (from aerosol can) and stainless steel shield. All items have been carnauba wax polished*

A miscellany. From left to right: *lamp shaped biscuit jar in oak, utilising a starboard lamp lens, with brass ring, lacquered; knicknack jar in lateral grain Australian jarrah with ash lid, French polished; condiment shaker in ash, carnauba wax polished*

CHAPTER FIFTEEN

Some New Tools, Devices, Jigs, etc.

In the following pages I describe various tools, devices, projects and techniques which I have formulated over the years in meeting problems which have arisen. They have all withstood the test of time, and should make a useful addition to any keen and painstaking amateur's inventory.

THE SPEARPOINT GENERAL PURPOSE TOOL

I call this tool a general purpose tool because it can be used effectively in so many different ways, many of them already covered in the foregoing chapters.

It is ideal as a parting tool because, being a mere $\frac{1}{16}$in (1.587mm) across the blade it penetrates quickly, makes the narrowest cut, and can be sharpened in a mo-

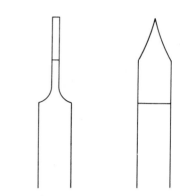

A sample piece showing a variety of forms cut entirely with the spearpoint, and touched by no other tool or abrasive

Diagram of the spearpoint general purpose tool

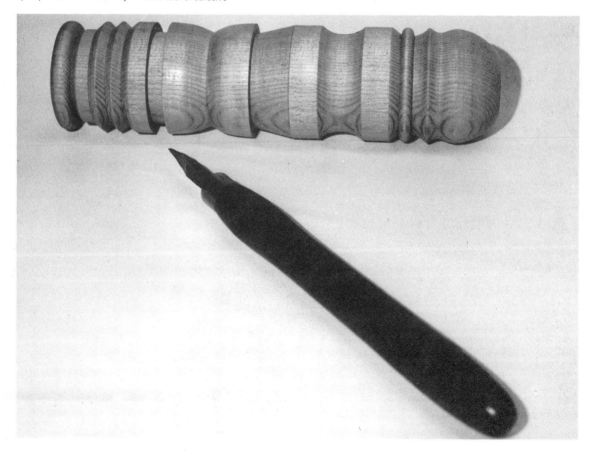

ment. Used skew chisel fashion for roughing down it will rapidly remove waste in spindle turning, slicing under the grain as no other chisel will, and in areas too confined for a gouge to be used.

It is perfect for very small spindle turning or bead cutting, and in faceplate hollowing out is quicker and less fatiguing than any other tool, with less risk of pulling the work from the screwchuck.

Using the V-cutting technique described in Chapter 16 it will lift waste out of bowls with the minimum of effort. It will centre hole for the screwchuck accurately and cleanly, ready tapered for the screw. (See Chapter 11.)

With the blade in the vertical plane, it will skew cut clean and deep, square off ends, undercut shoulders and round bosses and big beads with a swing of the handle, leaving a shining smooth surface. It is a really versatile tool, and one I use more than any other.

As the name implies, the spearpoint, square in section, is hollow ground on all four sides to a flat edged spearpoint. It has two short and two long bevels, the edge being formed by the junction of the two short bevels. The long bevels are ground to give a parallel projection of approximately 1in (2.54cm) long by $\frac{1}{16}$in (1.587mm) thick, the width at the edge.

Because of the short bevels, it has considerable strength when used in the horizonal plane, and for this reason is particularly useful for the rapid removal of waste in hollowing out operations. In this position it is also ideal for sizing cuts, parting off up to depths of 1in (2.54cm), roughing down short lengths and trimming the corners from faceplate work by penetration at right angles to the face. It can also make finishing cuts on very small diameter work.

Turned through 90° to bring the edge into the vertical plane it is ideal for marking out cuts, squaring or rounding the ends of spindle work or for V cuts. In either plane it is a ready means of spotting centres in faceplate work for reversing on to the screwchuck, penetration to about $\frac{3}{8}$in (9.525mm) giving a tapered hole shaped to the screw.

My spearpoints are made from 10in (25.40cm) square files, ground smooth on all sides, lightly chamfered on the corners, and hollow ground on a medium grit 6 × 1in (15.24 × 2.54cm) carborundum wheel. Care is taken not to overheat the steel, particularly as the final edge is formed. Because of its narrowness, and the short hollow grind forming it, the edge can be honed on the oilstone in just a few moments.

The extension of the $\frac{1}{16}$in (1.587mm) blade is maintained as a parallel section so that in subsequent regrinds the width of the blade is not reduced.

With the necked-in type parting tool – described and recommended in some books – as the edge is repeatedly resharpened over the course of time it moves further and further back into the narrower necked in area until finally it is useless for parting purposes. Thereafter only a major regrind operation will restore it to an effective shape. With the parallel bladed tool, however, if care is taken in regrinding, it will be effective until finally ground away to a mere 1in (2.54cm) or so in length.

When used for rounding the ends of spindle work the tool is held horizontally, with the edge in the vertical position, the blade pointed in the direction the curve will take and the tool rest at centre height. The cut is made by a straight thrust of the tool, the handle being swung round to set the degree of curvature required. The bevel is rubbing from the moment the tool cuts in, and a dead smooth, even shining surface results.

A TOOL FOR ASSEMBLING ADAPTERS IN LAMPS

The tool being described is for assembling the plain brass threaded sleeve or adapter commonly used to attach the light fitting to standard lamps.

The hole prepared in the lamp for the adapter, which is 1$\frac{1}{2}$in (3.81cm) long and threaded externally $\frac{1}{2}$in (12.7mm) BSB (26 TPI), is counterbored $\frac{3}{8}$in (9.525mm) to a depth of 1$\frac{1}{4}$in (3.175cm) and tapped out using a No. 2 taper tap of identical size to the adapter.

If the hole is first liberally lined with sealer and given time for this to dry after thoroughly saturating the wood, the cutting action of the tap will be facilitated and the fibres of the wood prevented from shredding.

The tool itself is simple enough, consisting of a piece of galvanised piping of $\frac{3}{8}$in (9.525mm) internal diameter, 4–5in (10.16–12.7cm) long. One end is tapped internally to a depth of $\frac{1}{2}$in (12.7mm) with the $\frac{1}{2}$in (12.7mm) BSB (26 TPI) No. 2 taper tap, and the adapter tested for a free fit in the pipe.

Following this the pipe is drilled transversely $\frac{3}{8}$in (9.525mm) in from the threaded end with a drill of a suitable size to allow free passage of a 4in (10.16cm) round head nail. The nail now has a flat approximately $\frac{1}{8}$in (3.175mm) wide filed along the full length of one side, after which it is passed through the hole and has the last inch away from the head end turned through an angle of 90° to retain it in the pipe. The tool is now ready for use.

In operation the nail is turned so as to present a rounded face to the adapter screwed down on to it. The adapter, now screwed into the tool, is entered into the threaded hole in the lamp and, using the tool with its nail as a tommy handle, is turned into the hole until the face of the tool butts against the end of the lamp. At this point the nail is rotated to bring its flat surface towards the adapter, so freeing the tool and allowing it to be removed without disturbing the adapter in the lamp.

The adapter will now protrude about $\frac{3}{8}$in (9.525mm) from the top of the lamp, providing ample support for the light socket, which should be checked to ensure that it seats down on the end of the wood.

The adapter assembly tool. Note the flat filed along the side of the nail

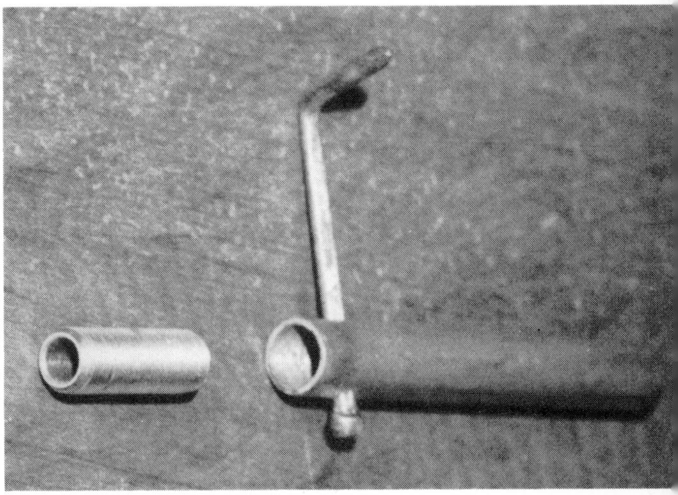

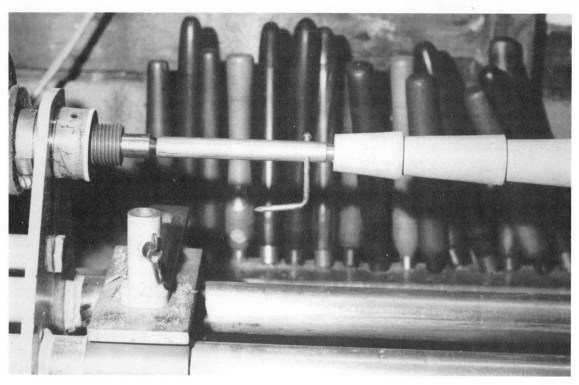

The adapter tool in use, lined up by means of centres at head and tailstock

A TEMPLATE FOR CENTERING IRREGULAR SHAPED TIMBER FOR FACEPLATE AND SPINDLE TURNING

Occasions arise when the selected piece of wood for faceplate or spindle work is of such irregular shape that fixing the centre is a problem, as in pieces cut from tree trunks or branches. In such situations this device is the answer.

First set up a piece of scrap wood on the faceplate large enough to take an 8in (20.32cm) square of $\frac{1}{8}-\frac{1}{4}$in (3.175mm–6.35mm) thick Perspex. Dress the face of the wood flat and true and secure the Perspex to it. This can be done by driving screws through the four corners, after centering the Perspex within a circle scribed on the wood. Alternatively, the Perspex may be held by strips of wood across its corners, these being nailed or screwed on, so avoiding unnecessary holes in the template.

When secure, a small hole, no more than $\frac{1}{16}$in (1.587mm) diameter, is bored through its exact centre, and from this, taking care not to enlarge the hole, a series of circles, $\frac{1}{4}$in (6.35mm) apart, are scribed with the dividers across the whole face of the Perspex. Once lightly marked with the dividers the rings are positively engraved with a bruzz or the sharp corner of the skew chisel.

Alternating rings are coloured red and black with wax crayon or felt tip pen, and the centre hole is countersunk from the opposite face. The reason for this is to have the small centre hole against the surface of the wood, whilst the countersink gives clearance to the tool used for marking the centre through the hole. At the same time the engraved rings are also against the wood, giving a much clearer definition than if they were on the surface towards the operator.

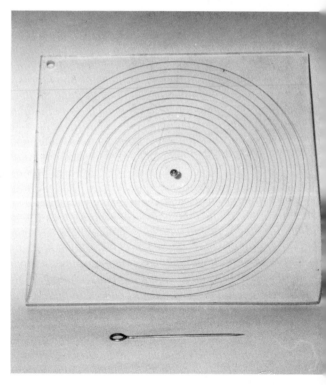

The centering template for irregular shaped wood, with pricker

The template in use

In use, the template is laid on the surface to be centered, and moved about to bring the whole area of the wood within one of the circles on the template. The centre is then pricked through the hole.

A TOOL FOR CENTERING FACEPLATE WORK

A problem often encountered in faceplate work is getting the workpiece accurately centered on the faceplate.

A method commonly used is to scribe a circle or series of circles on the face of the work, positioning the faceplate within the circle nearest to its size, and marking the screw positions through from the back of the faceplate. This method has the disadvantage that unless the two items are clamped together a slight undetected movement of the faceplate can result in an error in marking the screw positions on the wood.

A superior way to do this, where the scribed circle intersects the screw holes and one screw located on the circle secures the faceplate whilst the position of the remaining screw holes is marked on the line through the faceplate, is fully described in Chapter 8.

An even quicker, though equally accurate method is to use a simple centering device. To make this, turn a cylindrical length of hardwood 4in (10.16cm) long to be a sliding fit in the mandrel hole of the faceplate, and square one end. Into the centre of this drive a short nail. Cut it off leaving ⅛in (3.175mm) protruding and sharpen this to a point.

The device is now ready for use, so proceed as follows. Centre the workpiece, mark it with the centre punch, and lie it centre mark upwards on the bench. The faceplate, with the centering plug point protruding at its front, is now positioned to bring the centre point into the centre punch hole. When these two are married the faceplate is accurately centered, so the screw hole positions can be marked through the back of it. Whilst the nail is located in the wood the faceplate cannot shift, so all risk of error is eliminated.

The faceplate centering tool, with the workpiece centered with dividers and centre punch

The centering tool in use. Pilot holes can now be drilled and screws inserted from the back of the faceplate

Diagram of celluloid sheet marked out ready for cutting

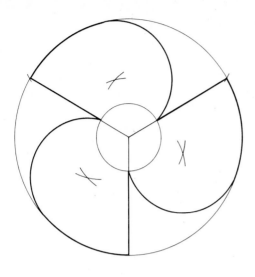

The 120° template positioned ready for 120° marking to be made

A TEMPLATE FOR MARKING OUT 120° POSITIONS ON FLAT SURFACES

The accepted way to find 120° positions around a centre is to scribe a circle and lay off the radius around the circumference, the intermediate points being 120° apart. As this is not always a convenient method to use, a template as described is a simple, quick and accurate alternative.

Cut a circle of 7in (17.78cm) diameter from celluloid or flexible plastic, and scribe three lines, 120° apart, from the centre to the edge. Next scribe a circle of 2in (5.08cm) diameter at the centre. With your dividers set at 1¾in (4.445cm), strike an arc from the point where the radial lines intersect the 2in (5.08cm) circle, and a second intersecting arc struck from the centre of the 2in (5.08cm) circle. Now, using the intersecting arcs as a centre, strike an arc of 1¾in (4.445cm) radius, starting at the point of intersection of the radial line and the 2in (5.08cm) circle, and finishing at the outer edge of the 7in (17.78cm) disc. The area between the radial lines and the curved line nearest to it is now cut away, exposing the radial line as an edge against which a pen or pencil can be used to mark the 120° positions.

In use, the template is positioned by having a pointed tool passed through the centre hole into the centre of the workpiece, and the three 120° locations marked on it by means of the radial edges.

A SIZING TOOL FOR REPETITION WORK

A simple tool for reducing ⅜in (9.525mm) diameter leg stubs to an exact size in repetition work is made from a 6in (15.24cm) length of 1in (2.54cm) wide by ¼in (6.35mm) thick mild steel bar.

Start by drilling a ⅜in (9.525mm) diameter hole through the bar, half-way across and ½in (12.7mm) from one end. Scribe two lines ⅜in (9.525mm) apart from the sides of the hole to one edge. Carefully hacksaw *inside* the lines to make a slot from the hole to the edge. Now open up the slot a little at its outside end and accurately file the sides of the slot back to the scribed lines, taking care to keep the two surfaces square and true.

In use, the tool is pressed over the stub or pin after it has been turned down to a full ⅜in (9.525mm), the diameter being reduced to a standard size by the compression of the fibres of the wood.

General view of double ended sizing tool. It has been painted with rustproof paint

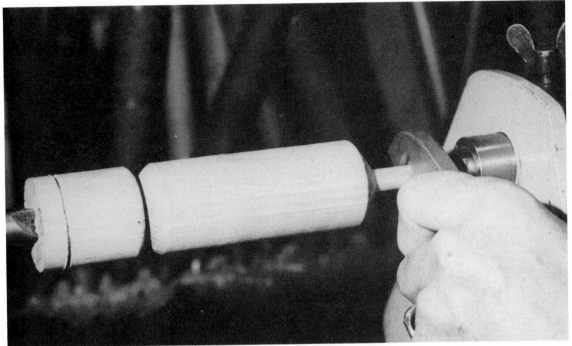

The sizing tool in use on the punch for shaping the copper tray described in Chapter 11

SCRAPERS THAT ARE DIFFERENT

A lot has been written about scrapers, and they are generally regarded as a necessary evil to be used only by nervous students, unimaginative plodders with no urge to master the true art of turning wood and perhaps, where absolutely unavoidable, by the professional. I must admit that the illustrations and descriptions of scrapers made from old files, often quite large ones, would have deterred me from their use long ago, had I not followed my own bent. In fact I use round nose and side scrapers in the final stages of turning all my hollow ware, not excepting large bowls, but they are scrapers with a difference, and used in conjunction with a modified tool rest which supports the tool right up to its cutting edge. (See the next section.)

Let me describe them. First there is a ½in (12.7mm) wide round nose scraper which started life as a trade supplied square ended chisel. As I had two of these already I converted it. The end was ground circular, and against all the accepted rules a hollow ground bevel of about 30° angle extending back about ½in (12.7mm) from the edge was ground off. I then committed the ultimate heresy, and put a second bevel with the oilstone, right at the edge, just enough to take the rag off from the grinder. If the tool is supported flat on the tool rest described, right up to within ½in (12.7mm) of its cutting edge, then that cutting edge can be made as fine as the quality of the metal will allow.

Another scraper is made from an 8in (20.32cm) hand safe edge file, which again has a long bevel around the end and side. Carefully ground, its teeth all removed and with its flat surfaces shining and corners bevelled, it can take its place unnoticed amongst the trademarked tools in the rack.

Then there are two others, 6in (15.24cm) and 8in (20.32cm) half-round files, ground off and polished like the rest, approximately ¼in (6.35mm) and ½in (12.7mm) wide at

their respective ends, but with the long bevel ground on the curved face and a shorter bevel brought around the side. In use they rest on their curved surface, which is no disadvantage in cutting with the end of the tool, and can be a positive help when side cutting as the curved back laid on the rest allows the cutting edge to be raised or lowered by simply rotating the handle.

Another very useful round end scraper, barely $\frac{1}{16}$in (1.587mm) across its tip, and very handy for forming decorative rings on pot lids and similar articles, is made from a 6in (15.24cm) square file. It is tapered in on two sides to $\frac{1}{16}$in (1.587mm) across the end, which is then carefully rounded, with a bevel of about 60° taken right down to its opposite side and around the flanks.

Whereas the scrapers described earlier are sharpened by a few passes across the secondary bevel with a slip stone, held in the hand, the $\frac{1}{16}$in (1.587mm) round nose is re-

Sketch of front and side view of scrapers:

1, end and side; *2, round end*

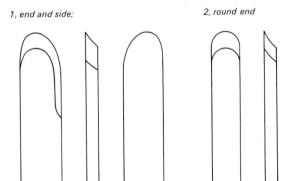

A variety of side and end scrapers ground with long bevels and a minimal chamfer at the edge

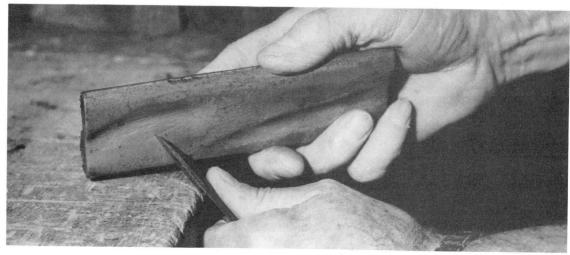

Sharpening a round end scraper against the bench. With such a fine edge only two or three passes of the stone are necessary

The internal tool rest. The corners are ground off

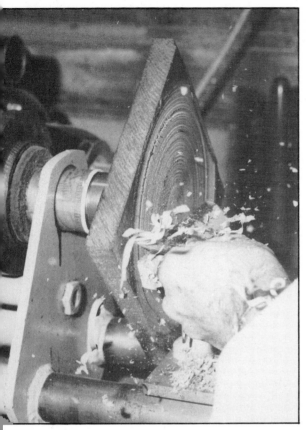

A round end scraper making the shavings fly

The internal tool rest in use

edged by rubbing its flat upper face on the oilstone at the bench.

All these scrapers will take really heavy cuts in quite hard Australian and New Zealand woods such as jarrah, kauri, matai, totara, manuka, pururi and blue gum, producing streams of shavings without over-heating, despite their fine edges, because the tool rest, coming close up behind the cutting edge, absorbs the heat generated. Support so near the cutting edge of the tool also virtually eliminates vibration.

AN INTERNAL TOOL REST

As I have mentioned earlier in the book, the standard tool rest has severe limitations when it comes to hollowing out narrow mouthed containers, so I suggest you do as I did many years ago and have a simple tool rest made up as follows by your friendly neighbourhood garage or engineering workshop.

A 6in (15.24cm) length of 1 × ¼in (2.54cm × 6.35mm) angle iron is welded at one end to a post of the same diameter and length as the shank of your tool rest. The angle iron is attached to the post with the edge of its top horizontal face towards the operator when the unattached end of the angle iron is directed towards the head-

stock, the post being welded to the inside vertical face. The unattached end of the tool rest is rounded on its two corners to clear the wood when fully home. In use the unattached end is pushed into the mouth of the hollow ware, so that it is close to the bottom of the hole, and the edge is close against the side at the normal cutting height for scrapers. The scraper, described in the previous section, is laid flat on the full surface of the tool rest, and so supported right up to its cutting edge. The tool rest is moved forward and sideways as the hole is deepened and widened, so that the tool has maximum support throughout the operation.

In my view a rest of this kind is essential for safe, smooth and accurate hollowing out work, and should form part of the lathe's standard accessories.

A TAIL END JIG TO SUPPORT OPEN ENDED WORK

Occasions arise from time to time in spindle turning operations when work on the tailstock end is precluded by the necessity to support the work with the dead centre. I refer to such jobs as cleaning up the top of a handle after parting off, supporting shakers or pepper mills during boring and opening up operations, or shaping or embellishing the tops of them.

*The tail end jig, with selection of collets or sleeves, some in heavy
leather, the others in wood. One has a leather lining*

A shaker mounted in the tail end jig having its hole drilled. A shaped driving chuck is being used

For small diameter work, up to say 1¾in (4.445cm) diameter, the problem is overcome as follows. From a car wrecker or similar source obtain a serviceable ball race of 2in (5.32cm) internal diameter. Mount this as a press fit in a heavy ply fame, and screw discs of hardboard or ply say ³⁄₁₆in (4.762mm) thick on the front and back faces of the frame to retain the ball race in position, leaving the centre 2in (5.08cm) diameter hole clear.

Adapt the base of the frame to fit the bed of the lathe, with the centre of the hole on the centre line of the head and tailstock. Finally, turn wooden sleeves or collets with a small flange at one end to be a sliding fit in the hole of the bearing. As required, a sleeve is shaped internally to fit the article to be worked on, and sufficient projection allowed through the jig for the operation to proceed. The sleeve is then slit along one side, to allow it to expand sufficiently to grip the ball race, so that the article, sleeve and race rotate as one.

When ready, the workpiece is set up on the driving centre, its rear end seated in the jig with the flange of the sleeve towards the headstock, and the jig secured so that pressure by the workpiece against the driving centre is maintained. The tool rest is then brought into position against the end of the workpiece, and the projected task completed.

A REVOLVING DEAD CENTRE MADE IN THE LATHE

Although not intended for sustained heavy work, this device will prove invaluable for a variety of purposes where friction free pressure or support is required. It consists primarily of a ball race set in a housing shaped to fit the tailstock

poppet. Into the ball race a variety of adapters designed to suit the job in hand can be fitted, being simply pressed home into the hole of the race.

To make the device, obtain from any available source two identical small ball races of say ¾–1in (19.05mm–2.54cm) outside diameter, with a hole diameter of ¼–³⁄₈in (6.35–9.525mm). From hickory or beech turn a housing shaped to fit into or over the tailstock mandrel, and recessed at its forward end to take the two ball races, one on top of the other, as a tight press-in fit, the upper race being flush with the end of the housing. Now select a bolt with its shank a sliding fit in the bearing hole, and of a length to seat in both races without fouling the bottom of the hole. Set up the bolt in the Jacobs chuck, and file the head to a conical shaped point.

The revolving centre is now complete. By making various other shaped fittings in wood, with shanks a press fit into the housing, the device can be used for supporting workpieces with rounded, flat or hollow ends, as circumstances demand.

Section diagram of the revolving centre

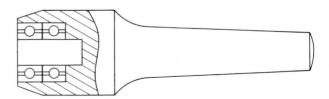

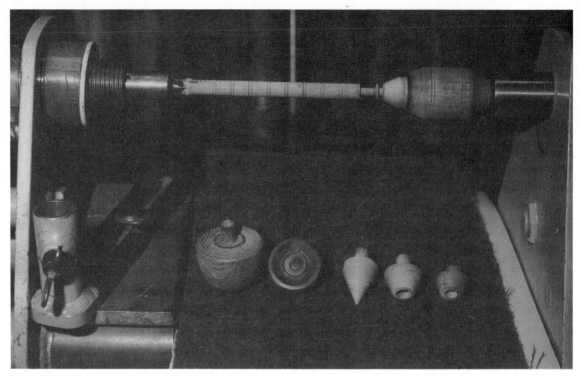

The revolving centre with adapter supporting workpiece, and various shaped adapters in the foreground

A SPARE WOODEN SCREWCHUCK MADE IN THE LATHE

As an extra accessory, a screwchuck in wood, with a tapered shank to fit a hollow mandrel, a screwed boss for a threaded mandrel, or designed to screw into or on the faceplate, can be made as follows.

Tapered shank type

Turn a form in beech or other dense wood, 3in (7.62cm) across the face, 1in (2.54cm) in thickness, with a tapered Morse shank to make a solid seating in the headstock mandrel. On its face turn a raised ring of 2in (5.08cm) outer diameter, $\frac{1}{4}$in (6.35mm) wide and $\frac{1}{8}$in (3.175mm) high, with slightly tapered sides, leaving the remainder of the face quite flat. Strike a circle of $\frac{1}{2}$in (12.7mm) diameter on the face, and lightly V-cut it. On this circle drill two $\frac{1}{16}$in (1.587mm) diameter holes, directly opposite each other, to a depth of $\frac{1}{2}$in (12.7mm). After this, select a nail to be a tight fit in the $\frac{1}{16}$in (1.587mm) holes, and approximately 1$\frac{1}{2}$in (3.81cm) long. Cut off its head, chamfer the stump, then bend it into a flat bottomed U shape, the base of the U being $\frac{1}{2}$in (12.7mm) across, and the arms no longer than $\frac{1}{2}$in (12.7mm).

The metal U is now driven into the holes prepared in the face of the chuck, care being taken to avoid setting down the centre part of the U bottom. Before it is fully home, carefully file the U along its base, bringing it to a narrow edge locking bar which will fit snugly, screwdriver fashion, into the slot of a 1$\frac{1}{2}$–1$\frac{3}{4}$in (3.81–4.445cm) 10 gauge countersunk head wood screw. After filing, drive the U fully home.

Following this, turn a 3in (7.62cm) diameter disc of 1in (2.54cm) ply or hardwood, and cut a 2in (5.08cm) outer diameter groove on one face, $\frac{1}{4}$in (6.35mm) wide by $\frac{1}{8}$in (3.175mm) deep, with tapered sides to match the raised ring on the face of the chuck. When brought into face-to-face contact there must be no side movement. At the centre of the disc, on the same face, turn a $\frac{3}{4}$in (19.05mm) wide recess deep enough to clear the chuck's locking bar when chuck and disc are face to face.

Now bore a hole at the exact centre of the disc to be a snug fit on a 10 gauge screw, and countersink the hole on the side towards the locking bar sufficient only to allow the chuck and disc to close face to face when the locking bar is fully engaged with the slot of the screw. Finally, drill three holes of a diameter to clear a 10 gauge screw, located centrally in the groove of the disc at 120° intervals. Countersink these holes on the face away from the chuck, ensuring that the heads of the screws are not above the surface when screwed fully home.

Clamp the chuck and disc together, then screw the disc to the chuck, with the centre screw in place, engaged with the locking bar, checking to see that the screw is positively locked and the surfaces of the chuck and disc are closed together.

It now only requires a deep V to be cut lengthwise at the side of the assembled chuck to ensure correct reassembly whenever it is stripped down for a changeover of the centre screw.

The screwchuck before assembly. Note the locking bar in the face of the left hand part

The Morse screwchuck assembled, with double sided sandpaper clutch. There is an index mark along the side of the chuck to ensure correct reassembly

Screw-in type chuck for threaded mandrel

As this type of chuck will be screwed into the mandrel it will take a somewhat different form, so first acquire a bolt which will fit the mandrel, and of a length permitting full entry of the threaded portion, plus 1in (2.54cm) of plain shank.

Turn the form for the chuck from beech or other hardwood, with a face of 3in (7.62cm) diameter by 1in (2.54cm) thick, shaped back to a boss of 1½in (3.81cm) diameter by 1in (2.54cm) long. Blind bore the boss to a depth of 1in (2.54cm), the hole to be a tight fit on the shank of the bolt, which is then chamfered on its plain end and pressed home into the hole. Drill a transverse hole ½in (12.7mm) from the end of the boss, through the wood and metal, and drive a tight fitting nail into it, filing the ends off flush. Following this, assemble a flat steel washer over the threaded portion of the bolt, drill and countersink two opposed holes through the washer, and screw it to the boss of the chuck. This washer will serve as a bearing surface against the flange of the mandrel, and minimise wear between the parts. The chuck is now screwed into the headstock, faced off true, and all the operations previously described completed.

Screw-in type for faceplate

For screwing into the faceplate the disc from which the chuck is made needs to be 1½in (3.81cm) thick, to allow ½in (12.7mm) for the length of the spigot, which is turned to be a tight screw-in fit into the mandrel hole of the faceplate, as described in Chapter 16. In all other particulars, the making of the chuck follows the previous instructions.

The screw-in type chuck, showing the pin in the boss locking the thread, and the steel washer to bear against the flange of the mandrel

Cutting the slot for the channelling tool, using the modified tenon saw

Screw-on type for faceplate

For screwing on to the faceplate the normal centering procedure is followed, whereafter the making of the chuck remains the same.

A TOOL FOR CHANNELLING

For those occasions when a groove or slot is required to carry flex within a split turned standard lamp, or across its base, a simple tool, easily made, and used in conjunction with suitable preliminary preparations, can make all the difference to the quality of the finished job.

Having laid out the position for the channel by, if possible, scoring a deep central line with the marking gauge or a rule and trimming knife, cut in on the line with a fine toothed tenon saw. Cuts of this kind are started much more easily if the end of the saw blade has been shaped to a convex curve from the edge to the back strap and the teeth cut around it in continuation of the original edge.

The curved portion of the blade can then be applied at any starting position along the surface to be slotted, lowering the handle to bring the full cutting edge to bear when entrance into the wood has been made. The depth of cut required, approximately $\frac{1}{8}$in (3.175mm), is controlled by clamping a strip of ply or hardboard on to the blade, parallel to the edge, and by waxing its contact face the operation is that much easier. Once the saw kerf, which must always follow the grain, has been made, the channelling tool can be brought into play.

It is made as follows. Select a piece of sound timber $1\frac{1}{2} \times$ 2in (3.81cm × 5.08cm) × 6in (15.24cm) long, plane one narrow face flat and true, and mark a line lengthwise through its centre. Measure off $\frac{1}{2}$in (12.7mm), 1in (2.54cm), 3in (7.62cm), 5in (12.7cm) and $5\frac{1}{2}$in (13.97cm) from either

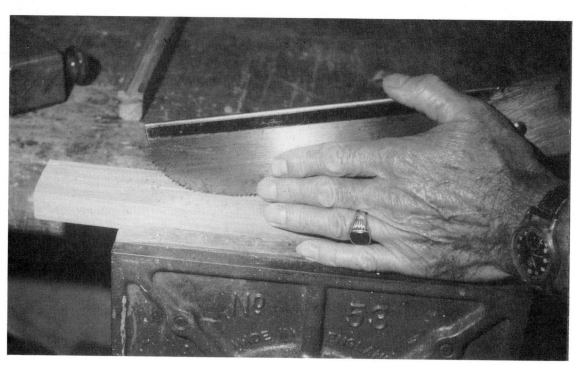

end, and drill holes accurately on the line to take five 1¼in (3.175cm) No. 10 gauge round head steel wood screws.

Screw the second, third and fourth screws within 1/16in (1.587mm) of the surface of the wood, with their slots crossways to the length of it. Next take a fine tooth hacksaw and cut down the screw slots to just short of the surface of the wood. Following this, cut through the base of the screw heads, from the front, without damaging the wood.

It will now be seen that the half screw heads remaining, all facing in one direction, form semi-circular faces. The heads of the two outer screws are removed completely, leaving their stubs ⅛in (3.175mm) higher than the tops of the modified screw heads. The stubs can now be filed into wedge shaped guides for locating in the saw kerf, their top edges reduced to approximately 1/32in (0.794mm) wide, running lengthwise to the long axis of the wood.

When the tool is positioned in readiness for channelling, the two guides, situated at the outer ends of the tool, will sit in the prepared saw kerf, and guide the cutters in shaping the channel for the flex, simultaneously deepening the saw kerf as the cut progresses. To this end, the guides should have a very slight rake on their upper surfaces, but their forward faces should be left in the round to avoid scouring out the sides of the saw kerf. The end of the tool away from the cutting faces can now be rounded up with rasp and sandpaper to fit the hand, and if desired a turned stub handle fitted to the upper front end.

Apart from a coat of sealer this completes the tool which, in use, after the saw kerf has been made, is entered in the slot and used plane fashion to cut the rounded channel for the flex until the plane bottom rests on the surface of the workpiece, when the full depth of cut will have been reached. As the cutters wear they are lightly filed on their front faces to restore their cutting action.

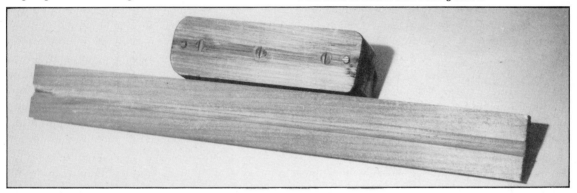

The finished tool showing the underside, with a channelled sample in foreground

The channelling tool in use

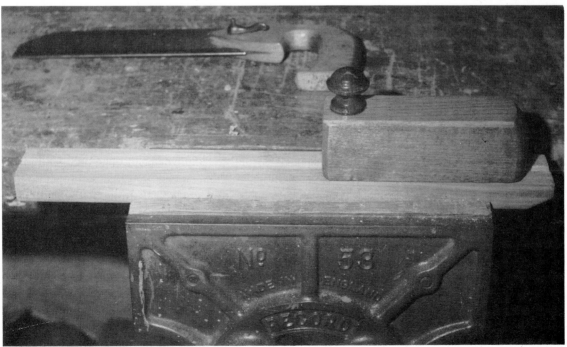

A STRAP WRENCH FOR ROTARY LEVERAGE

This tool will be found to be particularly useful in any situation where rotary leverage is wanted on a smooth, round surface offering no hand grip. Used in conjunction with the screw-in assembly method of securing wood to the faceplate, as described in Chapter 16, a really solid face-to-face coupling can be made.

For the lever select a piece of oak, ash or beech 14in (35.56cm) long by 2¼in (5.715cm) wide by ¾in (19.05mm) thick, planed on both wide faces, and mount it between centres. Square both ends, leaving ½in (12.7mm) waste at the headstock, and from the tailstock mark off at 6½in (16.51cm). Using the shallow ⅝in (15.875mm) gouge, form a handle shape between the tailstock and the 6½in (16.51cm) mark, and round the edges between there and the headstock. Sand and seal overall, and part off at the headstock.

Next acquire a 6½in (16.51cm) length of steel rod or wire, of 3/16in (4.762mm) diameter, and form it into an oblong, square cornered loop of 1¾in (4.445cm) inside length, by 1in (2.54cm) inside width, with the ends abutting half-way along one long side. Cut a groove across the wide face of the handle ¾in (19.05mm) in from the wide end, to allow the metal loop to bed into it, flush with the surface, and round the end of the wood in an arc from the groove up to the opposite corner.

Following this, step in the sides of the wood from the groove to the top, to clear the 1¾in (4.445cm) inside dimension of the loop, and cut the angle of the step to conform with the arc of the curved top. When satisfied with the fit of the loop, obtain a piece of tough oxhide or very heavy strap leather, of 1¾in (4.445cm) width by ¼in (6.35mm) thickness, and at least 15in (38.10cm) long.

To secure this and the loop in position, cut a piece of ⅛in (3.175mm) steel or brass plate to a rectangle 2in (5.08cm) long by 1¼in (3.175cm) wide, and drill four 3/16in (4.762mm) countersunk holes ¼in (6.35mm) in from each corner. Position the plate to cover the groove, straddled by the four screw holes, with the end of the strap completely under the plate, dressed side upwards and drill ready for the screws.

Assembling the wrench can now begin so first encircle the handle with the metal loop and bed its split side in the groove, its free side away from the wood. Next glue the strap in its position under the plate, and screw the plate home using ¾in (19.05mm) No. 8 gauge steel countersunk head screws.

Once the glue is dry the tool is ready for use, and is operated thus. If the article is being given an anticlockwise turn, say in unscrewing a frozen screwchuck, the handle would be held with the metal loop on the underside, and the strap passed over the top of the article and threaded back through the loop. Enough slack is left in the strap encircling the work to allow the strap to double back on itself, so trapping it between the handle and the work. Downward leverage is then applied, and the more pressure exerted, the more the work is gripped. To reverse the direction of rotation the tool is reversed, that is, it is applied from underneath, and levered upwards, or the operator moves to the opposite side of the job, whichever is most convenient.

The strap wrench parts before assembly

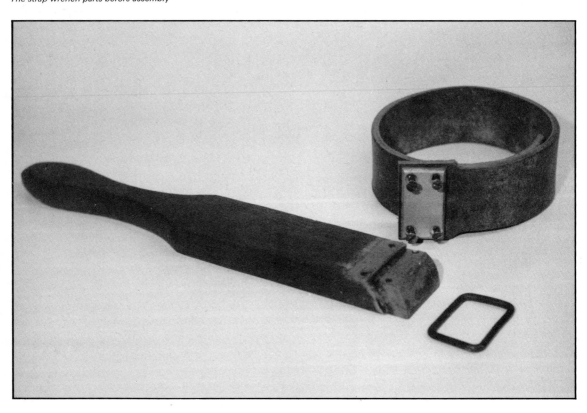

The assembled strap wrench screwing home a spigot chuck

HANDLES FOR TURNING TOOLS

Amongst the first things the beginner needs in his new hobby are handles: long handles for his turning tools, because perhaps those on the secondhand ones he bought are clumsy, or the new tool handles on that shop bought set are too small in the grip. Short handles too will be handy for the files he will use in bit sharpening and other workshop chores. There is nothing really new about the handles I shall describe, but their method of making has some novel features which you may like to try.

To start with a simple turning tool handle, select a piece of almost any reasonably dense wood 12in (30.48cm) long by 2in (5.08cm) diameter, fruit wood for preference.

The occasional small knots give them an individual identity, and the smaller limbs of apple, plum, pear or cherry are often just the right size. However, always add an additional ½in (12.7mm) on the diameter of these to allow for irregularities in the section shape. Also take care in centering up, as few limbs are straight for a full 12in (30.48cm).

Place the centres towards the edge on the hump side of a bent piece, and set it up in the lathe – without the tool rest! Switch on, and observe the wood as it flies round. There will be a solid area in the centre of the revolving mass, and a transparent area of wood around it. The solid image represents wood which would be touching the tool throughout 360° of movement, whilst the hazy outline is wood revolving out of centre, the extreme outer limit of the outline being wood which would barely touch the tool during one complete revolution.

Knowing this, you can gauge from the diameter of the core image whether a handle of 1½in (3.81cm) diameter could be turned from it on its present centres. If not, recentre the tailstock centre, checking the offset with a pencil held over the tool rest, and rotating the workpiece by hand. By

Fruitwood raw material for handles

recentering across the end of the wood, the optimum position can be found for extracting the maximum diameter from it.

Having done this, drive the fork centre hard into the workpiece on the bench, set up in the lathe, tighten and clamp the tailstock centre and position the tool rest just below centre height and clear of the eccentric hump of wood. With the lathe set at 1000 r.p.m., and using the ⅜in (9.525mm) deep gouge, skim lightly across the high spot. Once having got the tool angle just right, increase the depth of cut, moving out left and right from the high spot, until some part of the workpiece comes into the round.

At this point, if necessary, make a further change of centre to balance the workpiece between an area being cut and an opposite side not yet in contact with the tool. But don't move the wood too far: just half the distance the uncut portion is away from the tool. Of course, if the piece cannot be adjusted to provide 1½in (3.81cm) diameter over the 12in (30.48cm) length, then cut it in two and use for file handles. If a workable diameter has been obtained, round the wood down to a uniform cylinder of maximum diameter, remove the dead centre, and with a ¼in (6.35mm) jobbing drill chucked in the tailstock bore into the end of the cylinder to a depth of 2½in (6.35cm), clearing the chips from the hole as you go. So long as pressure is maintained on the tailstock handwheel the driving centre will rotate the wood, the drill acting in the role of a dead centre. But one word of caution: don't attempt to withdraw the drill before the motor is switched off and the wood is stationary.

The next step is to taper the hole for the tool to which it will be fitted, so sharpen the four corners of the tang of a large file (file tangs are soft and can be readily filed), or use the tang of the tool to be handled, sharpening it if need be. The file or tool can now be gripped in the vice and, by rotary pressure of the handle on the tang, the hole tapered out.

The conical hole thus formed in the handle will give a perfect seating to the tang of the tool when finally driven home, and is made at this stage to ensure that in subsequent shaping it will be concentric with the outside. Holes drilled after the handle is turned can run off course, and so spoil what might otherwise be a good turning job.

Having prepared the hole, re-mount the handle on centres, square the tail end, and measure in ¾in (19.05mm) with the dividers. At this point you will need a metal ferrule, so search your scrap box for a thin walled piece of brass or copper piping, of ¾in (19.05mm) or 1in (2.54cm) inside diameter, and saw off a full ¾in (19.05mm). (Always cut on the face of pipe nearest to you, moving the saw around the pipe so as to avoid cutting on the edge farthest from you; it will take the teeth out of your saw if you strike it.) Square one end of the ferrule, and chamfer inside that end with a half-round file.

Now cut in with the skew chisel on the ¾in (19.05mm) mark of the handle, and reduce from there to the end to the inside diameter of the ferrule, leaving the spigot of wood slightly oversize. Undercut the shoulder end of the spigot a fraction with the long point of the chisel and, if the metal ferrule is thin walled, reduce the diameter of the spigot at the shoulder also.

Put a very small chamfer on the end of the spigot, and ease its diameter down very gently with light skew cuts until the ferrule and spigot chamfers engage. Now remove the handle from the lathe, and press the ferrule home on the spigot, using the carpenter's vice, with a metal plate square across the ferrule end. Alternatively, place the handle upright on the flat surface of the vice or anvil, ferrule down-

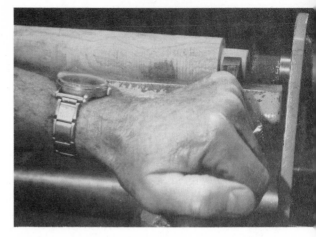

Shaping the ferrule end with the ½in (12.7mm) square end chisel. The ferrule is sitting on the dead centre ready for testing the fit

Reamering the hole in the tool handle using the tang of a file. The handle is still in an unturned state

wards, and using a mallet on the opposite end, drive the handle into the ferrule.

When it is fully home, with its end against the undercut shoulder, remount the handle in the lathe, its hole supported on the conical dead centre, and with the skew chisel supported close in to the end of the work use the square side of the bevel to scrape the metal of the ferrule back to the end of the spigot. Trim the sharp corner from the ferrule in the same way, and polish it with a piece of well worn, fine sandpaper.

Pressing the ferrule on to the handle using a steel plate in the vice

Spinning in a thin walled ferrule using a round sided screwdriver

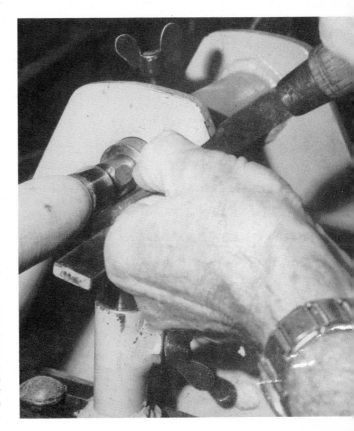

If a thin walled ferrule has been used, and a groove turned in the spigot by the shoulder, the metal can be spun into it so that they are locked together, and any future shrinkage of the wood will not allow the ferrule to come off.

To spin the metal into the groove, use the round side of a screwdriver blade, levered over the tool rest into the shoulder end of the ferrule, with a touch of oil to ease friction between steel and brass. But one word of warning. If unseasoned wood is being used allow an interval of at least four weeks before fitting ferrules.

Once the ferrule is fitted the handle can be shaped to suit you, using the $\frac{3}{8}$in (9.525mm) narrow gouge followed by the $\frac{5}{8}$in (15.875mm) shallow gouge. (If there are decorative knots in your handle finishing with the skew chisel is not advised as it may tear out areas of knotty grain, however sharp it may be. So be content then with a graded wet and dry paper finish.) Round down the headstock end to leave about 1in (2.54cm) waste, parting in to a stub of about $\frac{3}{8}$in (9.525mm) diameter. Sand the whole surface to a fine finish, rounding off with two or three decorative skew cuts on the largest diameter at each end.

Should you want to improve the appearance still further, try burning the decorations in with wire. This is very easy to do, requiring just 6in (15.24cm) of $\frac{1}{32}$in (0.794mm) steel wire, with a tear-off drink can ring attached to each end. The lathe is set at 1500 r.p.m., with a finger through each ring the wire is pressed into the skew cuts, making sure they are burnt completely out. If no skew cuts is made to guide the wire the position of the burn mark is almost impossible to control. As an extra touch a $\frac{1}{16}$in (1.587mm) diameter wire can be used for the centre line of three, after which the area is lightly sanded over to remove any surface scorching.

The handle may now be sealed to prevent dirt from penetrating into the grain, and if a really first class job is wanted it can be lightly steel-woolled to break the surface of the sealer, and carnauba wax polished. The finish won't last for ever, but it will look good at the time!

After parting off the waste, the handle can be mounted by its hole on a ¼in (6.35mm) coach bolt, head removed, and chucked in the headstock. It is then smoothed down with abrasive paper at its top end, the handle being supported with one hand whilst working with the other, and finally sealed and polished.

Taking such pains with humble handles will strengthen your resolve to excel in the more important projects you will tackle in the course of time. However routine the job, do it with all the skill and care you can muster. Never consider any task, menial or commonplace though it may be, unworthy of your best effort, but take pride in all you do.

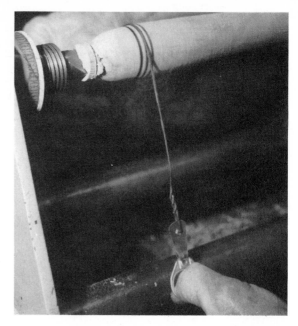

Burning decorative rings into the handle with steel wire. A tear-off drink's can ring is attached to the wire

A selection of handles made of plum, peach and citrus wood

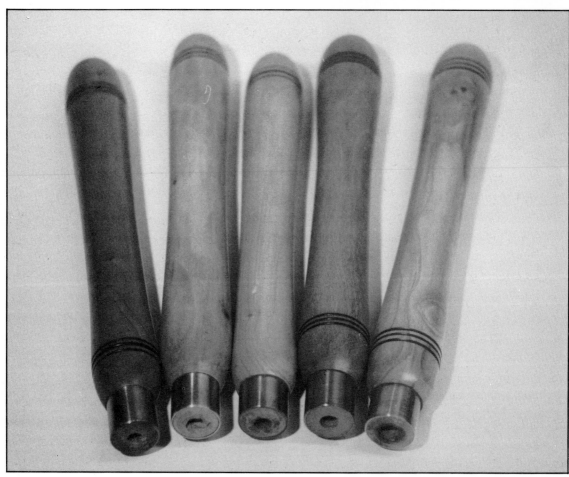

An assortment of file handles made of box and peach wood, and finished in clear lacquer

HANDLES FOR FILES, ETC.

In making file handles almost identical procedures are followed, the dimensions being adjusted to suit your requirements.

For files of 8–10in (20.32–25.4cm), a handle of 6in (15.24cm) would be suitable. For 6–8in (15.24–20.32cm) files 5in (12.7cm) is about right, and for anything smaller a 3in (7.62cm) handle would do.

For very small handles suitable for needle files and similar tools, 303-rifle cartridge cases cut up into ideal tapered ferrules. Intermediate sized handles, if no metal ferrules are at hand, can be made to look colourful and complete if fitted with detergent bottle tops of the flexible plastic kind, although of course they will not prevent splitting of the handle by excessive use of force. The holes in these handles would be tapered out as described earlier, thus greatly reducing the risk of splitting inherent in driving a tapered tang into a parallel hole.

MALLETS

These come in a variety of shapes and sizes, with rectangular heads for carpenters, doughnut shaped heads for sculptors and woodcarvers and cylindrical heads for judges and auctioneers, usually called gavels, and made rather light and ornamental. The mallets I shall describe can be made in two styles: formed all in one, head and handle together, or in the conventional way with the head turned as a separate part from the handle, the two then being dowelled together.

I find it quicker to turn my mallets in one piece from beech or fruitwood, such as peach or plum. Although the heads wear more quickly because the blows are taken on the side grain, by the same token the whole peripheral surface of the head can be used, and does not require positioning to strike in the way a double ended head does, besides having the useful space saving ability to stand on its head. Mine are in

constant use for all the normal functions of a mallet, and particularly for driving fork centres into the workpiece. They last usually for three or four years, so two or so hours spent making one is not time wasted.

The one piece mallet

Take a piece of 3½in (8.89cm) minimum square wood, say oak or beech, 9in (22.86cm) long, set it up between centres and round down to maximum diameter. Mark off from the tail end 5in (12.7cm) and part in to 2in (5.08cm) diameter. From the 5in (12.7cm) mark to the driving centre round down the head to leave a maximum diameter of 3–3½in (7.61–8.89cm), slightly bellied out and wider at the top, leaving ½in (12.7mm) waste at the driving centre.

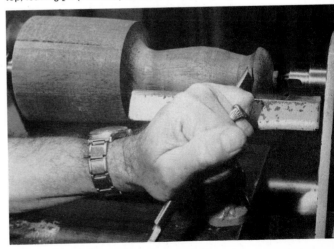

Roughing the one piece mallet to shape between centres, using the ⅜in (9.525mm) gouge

The turning is done with the roughing gouge, say the ⅜in (9.525mm) deep U, and finished with the skew chisel. Round all corners. Now turn the 5in (12.7cm) section back to the end into a handle shape, swelling it out to blend into the underside of the head, at the centre of the grip, and to form a check collar or flange on the end of the handle, where a ½in (12.7mm) waste is left for parting off the centre hole. Most of the handle turning is done with the ⅜in (9.525mm) deep U gouge, as a fair amount of wood has to be removed, and the finishing done with a ½in (12.7mm) shallow gouge. Test the grip as work proceeds.

With the turning completed sand and seal overall and part in to a diameter of ¼in (6.35mm) at the head and tail ends, widening the cuts to permit entry of a saw blade without marking the work. Saw off the two waste ends, and sand those areas on a sheet of garnet paper held on the bench top. Apply sealer to the sanded areas and stand the mallet on its head, ready for action.

The two piece mallet

The parts for the two piece mallet are both turned between centres, but may employ different woods. Beech is ideal for both head and handle, as is ash, or these in combination, but oak may be used for the head and hickory or fruitwood for the handle. Again, the head may be turned in a doughnut shape as in the one piece mallet described above, only with the grain running across the hole and not along it, or it may be turned cylindrical, with a striking face on the end grain at each end. For the reasons already given I prefer the doughnut shaped head, and with the grain running across the hole, its life should be considerable.

Take a suitable piece of hardwood of roughly 4½in (11.43cm) along the grain by 4½in (11.43cm) across by 4in (10.16cm) thick, and centre on the 4½in (11.43cm) square surfaces.

The block for the mallet head mounted ready for boring. The wood is supported on the fork centre and bit only, pressure from the bit maintaining the drive

The mallet head supported on the driving centre and the flanged plug at the tailstock, being rounded to shape

The mallet after finishing with sealer and a rub of linseed oil

Mount the workpiece on the driving centre and the point of a 1in (2.54cm) modified Irwin bit chucked in the tailstock, and with the lathe set at around 500–700 r.p.m. commence feeding in with the hand wheel as the lathe is switched on. Continuing pressure on the hand wheel will maintain the drive from the forked chuck, the hole being taken no nearer to it than ¾in (19.05cm) to ensure that the points of the bit and centre do not collide.

Next, turn a flanged softwood plug as a push fit in the open end of the hole, and remount the block between centres. Now turn the top and bottom surfaces of the head slightly convex and turn the striking surface sylindrical, but ¼in (6.35mm) larger in diameter at the headstock end and bellied out a little in the middle. Round the corners and sand and seal overall.

The remaining unbored portion of the workpiece is in turn opened up by the 1in (2.54cm) bit chucked in the headstock, the workpiece being supported by a waste wood pad

at the tailstock and fed on to the cutter by the hand wheel whilst being controlled with the other hand. (An alternative method is shown in the photo on p. 133) Follow this operation by opening up the mouth of the hole a little at the top, or wider, end of the head, using a 6in (15.24cm) half-round file. This will help to lock the head on when the handle is wedged later.

For the handle, centre and set up a piece of hickory, ash, beech or fruitwood of 1¾in (4.445cm) diameter by 10in (25.4cm) long and square it at the tailstock end. Mark in from here 4½in (11.43cm), and turn down this length to a tight fit into the head but with the corner at the 4½in (11.43cm) mark rounded into the full diameter of the handle.

Now shape the handle into the desired shape, including an expanded diameter or flange at the butt end to assist in retaining a grip when the mallet is in use. After tool work with the roughing and shallow gouges is finished sand seal

Boring out the remainder of the hole in the mallet head

Shaping the mallet handle

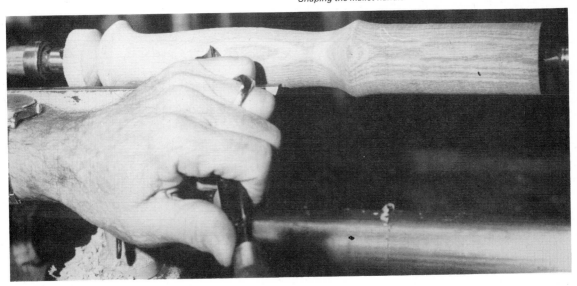

The two piece mallet ready for use

and polish the handle, parting off the stub of waste at the butt and sealing this in turn.

Cut a saw kerf across the grain at the top end to a depth of ¾in (19.05mm) and file its mouth open slightly. Now drive the head on to the handle, with the grain of the handle lying in the same plane as that of the head, by striking the butt of the handle with another mallet or plastic faced hammer. When the head is right home cut a wedge of oak or beech and drive it into the kerf as far as it will go, using the side of a chisel blade as a punch to force it in beyond the projecting shoulders of the kerf, adding a touch of glue to the wedge and slot before assembly. Once the glue is dry, the surplus wood of the handle can be cut back to the head, and the area sanded and sealed.

CENTRES FOR SUPPORTING BALLS DURING FINISHING OPERATIONS

After balls have been turned between lathe centres, as described in Chapter 9, a means is required to hold them whilst the stub ends are removed. Two cup centres turned in wood usually suggest themselves, and are made to suit the balls concerned. Centering cups made to the following detail will, however, accommodate balls of 1½–3½in (3.81–8.89cm) diameter, and will form a useful addition to your collection of lathe accessories.

Take a piece of beech of approximately 2¼in (5.715cm) diameter by 3in (7.62cm) long, plus the extra length needed for the type of drive suited to your lathe. An extra 3in (7.62cm) would be necessary for a No. 2 Morse taper, only ½in (12.7mm) for a spigot to screw into the faceplate as described in Chapter 16 and nothing at all if the screwchuck or fork centre is to be used. Of the last two methods, I would suggest the screwchuck, so as to give a positive control to the cup centre on the driving side.

Disregarding for the moment any extra wood included for fitting, mount the piece between centres using the ring dead centre and round down to 2in (5.08cm) diameter, smoothing off with the skew chisel. Next square the tail end, measure in 1½in (3.81cm) and part off on the mark. Mount a piece of softwood on the faceplate or screwchuck large enough to chuck the piece just parted off, and set it up in the chuck with the ring centre impression concealed, i.e. towards it. The reason for this will be seen later.

Square up the face of the disc with light cuts of the ½in (12.7mm) or ⅝in (15.875mm) shallow gouge, and scribe a circle of 1¾in (4.445cm) diameter on its face. Chuck a ⅛in (3.175mm) drill in the tailstock, and drill into the disc to a depth of ½in (12.7mm). Remove the drill (a careless knock will easily snap it), and bring up the tool rest at centre height.

Following this, using the skew chisel with its point towards the centre, scrape a funnel shaped hollow running from the 1¾in (4.445cm) scribed circle down to the bottom of the ⅛in (3.175mm) hole. Make the surface of the funnel smooth and flat in section, and remove the assembly from the lathe.

Now remount the main piece between centres, and shape one end to suit the intended method of driving it when in use. Once completed mount it in the intended way, dress its face flat and smooth and, as before, scribe a 1¾in (4.445cm) diameter circle into the centre to a depth of ½in (12.7mm) with a ⅛in (3.175mm) drill. Hollow out the centre as a funnel shaped taper, again using the point of the skew chisel.

When it has been made identical to the other half already done, cut a disc of worn garnet paper of 1¾in (4.445cm) diameter, remove a centre hole of ½in (12.7mm) diameter, and make four cruciform cuts from the hole to within ⅛in (3.175mm) of the edge of the paper.

As soon as it is ready glue the garnet paper disc centrally in the hollow face of the driving centre, where it will provide a positive drive to the ball when centered in the cup.

The centre chucked in the waste wood chuck for shaping the hollow face with the skew chisel. Note how the chuck has been left quite long for reshaping to suit future jobs. Because it is screwed into the faceplate there is no vibration, and it can be removed and reassembled repeatedly

The garnet paper clutch ready for glueing on to the face of the driving centre

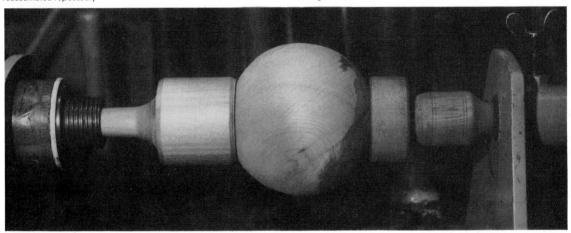

A large ball mounted between centres for final rounding

A small ball ready for final rounding. The tail half of the centre has been adapted to fit into the revolving centre

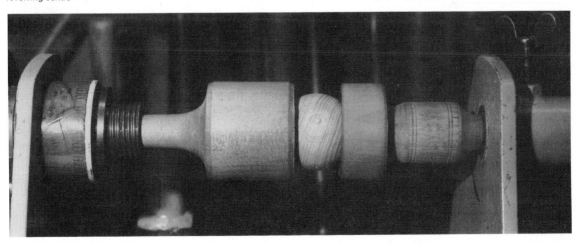

A TOOL FOR SCRAPING BALLS ROUND

This type of tool, long used in the engineering world for rough rounding balls in non-ferrous metals, can also be utilised when all of one's endeavours to turn a truly spherical ball in wood meet with failure. It cannot be called turning, and its use may be considered as a confession of ineptitude in one difficult area of the turner's craft, but I offer it to the reader merely as one way of making round balls.

Select a 12in (30.48cm) length of steel pipe, preferably uncorroded inside, its internal diameter approximately two-thirds the intended diameter of the ball. Cut the pipe square across one end, clean and smooth the inside of the mouth, and file it flat across using a fine file to leave a sharp inner edge.

This inside edge of the mouth of the tool acts as a scraper, so that by rotating it about its axis, and swinging it around the face of the ball, the wood is brought to a round shape, after all your efforts with the gouge and skew chisel have failed!

A TAPERED REAMERING DEVICE FOR CONICAL SHAPED CONDIMENT SHAKERS

This fitting was first made at a time when I was turning out a quantity of salt and pepper shakers in the modern tapered style. Most trade made articles had a 1in (2.54cm) diameter hole bored up the centre, and that was the full extent of their hollowing out. To me, as a non-professional, a shaker, like any other hollow ware, should have a side wall of uniform thickness – should, in fact *be* hollow – so I made them as described in Chapter 10. Having bored most of the waste out with a succession of graduated sized bits, the reamering tool which I shall now describe levels and smooths the inside surface to a uniform shape. The dimensions given relate to the external dimensions of the shakers described earlier in the book, so if you intend making your shakers of

The reamer body turned to shape, with a groove for blade pins being cut by a narrow round end scraper

a different size or shape you will need to modify the reamering tool accordingly.

It is made basically of wood, and designed to fit a hollow No.2 Morse taper tailstock mandrel, the actual cutting being done by hacksaw blades inset in the wood. Select a piece of beech 11in (27.94cm) long by 1¾in (4.445cm) diameter; set it up between centres and square one end. Round down the tail end to a No. 2 Morse taper if your lathe is so fitted, otherwise adapt the design to suit your lathe's tailstock mandrel. Reduce the remaining area up to the headstock to 1½in (3.81cm) diameter, and mark off at 3¾in (9.525cm), 4¾in (12.02cm), 5½in (13.97cm) and 10¼in (26.035cm) from the tailstock end.

From the 5½in (13.97cm) mark to the 10¼in (26.035cm) mark taper down to ½in (12.7mm) diameter, keeping the taper flat and smooth, and finishing with the skew chisel. The 3¾in (9.525cm) mark indicates the effective working end of the tool, the remaining portion back to the tailstock being shaped to suit the method of attachment to the tailstock poppet.

At the 4¾in (12.02cm) mark cut in with a very narrow round ended scraper to make a groove ³⁄₃₂in (2.381mm) wide by ⅛in (3.175mm) deep. If necessary, a scraper can be easily improvised from a heavy nail ground or filed to the shape required and fixed into a handle for this one job.

The tool rest is next set up at exact centre height and aligned close to the tapered portion of the workpiece, then used as a guide to strike a line along the full length of the taper using a scriber or other sharp ended tool. Now turn the workpiece through exactly 180° and repeat the scribing operation. Once marked out, part off the piece at the 10¼in (26.035cm) mark and remove it from the lathe.

Grip it in the vice in a horizontal position with a scribed line uppermost and, taking great care to follow the line and to cut radially into the wood, saw in on the line to a depth of ⅜in (9.525mm) using a sharp, narrow set tenon saw with a wooden stop clamped to the blade to control the depth of cut. (This is most important.)

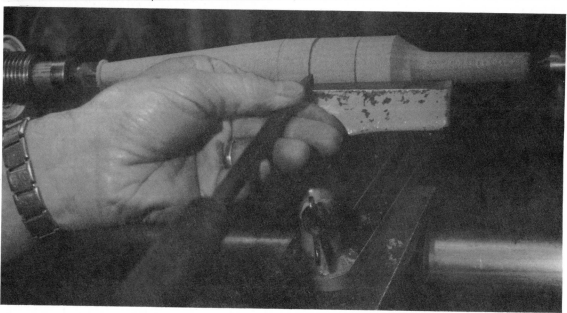

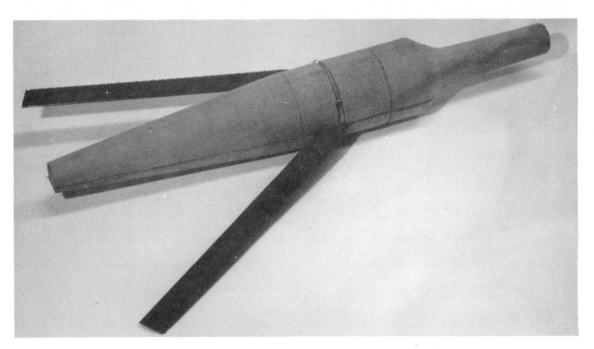

The reamer body slotted and the blades fitted. There is a stop pin towards the lower end

The finished reamer with sectioned samples of a shaker after reamering

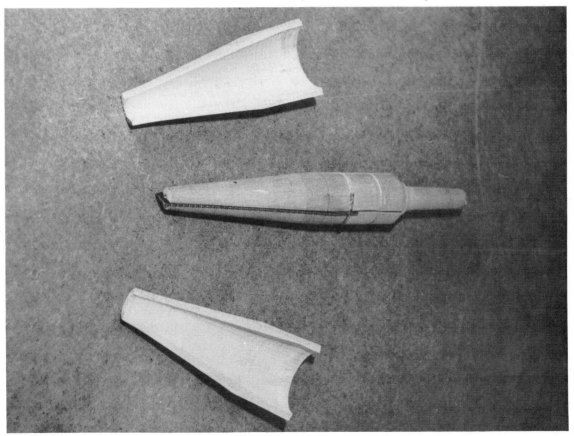

Having completed the first side, turn the wood over and repeat the cut from the other side, again taking great care with the direction and depth of cut. After this, obtain a new 12in (30.48cm) by 18 tooth hacksaw blade, either cast steel or flexible back, and break it into two equal parts. A flexible blade may have to be sheared in the vice with a square ended punch or a cold chisel, but the cast steel blade should be clamped at centre height and the half protruding above the vice jaws levered over with a piece of wood pressed flat against the whole surface. If this is not done it may snap into several pieces, and not even in the middle either! Success is, however, assured if a nick is first ground across the blade with the emery wheel. Once successfully cut, each half blade is pressed home in its slot in the wooden fitting, with its hole end aligned with the groove and, of course, its teeth outwards.

To secure the blades take two nails to be a tight fit in the groove, behead them, and set them to the curvature of the said groove. Insert each nail half-way through the hole of its blade and press it firmly home in the groove, using a hammer and punch finally to seat it. When the blades are now pressed home in their respective slots they should cross over at the bottom end to give a cutting width of approximately ½in (12.7mm). Whilst still in this position they are ground on the grinding wheel to give a square end to the cutter, projecting about ⅛in (3.175mm) beyond the wood.

Lastly calculate the position within the wood where the blades begin to cross over each other and bore a small hole through the wood at right angles to the blades at this point, to take a driven nail. Its purpose is to form a positive check to the saw blades settling back into their slots with repeated use. You will realise that the blades are very thin and so have only a small area of wood resisting the pressure imposed on them as they penetrate the tapered hole in the shaker. The nail stop is therefore quite essential, but great care must be taken to locate it in the exact position where the blades are in contact with it, but are not being forced out of their slots.

If a full size section drawing of the boring tool is made, the position for drilling the nail hole can be plotted exactly, and then marked out on the tool. I find on my reamer it is approximately 3¼in (8.255cm) from the centre of the groove.

Grind back the first ¾in (19.05mm) of the blades at their hole ends, to conform with the parallel portion of the wood. The outer edge of each blade should then be protruding about ⅛in (3.175mm) from its seating.

When it is finally assembled give the whole tool a liberal coating of sealer to resist the effects of moisture transferred to it by the heat generated during the reamering operation.

CHAPTER SIXTEEN

Some New Techniques Considered

FACEPLATE TURNING USING A MODIFIED SCREWCHUCK AND METHOD

If the screwchuck is suitably adapted it is possible, despite some expert opinion to the contrary, to turn platters and bowls up to 11in (27.94cm) diameter (the capacity of my lathe), to 6in (15.24cm) depth, on a 3in (7.62cm) diameter screw chuck using a No.10 gauge steel wood screw protruding ½in (12.7mm) from the face of the chuck. The only precaution necessary, dictated solely by common sense, is that the tools are sharp and excessively heavy cuts are not made.

Turn off a step of metal from the edge of the face of the chuck, approximately ½in (12.7mm) wide and ⅛in (3.175mm) deep, adjusting the width of the step to give a 2in (5.08cm) diameter to the raised face at its centre, and lightly chamfer the edge of the raised face.

Now glue sufficient worn medium grade sandpaper back to back to allow a ring of ½in (12.7mm) width and 2in (5.08cm) hole diameter to be cut from it and fitted to the step of the chuck. The disc of paper cut from the ring is now pierced through its centre and fitted over the screw of the chuck which, after the workpiece has been suitably prepared, is ready for use.

The next step is to secure the workpiece to the faceplate in the conventional way, and dress its face flat. Turn a 2in (5.08cm) diameter by ⅛in (3.175mm) deep recess into the centre, checking it for good fit on the raised face of the screwchuck, and piercing a hole for the screw. Whilst it is still in position on the faceplate round up the bottom and sides of the bowl and sand, seal and finish it. When ready, remove it from the faceplate and reverse it on to the screwchuck, where the raised face of the chuck will be a snug fit in the recess, with the sandpaper disc and ring making a firm contact between wood and metal.

The workpiece is now locked to the face of the chuck by means of the sandpaper clutch, the wood and metal moving as one with relatively little torsional strain on the screw, and no side strain possible with the stepped face of the chuck being seated in the recess of the base of the bowl.

The modified screwchuck with double sided sandpaper clutches and prepared base of bowl

A bowl mounted on the modified screwchuck ready for hollowing out

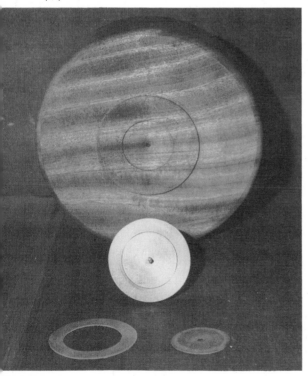

ORNAMENTAL PLUGS FOR SCREW HOLES

Reference has been made in various parts of the book to ornamental plugs or caps used to conceal screw holes in bowls, jars, lids, etc. Although requiring care and patience in the making, they do much when fitted to enhance the beauty of an article, and declare to one and all that here is a craftsman who aspires to a really high standard of workmanship.

Set up a piece of 6 × ½in (15.24cm × 12.7mm) square boxwood, the distinctive colour of which sets it off remarkably well, and round it down between centres to ⅜in (9.525mm) diameter using the ½in (12.7mm) shallow curve gouge. Square up the end with the spearpoint, edge in the vertical position, in one straight-in thrusting cut to the centre, the bevel aligned at 90° to the centre line of the lathe, and rubbing throughout the movement.

Once the end is true, the wood is marked off in ⅜in (9.525mm) and ⁷⁄₁₆in (11.112mm) alternating intervals along its length, using the vertical edge of the spearpoint, as before. The tool is then turned on its side to bring its edge into the horizontal plane, and is used to reduce the end ⅜in (9.525mm) section down to ⅛in (3.175mm) diameter. The bevel is rested well up on the wood, and eased back until shavings appear, as in a parting cut, except that the tool is traversed across the surface to reduce it evenly along its ⅜in (9.525mm) length.

As the cut progresses the tool is turned from time to time through 90° and the fibres under the head of the plug cut away. The handle of the tool is held a little off to the right for this, so as to make the underside of the head of the plug slightly concave. This will ensure a wood to wood contact at the edge of the plug, making it a really snug fit when finally in position.

After the shank and underside of the head of the first plug are completed the lathe is stopped and the conical centre exchanged for the rotating centre fitting described in Chapter 15.

An adapter, as shown in the photograph, designed as a push fit into the revolving centre housing at one end and blind bored ⅛in (3.175mm) diameter to a depth of ¼in (6.35mm) at the other, is then fitted to the revolving centre housing.

The tailstock is repositioned to bring the adapter on to the end of the workpiece, clamped, and the shank of the plug fed into the blind hole of the adapter as the revolving centre is screwed forward with the hand wheel. When the workpiece is again fully supported, the hand wheel is clamped ready for turning the next plug, and the lathe restarted. From this point on a series of operations is repeated along the length of the wood.

The spearpoint with its blade in the vertical plane is used to cut in the shank of the second plug, leaving a thickness of ¹⁄₁₆in (1.587mm) for the head of the first plug. Then, with the blade in the horizontal plane, the shank of plug No. 2 is reduced in the same way as for No. 1, with the fibres at each end being cut through with the blade in the vertical position as before, slightly undercutting the head of the second plug, and rounding the top of the head of the first plug. When the second plug shank is down to ⅛in (3.175mm), and the curving head cuts are done, the spearpoint is used to V cut and part off No. 1 plug from No. 2. The free hand encircles the work as the parting is completed, the No. 1 plug remaining in the adapter.

With the lathe switched off, the plug is removed from the adapter, which is fed forward with the hand wheel to engage the shank of plug No. 2, whereupon the complete cycle is repeated.

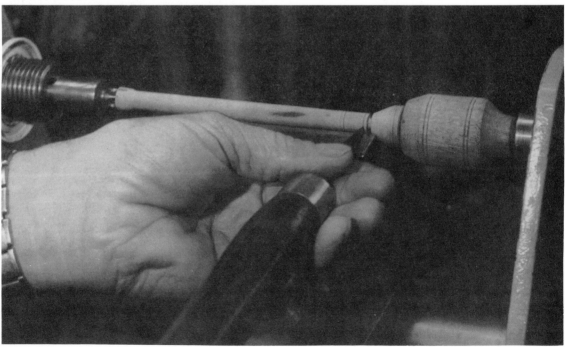

The boxwood dowel marked off and No. 1 plug being turned to size using the spearpoint GP tool and adapter in the revolving centre

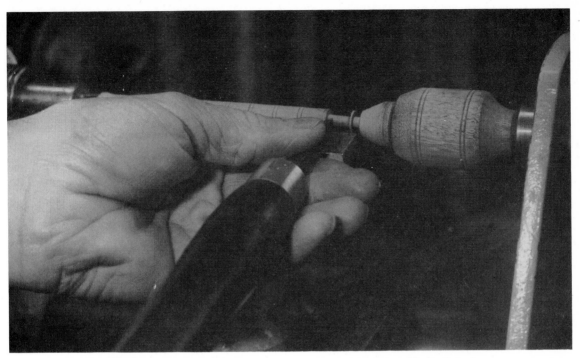

The finished No. 1 plug supported by the adapter of the revolving centre whilst No. 2 plug is shaped

A selection of finished plugs of various sizes plus sleeves for flex holes in radially drilled lamp bases

When sufficient plugs have been made for stock I chuck them in the Jacobs ½in (12.7mm) chuck and finish off the tops with a fine grade of paper. Later they are sealed and rechucked for carnauba waxing. A labour of love you may say, but to me well worth the end result.

CUTTING CIRCULAR DISCS ON THE FACEPLATE

If the workpiece is an irregular shape – square perhaps – it can be brought to round by using the spearpoint tool previously described.

After the workpiece has been centered by one of the means already suggested, it is mounted on the screwchuck, and a circle of the desired diameter scribed with dividers, care being taken to present the point gently and at a downward angle over the edge of the tool rest.

With the circle clearly marked the spearpoint is presented, blade in the horizontal plane, on the waste side of the line at centre height, the tool held parallel with the top of the bench.

The cut is widened on the waste side as penetration proceeds until the tool is within $\frac{1}{16}$in (1.587mm) of the back of the workpiece, when the lathe is stopped and the corners broken off by hand, or removed by sawing round the cut with a hacksaw blade. If, however, a disc of ply or hardboard has been interposed between the faceplate and the workpiece, then of course the cut can be taken right through, but watch out for the severed corners flying off in all directions!

The edge is completed by swinging the tool rest round to the side and finishing with the $\frac{3}{8}$in (9.525mm) or $\frac{1}{2}$in (12.7mm) gouge in the usual way.

ROUGH HOLLOWING OUT OF BOWLS USING THE SPEARPOINT TOOL

The spearpoint is an ideal tool for removing the bulk of waste in hollowing out bowls, because unlike the gouge it takes but a moment or two to resharpen its $\frac{1}{16}$in (1.587mm) blade and, incidentally, makes far less mess too.

The tool is presented, edge in the horizontal plane, at right angles to the face of the wood and $\frac{1}{8}$in (3.175mm) on the waste side of the intended wall thickness, and entered to a depth of approximately 1in (2.54cm). It is then swung round at 45° to the surface, about 1in (2.54cm) to the waste side of the first cut, and directed towards it. The tool is thrust in until the second cut intersects the first, when a ring of wood of triangular section will part out of the workpiece.

Repeating the operation by alternating 45° penetrations of the tool will produce a series of triangular section rings of waste across the face of the work.

Continue the operation into the depths of the hollow until the bulk of the waste has been lifted out, and then finish in the conventional way with the gouge and scraper. Because of its narrow edge the spearpoint requires a minimum of pressure, creates practically no vibration and, as already mentioned, takes no time at all to resharpen.

ROUGH HOLLOWING OUT OF POTS, JARS, ETC

As with bowls, the spearpoint is a quick and easy means of removing the bulk of waste from all types of hollow ware, before finishing with the scraper, and is used as follows.

Having first bored the full depth of the hole with your largest centre bit, present the spearpoint at right angles to the face of the work, starting the cuts at the centre and moving one blade width at each penetration of 1in (2.54cm) towards the outer edge of the wood. Because the tool is cutting on its forward edge, along the axis of the lathe, there is no side strain on the workpiece, so heavy cuts can be made.

After the bulk of the waste has been cut away, the inside surface is levelled with scrapers in the usual way.

The spearpoint GP tool cutting a disc on the faceplate. Note the narrow kerf made by the $\frac{1}{16}$in (1.587mm) wide edge of the tool

The bowl after the spearpoint GP tool has cut away the first ring of waste

Above: Hollowing out with the spearpoint completed. A large amount of solid waste is removed, so reducing litter, and wear and tear on the tool

Below: The spearpoint hollowing a jar. (This tool is newly made from a 10in (20.54cm) square file)

A METHOD OF SECURING MATERIAL TO THE FACEPLATE WITHOUT THE USE OF SCREWS

When the faceplate has its mandrel hole threaded through to the front, it can be used for securely mounting both faceplate and spindle turned projects without the use of screws.

Square one end of the workpiece between centres, slightly concave, and leave a central spigot of $\frac{3}{8}$in (9.525mm) length, with its edge chamfered and its diameter a tight fit in the hole of the faceplate.

Then fit a distance washer of hardboard, plywood or metal (preferably metal) behind the boss of the faceplate so that when it is screwed home on the headstock mandrel there is about $\frac{3}{8}$–$\frac{1}{2}$in (9.525–12.7mm) of the internal thread

of the faceplate exposed at its face. If the spigot of the workpiece is now aligned squarely with the faceplate hole by means of the tailstock centre it can be screwed into the faceplate until they abut tightly together, a drop of oil assisting the union.

By this means hollow ware up to the full diameter of the faceplate, and 6–8in (15.24–20.32cm) depth, may be turned, besides normal spindle work of up to 12in (30.48cm) length, unsupported at its outer end, as for serviette rings or egg cup projects. As an additional advantage it is a very handy method of mounting softwood spigot and hollow chucks used in repetition work which can be fitted and removed repeatedly, yet always run true on re-assembly to the faceplate. Any initial tightness necessary to a really solid assembly is readily overcome by means of the strap wrench described in the previous chapter.

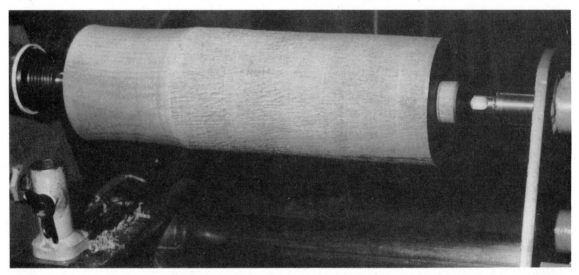

A spigot turned on the workpiece, having been callipered to size

The workpiece aligned with the faceplate from tailstock end, and partially screwed home. The distance collar is fitted behind the faceplate

The workpiece solidly mounted on the faceplate

Showing the thread formed on the spigot by the faceplate, allowing repeated reassembly, and the distance collar used behind the faceplate to allow the spigot to enter fully into the faceplate hole. The wood is stained from oil used to lubricate the spigot

CHAPTER SEVENTEEN

Carnauba Wax Polishing and Some Thoughts on Sanding

Using the tow or cotton wool pad in wet sanding. Note the plastic sheeting to catch surplus water, and trailing position of the hands, tow hand above the sanding hand

Carnauba wax polishing is a well known method of finishing work which will not be handled overmuch, and features in most woodturning manuals. Different people apply it in different ways: some as it comes in its dense, solid state, others in diluted preparations of their own devising. It is spoken highly of by some, whilst others express reservations: it chips too easily, is too difficult to bring to a uniform lustre, or will not withstand normal handling if in everyday use. The last criticism has some validity, but if the surface has been properly prepared before waxing, the fading polish develops a patina which can be equally attractive. To me, as a general purpose finish, it is the quickest, cleanest and easiest method of, at will, putting a high shine, matt shine or dull shine on wood of any that I have tried, and I prefer it to any other. However, for success, certain preliminaries must be carefully followed, so I will first consider a faceplate operation.

To begin with, having achieved the smoothest surface possible using the appropriate tools for the job in hand (gouge, chisel or scraper), thoroughly wet the surface to be treated. Then, using 280 gauge wet and dry paper in one hand trailing the direction of rotation, and holding a water saturated wad of tow or cotton wool in the other against the wood, run the lathe at say 1000 r.p.m. and thoroughly sand the surface. Keep the wood wet, and wash off the paper from time to time, preferably in a tin of water handy on the bench. Exercise restraint in the amount of water used, and by covering the tool rack with a folded sheet of tarred paper and the bed of the lathe with a sheet of plastic no undue mess need be made.

There is a good reason for using tow or cotton wool to apply the water. If by chance an end gets caught on the revolving work it will immediately pull apart with no harm done. If rag or cloth is used there is no guarantee that this will be so.

Follow the 280 paper with 360 grade if a particularly smooth surface is desired; for most jobs the 280 paper is completely satisfactory.

When the sanding is done thoroughly wash the surface, and with the lathe still running at 1000 r.p.m. press an old piece of clean towelling against the wet wood, moving pressure across the face of it as drying proceeds, until all is dry. The effect of this treatment is to produce a surface which is completely free of all sanding rings as it simultaneously raises and levels the grain and finally burnishes it ready for the next operation. (Water stain would be applied at this point if desired.)

With the lathe stationary and the wood thoroughly dry, apply sanding sealer to the prepared surface, stroking with the grain, and allow to dry.

Restart the lathe and, using a fine steel wool, lightly break the skin of the sealer. Dust off any resulting powder next, and with the lathe again in motion and still at 1000 r.p.m. apply a lump of carnauba wax with medium pressure to the surface of the workpiece, taking care that a flat area of the wax makes contact with the wood, as a sharp corner of wax can quite easily mar the surface. Traverse the wax across the face of the work, moving from the centre to the edge, and repeat the pass in the opposite direction.

Now take a piece of lint free gauze, and with it well padded on the forefinger traverse it from the centre to the edge of the face, applying sufficient pressure for friction to melt the wax but easing pressure progressively approaching the outer edge. In spindle polishing the pass would traverse the work from one end to the other with uniform speed and pressure.

Stop the lathe and examine the surface. Streaks or rings indicate incomplete melting of the wax; dull areas, that too much of it has been wiped away. Reapply the gauze or wax or both as necessary. Unless you apply hard pressure to an edge or projection, when burning can result, no harm can be done by repeated applications and wiping off of the wax, so just keep on trying until practice and patience reward you.

Just a word or two of caution. Always seal the wood before waxing, otherwise water accidentally splashed on the polish will leave marks which cannot be removed, and never leave brush marks in the sealer before polishing. The polish will never eradicate them; the only remedy is to steel-wool back to the bare wood and start again.

SOME PASSING THOUGHTS ON SANDING

Never commence sanding until the tool work is finished. Particles of grit lodged in the fibres of the wood will blunt any tool applied to it.

Never depend on abrasive paper to remedy defects in shape or surface left by the tool.

Never use a coarser paper than necessary to smooth the surface.

Move in graded stages from coarse to fine paper in sanding operations and use wet and dry if only at the end to raise the grain.

Two or three coats of sealer brushed generously on to the back of a good grade abrasive paper (such as Swedish 'Ekamant') will make it quite waterproof. Although not as flexible as wet and dry, it performs as well and lasts indefinitely.

Cut the paper into handy strips of 1–2in (2.54–5.08cm) width for both economy and convenience, using an old hacksaw blade along a fold in the paper or, if you have them, an old pair of tin snips. Any attempt to cut the paper with a sharp edged tool will blunt it at once.

Sand up into corners by backing the edge of the paper with a flexible 6in (15.24cm) steel rule, and use it also for squaring mouths of hollow ware or curving to suit a dished surface.

Lap the paper over the flat end of a cork to apply pressure at a given point, or around the body of a cork to spread the area of contact. If a groove is being worked on then round the other end of your cork on the sander and lap the paper around it for getting into the groove, or roll the paper around the body of the cork as described in Chapter 11.

Always trail paper with the hand under the revolving wood, the fingers following the direction of rotation.

After sanding to a smooth finish in the lathe, eliminate any minute rotary scratches by sanding the wood lengthwise along the grain.

When sanding resinous or waxy woods, which rapidly clog the paper, have your file scratch card handy and scour off the clogging particles with this.

Wet and dry paper can be used dry, as the name implies, but sustained pressure on any one area soon makes enough heat to remove the abrasive, so frequent movement over the whole surface of the paper is recommended.

Again, don't leave your wet and dry paper immersed in water when not in use, or at least not for lengthy periods, as the paper will deteriorate.

ALWAYS remove the tool rest before sanding operations begin!

Glossary

arc   Part of a circle.

bed   The base of a lathe to which the headstock, tool rest and tailstock are attached.

bell chuck   A hollow steel chuck which holds the work by means of bolts around its circumference. Requires caution in use.

bellied out   Bulged out.

between centres   Work held between driving centre at headstock and dead or revolving centre at tailstock.

bit   a tool used for boring holes, usually held in the Jacobs chuck.

blank   Material before being worked on.

blind bore   A hole closed at one end.

boss   A cylindrical projection.

bruzz   A tool V shape in section, for marking where details will come.

callipers   A tool for testing diameters. The work, having been turned to the correct size, just touches both legs as it passes between them. The spring jointed type is generally preferred.

centering   Setting up work between centres so that it runs true. Marking the centre.

centre punch   A punch with conical point. Used to make a seating for the point of the drill.

chamfer   A bevel or angle across a corner.

chuck   A device for holding the work or boring tool whilst being rotated.

chucking   The act of fixing work or boring tool in a chuck.

circumference   The outside of a cylinder.

clams   Protective faces for vice jaws. May be cork, leather or wood or, for metal holding, lead, copper, brass or tinplate.

counterbore   A larger hole drilled on a smaller.

countersink   A bevel or angle cut on the mouth of a hole. A tool used for this purpose.

cup chuck   A hollow steel chuck into which irregular shaped wood can be forced for driving between centres.

dividers   Similar to compasses but with two sharpened steel legs which are used for stepping distances around circles, or along spindle work.

drill chuck   A self centering chuck for holding drills. See Jacobs chuck.

drill jobbing   The common general purpose twist drill. Usually ground with a flat rake and centre point for woodwork.

faceplate   A circular plate screwed to the headstock mandrel, having equal spaced screw holes for holding work being turned.

ferrule   A metal sleeve fitted to prevent wood from splitting, as on tool handles.

flexible back   A hacksaw blade with only the teeth hardened.

flush with   One surface level with another.

fork chuck   A driving chuck with two fangs or prongs and a central point.

Forstner bit   A specialised bit with a projecting circular rim formed on its cutting face. This causes it to cut true, even when overlapping other holes.

four prong chuck   A driving chuck with four fangs, giving a more positive drive, especially in soft woods.

frozen joint   The situation where two metal surfaces seize together.

headstock   The main assembly at the left hand end of the lathe, supporting and driving the work.

horizontal plane   Level with the horizon.

HSE file   Hand safe edge file. Ground smooth on one edge.

indexing head   In engineering, a plate with a range of drilled holes. By means of a spring loaded pin a selected ring of holes will position the work accurately, as required.

Jacobs chuck   A self centering chuck for holding bits and drills. Called by the maximum size drill it will hold: $\frac{1}{4}$in (6.35mm), $\frac{3}{8}$in (9.525mm) or $\frac{1}{2}$in (12.7mm). Usually fitted with a Morse taper shank.

jig   A device made for the purpose of controlling the tool or work during the boring or cutting operations.

kerf   The groove cut by a saw or other tool.

L & S   Long and Strong gouge for heavier types of turning.

long cornered chisel   The skew chisel, with its cutting end at an angle.

long nose gouge   A gouge with a circular cutting end. Not square across.

mandrel or mandril   The main headstock spindle, usually hollow and threaded externally for the faceplate and certain chucks. It is tapered or threaded internally for Morse taper or screw-in driving chucks.

Morse taper   Engineer standard taper, progressing in sizes from No. 0 upwards.

non-ferrous metals   Metals other than iron and steel.

offset turning   Turning done on centres offset from the original true centres.

parting tool   Narrow ended chisel for cutting through spindle work.

periphery   The circumference or outside of a cylinder.

pilot hole   A small hole drilled first to guide a larger drill.

poppet   Part of the tailstock controlled by the hand wheel. Supports the work by means of the dead centre. Also called the tailstock mandrel.

prong chuck   Alternative name for the fork chuck.

proud   Said of a surface standing above an adjoining one.

radial   On a line from the centre.

radius   Half the diameter of a circle, and one-sixth of its circumference.

rake   The angle back from the cutting edge of a tool.

rebate   A step or shoulder.

rest   A support for the tool.

revolving centre   Tailstock centre fitted with ball bearings, which revolves with the work.

ribbing   A spiral formed on spindle work as a result of vibration or whip in the workpiece. (See Chapter 9.)

right angle   An angle of 90°.

saw tooth bit   Boring bit with saw teeth on its circular rim. Fast cutting and holds on course. (See Forstner bit.)

scrapers   Tools with ends of various shapes for some faceplate work. Because the metal is of the right hardness, old files with the teeth removed are often used as scrapers.

screwpoint chuck   A small chuck which holds the wood by means of a central screw. This may be fixed, but in some chucks is adjustable.

section   In drawing, the surface exposed when an object is cut through.

shell bit   A boring tool having a grooved shank for clearing the waste, and a cutter half across its end. Used in long hole boring.

skew chisel   A long cornered chisel.

sleeve   A hollow cylinder.

spigot   A projecting end with a formed shoulder, the spigot fitting into a matching hole in another part.

spoon bit   A boring tool with a grooved shank for clearing waste, and a sharpened end shaped like a spoon. Used in long hole boring.

tailstock The main assembly at the right hand end of the lathe. Has an adjustable poppet carrying the centre which supports the work.

taper centre The conical dead centre.

ticketer A rod of hardened steel used to dub over the edge of freshly sharpened scrapers.

torsional strain The leverage around an axis; a twisting force.

transverse In a crosswise direction.

twist drill The jobbing or engineer's drill.

vertical plane At right angles to the ground.

Suppliers

U.K.

There is a large number of makers and suppliers of woodturning equipment throughout the U.K., most of whom advertise in the two popular magazines, *Woodworker* and *Practical Woodworking*

U.S.A.

The Cutting Edge
295 S. Robertson Blvd
Beverly Hills 90211
California

Wood-Crafter's Supply Center
1715 N. Sherman
Indianapolis 46218
Indiana

Amherst Woodworking & Supply
Box 464
Sunderland Rd
N. Amherst 01059
Massachusetts

AUSTRALIA

Lathes such as the Ezycut, Luna SP800 and SP1000, and the Woodfast, are currently available through:

Fletcher Machine Tools Pty Ltd
77 Queens Road
Sydney
and
46 Rutland Rd
Melbourne

NEW ZEALAND

Lathes such as the B-Line, Turnmaster and Tanner are available through:

The Farmers Trading Company
Hobson St
Auckland

The Myford ML8 is available through:

Shroffs Hardware
Hobson St
Auckland

The useful Teknatool TL100 is available through:

Latalex Ltd
Henderson
Auckland

INDEX

Index